The Bedside, Bathtub & Armchair
Companion to Jane Austen

The Bedside, Bathtub & Armchair Companion to Jane Austen

Carol Adams,
Douglas Buchanan,
and Kelly Gesch

continuum

2008

The Continuum International Publishing Group Inc
80 Maiden Lane, New York, NY 10038

The Continuum International Publishing Group Ltd
The Tower Building, 11 York Road, London SE1 7NX

www.continuumbooks.com

Printed in the United States of America

Library of Congress Cataloging-in-Publication Data

Adams, Carol J.
  The bedside, bathtub & armchair companion to Jane Austen / Carol J. Adams, Douglas Buchanan, and Kelly Gesch.
    p. cm.
  ISBN-13: 978-0-8264-2933-9 (pbk. : alk. paper)
  ISBN-10: 0-8264-2933-5 (pbk. : alk. paper) 1. Austen, Jane, 1775-1817--Handbooks, manuals, etc. 2. Women and literature--England--History--19th century. 3. Novelists, English--19th century--Biography. I. Buchanan, Douglas. II. Gesch, Kelly. III. Title. IV. Title: Bedside, bathtub and armchair companion to Jane Austen.

PR4036.A65 2008
823'.7--dc22
  [B]

                                                    2008021981

For Evander Lomke,
a reader for readers

Contents

First Impressions:
Letting Jane Austen Into Your Life

"Where shall I begin? Which of all my important nothings shall I tell you first?" So Jane Austen wrote to her sister Cassandra in 1808. But she did not write "important nothings," she wrote wonderful letters (and the letter of that 1808 day is such an example), and even more wonderful novels. Her dilemma, "where shall I begin?" is ours as well. Where to begin to describe this beloved author and her beloved works?

Of course, everyone has first impressions when meeting a novel or the author. Sir Samuel Egerton Brydges describes Jane Austen as "fair and handsome, slight and elegant, but with cheeks a little too full." He never suspected "she was an authoress."

And what of the poet W. H. Auden? He wrote:

You could not shock her more than she shocks me;

Beside her Joyce seems innocent as grass.

It makes me most uncomfortable to see

An English spinster of the middle class

Describe the amorous effects of "brass,"

Reveal so frankly and with such sobriety

The economic basis of society.

And then there was Kipling. For Kipling's characters in "The Janeites" on the Somme Front during World War I, it seemed entirely appropriate to name guns "General Tilney" and "The Lady Catherine de Bugg."

Austen consoles the lonely, makes happy the care-worn, and spreads joy and delight wherever she is read. We may cringe when Elizabeth misreads Wickham in *Pride and Prejudice* (and recognize that in that moment she is definitely her mother's daughter). We either completely understand Fanny Price in *Mansfield Park* or are absolutely impatient with her. But it doesn't matter: We trust Jane Austen to take us through a thicket of thorns, pricking us with anxiety felt over missed opportunities, only to return us safely home with our baskets filled with berries, like the strawberry pickers at Donwell Abbey.

Perhaps we are new to Jane Austen—having seen a movie or ten—and we want to get a little closer. Who is this Jane Austen? How did she write such wonderful novels? Why do so many people love her novels so? What did she really say?

The Bedside, Bathtub & Armchair Companion to Jane Austen has something for everyone: The newcomer can learn about Austen's life and her novels, about themes in the books, and their translations into film. Janeites and other Jane-readers and Jane-addicts can test their knowledge with our quiz, and learn along the way, too. There's some fun and there's some elucidation. (Just enough of both, we hope!)

As with all books in this series, we provide "Capsules" of the novels, but don't worry—in the capsules—we don't give away the "happily ever afters," nor identify for whom such things do not come to pass. And for those who know the plots, the capsules may introduce new ideas about the books and their themes. Yes, we know the movies have been watched, and re-watched and for some of you, the books are reread every decade (if not yearly). But for those who come to this book wanting to know about Jane Austen and who have not read her novels, we don't betray her plots in the capsules. How fortunate you are! How we envy the person who is opening *Emma* or *Pride and Prejudice* for the first time. Read her. Read her again. Keep her by your bedside, near your bathtub, and tucked into your armchair.

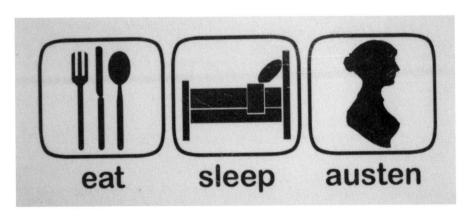

CAPSULE

Pride and Prejudice

If any of the families in Jane Austen were to be the characters in a dysfunctional evening sitcom, it would be the Bennets of Longbourn. There is Mr. Bennet, whose biting sarcasm wears thin the nerves of his wife, and whose nerves are in turn tried by his younger daughters. Mrs. Bennet is obsessed (understandably) with finding husbands for her children Jane, Elizabeth, Mary, Lydia, and Kitty. Jane is sensible and even-tempered; Elizabeth, independent and loyal, the favorite of her father; Mary, bookish, yet unwise in many things; and Lydia and Kitty, forever hounding young officers and new fashions. In short, the makings of Georgian family chaos.

In Pride and Prejudice, *we first meet Elizabeth Bennet working on the trimming of a hat. This hat was designed for the 1995 BBC/A&E* Pride and Prejudice. *Courtesy of Baronda Ellen Bradley.*

Since *Pride and Prejudice* is probably the most reread book in English, everyone knows that our sitcom begins when it is found out that Netherfield Park, the manor house three miles away, has been let by one Mr. Bingley. For Mrs. Bennet, the obvious course of action is to ensure her daughters receive due consideration in the race to matrimony. Mrs. Bennet's mind is seldom without connubial machinations: meetings and dances, plans and positioning—they are all directed toward marrying off one or another of her daughters.

While Mrs. Bennet is busy plotting marriages, the novel known for its "marriage plot" actually explores much different territory on its way to either please or disappoint Mrs. Bennet. *Pride and Prejudice* is as much about the education of a young woman—not book-learning education, not the education that is discussed one night at Netherfield, when Miss Bingley, wooing Darcy by mirroring what she believes to be his opinions, proposes, "A woman must have a thorough knowledge of music, singing, drawing, dancing, and the modern languages, to deserve the word [*accomplished*]." No, Lizzy's will be another education altogether.

Into every sitcom, some drama must come. The crisis that undergirds the novel, and that causes ongoing consternation to Mrs. Bennet, is that the Longbourn estate is entailed to a distant relative. Entailment ties up a landed estate for a generation ahead; so that the current owner is actually only a tenant for life, and thus has limited powers. Entailing an estate provided continuity of ownership of property. The tenant for life can't dispose of the estate. Through a will, the estate is left to the first male heir, but it is entailed on the heir's son. The heir's son becomes the heir "in tail."

The assumption of an entail is that the person who gains the estate from the dictates of the entail will do the same thing—granting to his son only life tenancy, and entailing it to the first son of his first son, thus guaranteeing the property stays in the hands of the family for two more generations. Mr. and Mrs. Bennet expected to have a son, and when he turned twenty-one, they were going to break the entail, to provide for Mrs. Bennet and the younger children. But after five daughters, and no son, the situation of the mother and the daughters was very unstable. Mrs. Bennet is not far wrong that with the death of Mr. Bennet, Mr. Collins (upon whom the estate becomes entailed as there were no sons) could toss them out. Despite Mrs. Bennet's poignant exclamations about her fate, because her character is so nervous and shallow, the depth of the critique of entailment may not be felt. It is left to the unpleasant and imperious Lady Catherine to voice the all-important position that there is "no occasion for entailing estates from the female lines." Such beliefs will not save the Bennet girls from being dispossessed.

Strangers and Journeys

The novelist John Gardner proposed that there are two basic story lines in a novel: a stranger comes to town or someone goes on a journey. Elizabeth Bennet, bright, articulate, sassy, sparkling, is the fortunate person to whom both of these things happen multiple times: three strangers (Darcy, Collins, Wickham) and two trips (to Charlotte in the spring, to Derbyshire in the summer). Largely told from Elizabeth's perspective, *Pride and Prejudice* shows us how she learns to evaluate information from a variety of quarters: personal experience, confidences shared by loved ones and strangers, and observations at home and as she travels. It turns out that when it comes to what makes a woman accomplished—and interesting to Mr. Darcy—Miss Bingley was wrong on many counts.

Yes, a love story is injected into this awakening of insight, a love story that is ignited by bad first impressions and whose flame is fed by misunderstandings, misreadings, and misrepresentations. Elizabeth has her work set out for her if she is to acquire the sort of education that matters, at least in this novel and to this novelist.

Jane Bennet, too, experiences both story lines—a stranger, a trip. And so does

Charlotte Lucas. Charlotte, in a speech Elizabeth cannot believe to be serious, suggests that "In nine cases out of ten, a woman had better shew *more* affection than she feels." Charlotte takes her own advice, and Jane, not born to duplicity or even simple flattery, will not. This creates both dramatic tension and comic relief. Why did Bingley go to London; why, when Jane goes to London, does he not come to see her? How does a man who has just professed "the violence of my affections" (as if!) to one woman, happily settle for another within three days?

Both the book and the heroine are exuberant. Jane Austen herself was proud of the book and the heroine, and proud of what she had accomplished after she "lop't and crop't so successfully." In early February 1813, she wrote to her sister Cassandra with some playful thoughts: "I am quite vain enough & well satisfied enough,—The work is rather too light & bright & sparkling;—it wants shade;—it wants to be stretched out here & there with a long Chapter—of sense if it could be had, if not of solemn specious nonsense—about something

Hero's recruiting at Kelsey's; or, Guard-Day at St. James's, *James Gillray, 1797.*
Courtesy of The Lewis Walpole Library, Yale University. 797.6.9.2.

The Charms of a Red Coat, 1787.
Courtesy of The Lewis Walpole Library, Yale University. 787.11.1.1.

unconnected with the story; an Essay on Writing, a critique on Walter Scott, or the history of Buonaparte—or anything that would form a contrast & bring the reader with increased delight to the playfulness & Epigrammatism of the general stile.—I doubt your quite agreeing with me here—I know your starched Notions." Austen is not serious here: she knew nothing was missing; she is the one who lop't it and crop't it.

With the introduction of the ——shire militia, the entire village of Meryton is turned upside down—an entire regiment of strangers coming to town! They don't know how to read character, or they are perhaps too hasty in doing so: They like Darcy; they dislike Darcy; they like Darcy. Of another it is reported, "All Meryton seemed striving to blacken the man, who, but three months before, had been almost an angel of light. . . . Every body declared that he was the wickedest young man in the world; and every body began to find out, that they had always distrusted the appearance of his goodness." Information in this town spreads quickly: "Mrs. Bennet was privileged to whisper it to Mrs. Philips, and *she* ventured, without any permission, to do the same by all her neighbours in Meryton." Gossip, after all, formed the current events of the day!

The youngest daughter, Lydia, is also given both story lines—a stranger (or several) arrive in town; she goes on a journey . . . and then another with one of those strangers.

Think of it: Austen has tackled both of John Gardner's basic story lines in fiction, not once, not twice, not thrice, but four times in one novel. Perhaps it was this ability to balance so many story lines into one secure plot that prompted one critic to declare: The "plot is a superb piece of machinery, and as with a Rolls-Royce, part of the proper pleasure that we take in the book lies in our appreciation of the quality of the engineering and the smoothness of the ride."

As a novel *Pride and Prejudice* matches the wit and sparkle of Elizabeth Bennet. It is *her* book. There has never been a heroine like Elizabeth, "as delightful a creature as ever appeared in print." (Those are Jane Austen's words when she received her first printed copy of the book in 1813.) Consider Lizzy, not just a "walker," as Miss Bingley disparages, she energetically jumps over stiles and springs over puddles. She is energetic in all she does: She argues, laughs, reasons, resists. She is witty and courageous; she holds her ground, but, importantly, she can also change her mind. She takes lemons and makes lemonade. But of her it would not be said what Bingley felt about Jane: "he could not conceive an angel more beautiful." True, there are times when she speaks her mind and we rejoice; but there are also times that she should hold her tongue, and she doesn't. We cringe when Elizabeth, breaching propriety yet again, shares her opinions about Mr. Darcy with another stranger, Wickham.

Some say *Pride and Prejudice* is a didactic novel; that it is trying to teach a lesson and is therfore conservative in its impulse. Perhaps they are reinserting what Austen "lop't and crop't" out of it, for the two people who are the most didactic—Mary Bennet and Mr. Collins—are both shown to be fools. At a moment of extreme anguish for her family, Mary spouts platitudes. Mr. Collins's proposal sounds more like a business arrangement, and to his mind it very well might have been.

Men, Marriage Proposals, and Misreading

Although Mr. Collins manages to gets his proposal out before he is "run away by his feelings" (as if!), Lizzy certainly wants to run away after hearing him. Unlike "Slick Wick," Mr. Collins unfailingly puts his foot in his mouth. As Lizzy tells Jane, he is "a conceited, pompous, narrow-minded, silly man." She might very well have added that he repeats himself, uses a limited number of clichés ("the offered olive branch"), and is a sycophant and hypocrite. There he goes, a clergy advocating morals who dances *and* plays cards. Perhaps his sense of morality is rather untrustworthy. When he becomes the spokesperson for Fordyce and all those others who would limit women's lives, we understand this, too, is not to be trusted.

Yes, we hear about Mr. Darcy, but only in general, and except in the first part of the novel, we are not given access to his *thoughts*. We know he believes it will be difficult for the Bennet girls to marry well. We know he believes there are not six women he would consider accomplished. We know these things only because he voices them. As with Elizabeth, it may be hard to get Darcy's measure, we hear so much conflicting information on him!

When Darcy is overheard saying "*You are dancing with the only handsome girl in the room,*" this is heard as petulant ill humor. Does it represent his character or is he just having a bad night? Is Darcy miffed that Bingley has the nicest looking girl despite Darcy's higher social status? Often Darcy's behavior can be interpreted generously or meanly. Lizzy's mistake (her prejudice) is to interpret it meanly; for instance, that he is rude rather than shy, or that he is proud rather than in a bad mood. For instance, why does Darcy tolerate Bingley's sisters? Lizzy might have seen Darcy's patience and forbearance there.

Lizzy is a bad detective. Col. Fitzwilliam tells her Darcy keeps postponing his departure from his aunt's at Rosings. Why does Darcy do this? Though she tells Darcy what part of Rosings is her favorite walk so he will avoid it, instead he continues to run into her there. Indeed, Lizzy has much to learn.

Fathers and Disappointments

In many of Austen's novels, fathers are a disappointment. A pleasant evening with General Tilney? Impossible. Before our eyes, Mr. Woodhouse would have our asparagus and sweetbread whisked from the table for failing to meet his arbitrary standards; and the fire would be so warm we'd be drenched in sweat. Sir Walter

The frontispiece to the 1833 edition of Pride and Prejudice, *published by Richard Bentley. "She then told him what Mr. Darcy had voluntarily done for Lydia. He heard her with astonishment." Courtesy of the Burke Jane Austen Collection, Goucher College Library.*

Elliot? Most of us would rather chose to walk three miles and muddy a petticoat—or two—rather than sit with him and Lady Dalrymple. But Mr. Bennet? Mr. Bennet, "so odd a mixture of quick parts, sarcastic humour, reserve, and caprice," would be entertaining. How long, though, would it last? Especially if we are as interested in human nature as Lizzy? Would we not see the human cost to Mrs. Bennet of his humor that deprecates and misdirects? He aggravates his wife's nerves rather than relieving them. He can never come right out and say anything directly, "I will go see this stranger at Netherfield." "I have gone to see this stranger at Netherfield; he is very nice. His name is Bingley." He sports with her. Countering her worries about what will happen to her and her children if he dies, he admits to a different fantasy, "Let us hope for better things. . . . that I might be the survivor." Ouch. It is not for nothing that Martin Amis calls Mr. Bennet the "most cynical character in all Jane Austen."

We like him at first; we are laughing with him in the first chapter and those that follow, but soon we realize his is a dangerous cynicism, at least if one wishes to be an effective parent. The cynic speaks from an emotionally remote distance. Lizzy points out the effects of this on Lydia: "She has never been taught to think on serious subjects. . . . She has been given up to nothing but amusement and vanity. She has been allowed to dispose of her time in the most idle and frivolous manner." (Sounds like the feminist critiques from that time!)

Lady Catherine confronts Elizabeth in the first illustrated edition of Pride and Prejudice *published by Richard Bentley in 1833.*
Courtesy of the Burke Jane Austen Collection, Goucher College Library.

Three Refusals

Elizabeth *does* learn from her father. She has learned how to stand up for herself.

Lizzy (so very articulate in refusing) actually gets the opportunity to refuse three times (Collins, Darcy, Lady Catherine). These refusals indicate, as political analyses of the novel suggest, that *Pride and Prejudice* refuses to toe the line in terms of the conduct expectations for young women. Elizabeth will not marry without love; she will not respect the hierarchy of rank and class. For her misguided "journey," Lydia is not cast out of the house. Lydia, who is also "exuberant," in her "wild giddiness" makes Elizabeth's impertinence acceptable. But Lydia undergoes no education; she refuses the benefits of self-evaluation. Even when her aunt Gardiner speaks to her about serious matters, Lydia ignores her. Lydia laughs and feels no regrets; Elizabeth, self-reflecting, cannot always laugh and *will* feel regret.

Jane Austen magnificently juggles all of these story lines: the strangers coming to town, leaving town (sometimes precipitously, sometimes overstaying their welcome) alternately provoking confusion and happier feelings; the heroines going on journeys, to London, to Hunsford, to Devonshire, to Brighton. Almost a century ago, Reginald Farrer declared that *Pride and Prejudice* is "the greatest miracle of English literature." Austen created a novel not unlike Pemberly itself, Darcy's well-kept but unostentatious Derbyshire estate: "neither gaudy nor uselessly fine." Would Elizabeth ask us if we fall in love with the novel for its impertinence or for its liveliness of mind? We'll have to go back and reread it another time to see. Happy thought, indeed!

Shelves in the closet
Happy thought indeed

www.cafepress.com/Giftature

THE Sentence.

It is a truth universally acknowledged that Jane Austen kicks ass.

It is a truth universally acknowledged that the beginning line of a good novel will be endlessly copied. One of the best imitations out there—"it is a truth universally known that Everything is Funnier with Monkeys"—is the opening line of a book review by Paul Collins in the January 14-20, 2004, edition of the *Village Voice*. Mr. Collins reviews a reprinted Victorian sexual education manual starring a suit-wearing primate—something the Austenian Mr. Collins would have blushed quite deeply at, in fear of it offending his patroness.

A quick search on Google reveals that possibly no other sentence in English literature has suffered the flattery of imitation as often as the opening sentence of *Pride and Prejudice*. The *New York Times* alone has recycled the line in countless ways, causing its brightness to fade under the unoriginality of its successors.

From that first sentence we know that Jane Austen is challenging us to read beyond the words. After all, it is not a truth universally acknowledged that a single man in possession of a good fortune must be in want of a wife, except perhaps for mothers in possession of an excess of marriageable young girls. It is the best scene setter in the world, telling us: don't expect the whole truth, and I'm not starting with one.

In one sentence, Austen sweeps away generalized statements taken for fact. Her readers would recognize the style from many eighteenth-century moralists who offered sweeping statements.

Did Austen take the idea from one of her favorite writers? In Samuel Johnson's *Rambler*, Hymenaeus, a young bachelor, complains about the "vultures" who employed eloquence and artifices to promote their schemes of attracting him to their daughters, saying "I was known to possess a fortune, and to want a wife." Literary critic Ellen Moers points out that "All of Jane Austen's opening paragraphs, and the best of her first sentences, have money in them." The opening sentence to *Emma* reads: "Emma Woodhouse, handsome, clever, and rich, with a comfortable home and happy disposition. . . ." And *Mansfield Park,* "About thirty years ago, Miss Maria Ward of Huntington, with only seven thousand pounds. . . ."

But the opening sentence of *Pride and Prejudice* is importantly paired with a second sentence, often dropped from consideration when under discussion.

> It is a truth universally acknowledged, that a single man in possession of a good fortune, must be in want of a wife.

> However little known the feeling or views of such a man may be on his first entering into a neighbourhood, this truth is so well fixed in the minds of the surroundings families, that he is considered as the rightful property of some one or other of their daughters.

Upon the rhythm of these first two sentences, Richard Jenkyns sees the influence of the weekly public reading of the Psalms in church. With a father who was rector of Steventon, Austen would have been a regular churchgoer. Jenkyns proposes,

> She will have heard readings from the Psalms in church almost every week of her life: their rhythms, with verse answering to verse, or half-verse to half-verse, echoing, amplifying, or

explaining, were bound to sink deep into her consciousness:

> The heavens declare the glory of God; and the firmament sheweth his handiwork.
> One day telleth another: and one night certifieth another.

Such are the rhythms that open *Pride and Prejudice.*

The rhythms are lost when the novel is made into a movie. Then the ironic tone of the narrator must be picked up by one of the characters. In the 1980 BBC miniseries, Elizabeth speaks the line to Charlotte Lucas. In the 1995 BBC version, Elizabeth speaks it to her sisters after church, upon hearing her mother tell her father of Bingley's moving to Netherfield. And in the 1940 and 2005 versions, it goes missing in action. Bridget Jones, contemporary manifestation of Elizabeth Bennet, proclaims, "It is a truth universally acknowledged that when one part of your life starts going okay, another falls spectacularly to pieces." In *Reading Lolita in Tehran,* we find it rewritten as "It is a truth universally acknowledged that a Muslim man, regardless of his fortune, must be in want of a nine-year-old virgin wife."

Austen wants us to rewrite that sentence. Emily Auerbach in *Searching for Jane Austen* suggests: "If we deduce that single women want husbands with fortunes, we simultaneously must conclude that ironic authors want readers with perception. From the start, Austen asks us to approach her novel in the spirit of intelligent and subversive questioning."

The Importance of a Good Carriage

For Regency gentility, carriages in all their forms were a big deal. Transportation was on the rise during Jane Austen's life, and for the first time tourism was becoming a lucrative industry. Trips to the healing waters of Bath, the metropolis of London, and other sites became more frequent, demanding not only more carriages but better roads. In an effort to make some money from the interest in travel, and to improve the rutted and bumpy carriageways, toll roads and turnpikes were constructed. Taxes were also placed on most carriages as a means to support the war effort.

This meant that owning any sort of vehicle was costly. In turn, this meant that carriages were not only means of conveyance, but were demarcations of social status as well. For an instance of expense, take the Bennets' coach. This was the ideal vehicle for a family of their size. It could seat six inside, three each on the rear and front benches, plus one

How to Gammon the Deep Ones, or the Way to Overturn a Coach, *Isaac Cruikshank, 1791. Courtesy of The Lewis Walpole Library, Yale University. 791.1.1.5.*

on a seat that could be pulled out. More could sit on top and, and one next to the coachman in the "box," or coachman's seat. A coach was typically pulled by four horses—which meant that the owner had to pay for the coach, the tax on the coach, the coachman, the coachman's clothes, the horses, and servants to care for the horses. Imagine paying this—in addition to supporting a household of five daughters, a wife, servants, and cooks—and still being considered to be at the low end of the area's wealth! This would mean that Mr. Clifford of Austen's juvenilia, who owns "a Coach and four," as well as "a Coach, a Chariot, a Chaise, a Landeau, a Landeaulet, a Phaeton, a Gig, a Whisky, an italian [sic] Chair, a Buggy, a Curricle and a wheelbarrow," was rich beyond measure—a Bill Gates of the Regency. The tale he appears in is a comic fantasy; only members of the monarchy would have had enough to support all these carriages. On the other end of the spectrum—impropriety aside—the cost of keeping a horse means Marianne cannot accept "Queen Mab," a mare Willoughby wanted to give her.

A newly married couple would start their lives together with a new carriage. When Mrs. Bennet believes she will soon have a daughter married, part of her fantasies include "the necessary preparations of settlements, new carriages, and wedding-clothes."

"Carriage" was the general term that applied to all means of conveyance. In construction terms, it referred specifically to the mechanism connecting the wheels together underneath the main body and is still used in automobile terminology today. There were many types of carriages in use at this time, as can be seen by the fictional Mr. Clifford's sizable collection above. Most carried with them certain social connotations. A gig and a curricle were both light, roofless, two-wheeled vehicles that could seat two passengers. Mr. Collins, Sir Edward Denham, and John Thorpe drove gigs. A curricle, however, is made to fit two horses. The curricle owner, then, would typically be seen as having more money than (and being socially superior to) the owner of a gig, who could only afford a single horse. Darcy, Bingley, Willoughby, Henry Tilney, and Charles Musgrove all drove curricles.

The barouche was the most expensive vehicle of the day. It was so expensive that no luggage rack was included—it was assumed that anyone who would buy a barouche would be sending their luggage in a separate cart, replete with more horses and crew, along behind them. Though Lady Catherine de Bourgh owns a barouche, she arrives at Longbourn in "a chaise and four." In *Emma,* Mrs. Elton continually chatters on about her friends the Sucklings' barouche-landau, a sort of "convertible" barouche—but no other specific types of carriages are noted in the novel! Every other instance of transportation is generalized. It is only Mrs. Elton, who makes much too much of social standing and small details, who is obsessed with the types of carriages. Of Emma's several complaints about Mrs. Elton, one is of her officiousness regarding Jane Fairfax. Emma has caught the

[Boy Bringing Round a Citizen's Curricle.] *As curricles actually used two horses and gigs only one, this gig may have been misclassified.*
Thomas Rowlandson, 1787. *Courtesy of The Lewis Walpole Library, Yale University 787.12.15.1.*

"name dropping" and in her analysis of Mrs. Elton to Mr. Knightley and Mrs. Weston parrots them back: "I cannot imagine that she will not be continually detailing her magnificent intentions, from the procuring her a permanent situation to the including her in those delightful exploring parties which are to take place in the barouche-landau."

In *Mansfield Park,* Sir Thomas sends Fanny in the carriage when she is invited to the parsonage to eat with the Crawfords. This shows that, newly back from Antigua, Sir Thomas has figured something out about Fanny—that she is marriageable.

Mary Musgrove, in reasoning out the results of her sister Anne's future happiness, imagines her "the mistress of a very

pretty landaulette." This was a one-horse chaise that could hold two people and was often thought of as a "lady's vehicle."

Oftentimes, as in the cases above, Austen will make pointed choices as to who drives what. Those of youthful vigor are often seen driving gigs and curricles, which allow the driver and passenger to show themselves off. These are also faster vehicles, thereby making them more perilous. Carriages were often in danger of becoming stuck, overturning upon hitting large bumps or rounding tight corners, and having wheels fall off—not to mention the threat of highwaymen.

These dangers were often overlooked, however, for the convenience of travel. Even those who could not afford carriages of their own could still travel by stage-

Return From Brighton, or A Journey to Town for the Winter Season, *Dent, 1786.*
Courtesy of The Lewis Walpole Library, Yale University 786.10.23.1.

coaches, though many commoners would go their whole lives without once stepping onto a carriage. Mail coaches were the most fashionable choice by any who had to travel this way, and the hackney coach the least fashionable. The mail coach had the benefit of being faster, as it had to keep a tightly scheduled route, and was protected by a guard. The hackney coach, on the other hand, had no horses of its own, and instead had to rent horses out from inn to inn. No reputable young lady would have stepped onto a hackney coach unless otherwise forced, or unless she was a certain young lady from *Pride and Prejudice.* In this case, she and Wickham switch from a chaise to a hackney coach (which provides anonymity and often the opportunity to have sex).

Carriages were not only how people traveled but also, for the young women who people Austen's novels, the means for experiencing the world outside their small village. Young ladies could not travel alone; even Jane Austen herself awaited the arrival of one or another of her brothers to begin her trips. A chaperone and a carriage together bring about the travels of Catherine Morland to Bath, Lizzy Bennet to Derbyshire, the Dashwoods to London. Sandra Gilbert and Susan Gubar in *The Madwoman in the Attic* believe the liberation provided by such travels accounts for "a recurrent interest in the horse and carriage" from the juvenilia to Austen's post-humously published fragments. Runaways, too, abound in her fiction: "young women whose imaginations are tainted by romantic notions which fuel their excessive materialism or sexuality, and who would do anything with anyone in order to escape their families." They catalog seven young women "runaways" in the novels, but we won't reveal those young women's secrets—we'll leave that to Austen.

A great example of the symbolism of carriages in a novel is the way the Crofts share driving responsibilities, the one balancing the other. Anne Elliot observes them as she rides with them in their gig. Mrs. Croft calls to her husband:

"My dear Admiral, that post! we shall certainly take that post." But by coolly giving the reins a better direction herself, they happily passed the danger; and by once afterwards judiciously putting out her hand, they neither fell into a rut, nor ran foul of a dung-cart; and Anne, with some amusement at their style of driving, which she imagined no bad representation of the general guidance of their affairs, found herself safely deposited by them at the cottage.

Missed Moments of Importance in the Life of Carriages:

- *Not* running into the post with Admiral and Mrs. Croft and Anne.
- *Almost* being purchased by the apothecary in *Emma*.
- Being refused for Jane Bennet to go in to Netherfield; being refused by Lizzy Bennet to take her to Netherfield; being refused by Mrs. Bennet to pick up Lizzy and Jane from Netherfield.
- Being refused to be ridden in by Lizzy when Lady Catherine De Bourgh offers her a ride back from Rosings to Longbourn.
- *Almost* succeeding in killing Willoughby.
- Jane Fairfax will probably never ride in Mr. Suckling's barouche-landau.

"Pray forgive me, if I have been very presuming, or at least do not punish me so far, as to exclude me from P. I shall never be quite happy till I have been all around the park. A low phaeton, with a nice little pair of ponies, would be the very thing." Mrs. Gardiner *in* Pride and Prejudice.

Two young ladies in calico gowns, *from* Gallery of Fashion *by Humphry Repton. Victoria & Albert Museum, London, UK/The Bridgeman Art Library.*

Why I Married Her. By Mr. Bennet.

Our authors speculate on the strange history that must certainly have predated the marriage of Mr. Bennet and the once-upon-a-time Miss Gardiner. He is seldom forthcoming with his wife: "Not all that Mrs. Bennet, however, with the assistance of her five daughters, could ask on the subject was sufficient to draw from her husband any satisfactory" response to most questions she put to him. We imagine him in a more garrulous state, explaining one of the greatest mysteries of all in *Pride and Prejudice:* How he fell in love with her.

From a Set of Rowlandson's Etchings. *1790.*
Courtesy of The Lewis Walpole Library, Yale University. 790.6.27.1.

Her seeming imprudence was matched perhaps only by my seeming sagacity; to meet someone who would boldly place down an exorbitant amount of money for a bonnet whilst I would hem and haw over the shilling difference between cold meats for the month was reckless excitement for me—evidence of the stimulating life found in the social circles I inhabited. I very much fancied myself the sober gentleman, despite the fact that on certain nights I could be found to be quite the opposite. I suppose that in the days of my youth I was wont to have a habit of spending too much of my income at a go, and then have to tighten my purse for the remainder of the month. My future wife's proclivity for repeated, though moderate, expenditures was at least constant in its injudiciousness.

She was possessed at once of all the delights and indelicacies of youthful exuberance, and my attempts at rectitude were quickly broken down. I can still recall perfectly her first flirting smiles when we were introduced, and her eagerness to accept my hand at our first dance. What a lively person she was; I see it in Lizzy now.

My acquaintances at the time—barristers mostly—were quite dull and insisted on frequent dinner parties. I had a habit of making guarded comments to the soon-to-be Mrs. Bennet, poking fun at those who we were invited to sit at table with. They, with their straight laces, did not pick up on my jests, but my wife-to-be would typically fall into a coughing fit as she tried to suppress her laughter at our hosts' expense.

It was not very long after we met that we entered a very short engagement. She had fallen instantly in love with me; once an idea occupies her thoughts, it cannot be loosed by even the most titanic effort, and her loyalties to those she chooses can become quite fierce. For my part, I loved her, too, though perhaps not with the same ardor that she experienced for me. Her charms were great, her affection unequaled, and she was quite becoming—I was also entranced by the fact that anyone could love someone so dry as myself.

I do not mean to sound that I had settled for her by any means. Her care and excitement complement, I believe, my tendency towards sedate study and reserve. She is, and always has been, genuinely heartfelt, and expresses as much as is in her heart; though the contents of that organ have been known to change markedly from moment to moment. There is also a single-mindedness of action and thought about her, which is alternatively charming and infuriating. One can imagine her as a wayward flood burst from its dam, and I, in those unfortunate sometimes, am that dam.

Admirers: An Interview with Joan Klingel Ray, author of *Jane Austen for Dummies*

Q: First, why Jane Austen?

A: Why not? Seriously, Jane Austen is clearly one of the greatest novelists to write in English. After her death, British men and women of letters started to write about this hitherto anonymous novelist and her novels, recognizing her skill in characterization, her mastery of dialogue, and even her satirical streak. All of these aspects of her writing appeal greatly to me, and clearly to many other persons who have made her the most popular classic novelist in the English-speaking world.

Q: To what do you attribute the current fascination with all things Austen?

A: Austen is unique in that while she is a classic novelist who is studied by academics and taught in universities, she also appeals to what we might call the "common reader"—the ordinary person who picks up her novels simply for the pleasure of reading them. Austen has a certain cachet because she is highly respected by the critics. And because she is very popular but her works are in the public domain, anyone can write a screen script and take as many of her great lines as they need; likewise, they can write sequels and other takeoffs on Austen. But let's not kid ourselves: there is only one Jane Austen. And while *Emma* will be read by university students and "common readers" scores of years from now, the sequels and spin-offs will be forgotten.

Q: When did you first read Jane Austen?

A: I read *Pride and Prejudice* when I was about thirteen or fourteen.

Q: Do you remember what you felt reading it?

A: I felt what I imagine most thirteen-year-old girls felt when reading *P&P*: I admired Elizabeth Bennet for her nerve and cleverness, and I loved Mr. Darcy.

Q: What would you recommend to someone just discovering Jane Austen?

A: First, I would encourage newcomers *not* to see the films or TV versions of her novels: most scriptwriters tend to think they are better writers than Jane Austen. (Wait until you see the new "Mansfield Park" on *Masterpiece Theatre*; you'd think they would have learned something from the commercial and critical failure of Patricia Rozema's *Mansfield Park* film!) I would recommend reading the novels in this order: *Pride and Prejudice, Persuasion, Emma, Northanger Abbey, Mansfield Park,* and *Sense and Sensibility*. I think this order eases the reader into Austen's language and syntax, which is quite sophisticated. Also, I think this order draws readers into Austen's canon by the nature of the "stories." Readers should also be aware that Austen is a satirist and uses irony; readers need to be able to hear the narrator's voice for what it is.

Q: As the author of *Jane Austen for Dummies,* what sort of responsibility to Jane Austen did you feel you had?

A: When I was asked to do this book—and I had never written anything as a trade publication—I decided that readers did not need plot summaries; rather, I wanted readers of Austen to have a clearer picture of the cultural context of her novels that Austen, of course, expected her contemporary readers to understand immediately. Austen writes about human nature: people never change, but society's rules do. Readers of Austen need to know the rules of Austen's society so that the plots and the characters make sense. This is what I wanted to do with the book so that readers would have a clearer understanding of what they read.

Q: What was the most surprising thing you experienced or learned about Jane Austen or her novels as you worked on your book?

A: I was surprised to learn how many screen and radio adaptations of Austen's novels were out there.

Q: As President of the North American Friends of Chawton House library, tell us about Chawton House.

A: Jane Austen's brother Edward was adopted by their father's wealthy cousins, Mr. and Mrs. Thomas Knight. The Knights had extensive property in Hampshire and Kent, and having no children, wanted to be sure that the property stayed within the family. The Hampshire property was the Chawton estate, consisting of about 270 acres. Chawton House is the manor house on the estate; the house dates back to Elizabeth I. As generations of Knights (Edward Austen took the surname Knight) inherited the estate and the manor house, they could not afford the upkeep of the mansion or the taxes on the property. Sandy Lerner, a member of the Jane Austen Society of North America and the founder, with her husband, of CISCO Systems, rescued the estate and house from being turned into a golf resort when she bought the Chawton property in the mid 1990s. Sandy hired the best people to help with the restoration of the house and land: historical landscape designers and architects, keeping in mind that as a historical property, the mansion was under various preservation laws in England. Sandy has turned the mansion, Chawton House, into the Chawton House Library for the Study of Early English Women Writers—writers who influenced Austen, by and large. The CHL is a wonderful research library for scholars. And the grounds, which have been restored to the way Jane Austen would have known them, are likewise a wonderful information source for historians of gardening and landscape architecture. The mansion, itself, is an architectural historian's dream as it represents many different styles of building over the generations of owners.

Q: What would you advise a first-time visitor to Chawton House and other Austen-related landmarks to be sure to do?

A: Visitors should visit Jane Austen's House in Chawton: this was the bailiff's cottage on Edward's estate that he refurbished for his mother and two unmarried sisters (Jane and Cassandra) in 1809. The house is now a museum. While there, one can walk up the road to the Chawton House Library and first see St. Nicholas's Church, in the back of which are buried Jane Austen's mother and sister, the two Cassandras. Ordinarily, persons cannot just go into the Library as the mansion is a research library, and like all research libraries, it has rules and requirements for entering and using it. But then drive to Winchester—just about twenty minutes— and go to Winchester Cathedral to see Austen's tomb. In London, persons can go to the British Library, where Austen's writing desk is always on display. By the way, I devote a chapter in *Jane Austen for Dummies* to the "Ten Best Austen-Related Places to Visit—and How to Get to Them!"

Q: Have you ever been a part of a book club that read only Jane Austen? If so, what was it like?

A: No, but as a Professor of English at the University of Colorado, Colorado Springs, whose field is late eighteenth- and early nineteenth-century literature, I regularly teach a senior seminar on Austen. This is a popular course, and I have had students from all walks of life in that class. The most wonderful aspect is seeing and hearing how students (some are army veterans; some are twenty-year-old females; some are middle-aged housewives who are finally getting around to earning that English degree they always wanted) react to Austen's novels. We have wonderful discussions about the novels, and by the time we are halfway through the semester—we read the novels in chronological order of composition—the students are able to talk about Austen's style and skills with considerable sophistication. Interestingly, students who have seen the Austen-based films and TV shows all end up loving the novels much more than the screen versions.

Q: Why join the Jane Austen Society?

A: The Jane Austen Society of North America (JASNA) is comprised of nearly three thousand persons (mostly nonacademics) joined by a love of and respect for the work of Jane Austen. JASNA has about sixty-four regional groups around the United States and Canada that enable members who live near a region to meet with their fellow Austen fans to discuss Jane Austen. Members receive three newsletters annually, plus a journal called *Persuasions* that contains articles about Austen, her works, and her times. There is also *Persuasions On-Line*, which prints articles that have an even wider dissemination. People can find out about JASNA at www.jasna.org.

Q: What is the most startling thing someone has said to you about Jane Austen or her novels?

A: Actually, there are two events, both very different. One occurred while I was JASNA president (three terms, 2000-2006). I visited many of the regions to give talks and meet members. After spending an evening chatting with a JASNA region's leadership group, the local leader said to me, "I bet Jane Austen was like you!" The other event is with my students: I am always thrilled when they recognize how relevant Austen's writing is to their own lives.

Q: When did you last read Jane Austen?

A: I just finished teaching the Austen Seminar in mid-December, 2007, two weeks before answering this question.

Q: Is there a Jane Austen-associated gift that you treasure?

A: I have a unique gift that was presented to me by the JASNA regional group of Boise, Idaho: a beautiful hand-painted silk scarf with Austen's profile on it.

Q: How do you observe Jane Austen's birthday?

A: I celebrate December 16th with our local JASNA regional group: we have an Austen birthday tea and conclude it by toasting Jane Austen.

Q: If you have an opinion on it, what makes a Janeite? Do you think the name should be changed to "Austenite" or something else that uses her last name rather than her first?

A: The word "Janeite" was coined in 1895 and has come to mean someone who is wild about Jane Austen unquestioningly. I always find it interesting that folks refer to Austen as "Jane." With what other writer do we do that? We don't call

Shakespeare "William" or Hemingway "Ernest." Yet so many readers feel personally attached to Austen when they read her novels that they get to be on a first-name basis with her. So I think it is a mark of Austen's uniqueness in the way her readers relate to her that they want to call her Jane. I see nothing wrong with that. But when I speak of her, I speak of Austen. And I hope that Janeites have come to be well-informed admirers of Austen who understand her craft.

Q: In working so closely with Jane Austen, did you discover something about yourself, a sort of Austen-mediated self-revelation?

A: I did not see this at first, but I have had—since I first taught Austen nearly thirty years ago (I was twenty-seven) at the university level—students tell me that they see Elizabeth Bennet in me! When I asked them why, they say it is because I have great self-confidence, that I have a good sense of humor, and that I am quick with thoughts. When this occurred for about the third time, I was reminded of my first year as a graduate student at Brown in the PhD program in English: the Director of Graduate Studies met mid-year with each student in the program. When it was my turn to meet with her, she said that the faculty felt I had "incredible self-possession." As I look back on that, I see that Elizabeth Bennet's key quality is her self-possession. (Keep in mind that when I was in graduate school, I was not working closely with Austen.) This has led me, when I teach *P&P,* to remind students that "pride" can be both a good and bad thing. Granted, it is one of the deadly sins! But an honest sense of one's self-worth is important in life. I would like to see my students—all of them—develop "incredible self-possession."

Sense and Sensibility

Austen's *Sense and Sensibility*, the first of her novels to be published, often has the misfortune to be read as *Sense* **versus** *Sensibility*. Then, too, it is often situated as *Sense and Sensibility* **versus** *Pride and Prejudice*, as though it is the lesser sister. We protest the unfairness of both of these oppositions. Neither cold, hard sense nor the most sweepingly romantic sensibilities suffice on their own throughout this novel, as is evidenced by the close friendship and seemingly mutual dependence between the two sisters Elinor and Marianne. Each must realize the truth or correctness in some part of the behavior of the other in order to become successful and happy. As to the other count, if indeed the manuscript her father offered to a publisher in 1797 was an early version of *Pride and Prejudice* (it was rejected sight unseen), then *Sense and Sensibility* was accepted for publication more readily than its more famous sister, *Pride and Prejudice*. This fact may not alone determine its merit, but it enjoyed success as a novel and went into a second edition within two years. Numerous editions followed, and the novel was much beloved by both Jane Austen's close family members and by readers across the nation. It was highly praised, as it is today, for the reality inherent in its portrayal of human nature.

A claim of unfairness in the treatment of this novel seems appropriate,

The title page of the 1811 first edition of Sense and Sensibility.
Courtesy of the Burke Jane Austen Collection, Goucher College Library.

for the novel itself begins with just that unfairness. Mrs. Dashwood and her three daughters, Elinor, Marianne, and Margaret, stand to be driven away from their family estate after the death of her husband and their father, Mr. Henry Dashwood. The beneficiary of the old man's death is a son from a previous marriage, a Mr. John Dashwood. He and his ungracious wife Fanny do not even wait for the Mrs. and Misses Dashwood to vacate the house before moving in. In one of the most memorable depictions of avariciousness working on a pliable mind, Fanny Dashwood convinces her husband, John, not to honor his promise to his father to look after his loved ones. We read, transfixed, as together they decrease the original contemplated sum from £3,000 to none.

It falls upon Elinor to conjure anything like a polite reception for the new occupants of the Norland estate. Marianne and her mother most dramatically "gave themselves up wholly to their sorrow, seeking increase of wretchedness in every reflection that could afford it, and resolved against ever admitting consolation in the future." Margaret, only thirteen, figures much less in the novel than a filmgoer might suppose. Mrs. Dashwood lingers at her beloved Norland long enough to witness a favorable turn of events for her eldest daughter, Elinor. The arrival of Fanny Dashwood's brother, Mr. Edward Ferrars, constitutes the beginning of a marked friendship between the two young people, and Mrs. Dashwood is optimistic enough to hope for a match.

Edward, currently a gentleman of no profession, harbors some desire to become a clergyman. This would mean a nice, but certainly not extravagant sort of living for himself and Elinor if they were to be married. Mutual affection shows, though certainly not enough for Marianne's taste. Too much, however, for Fanny Dashwood, who takes the first opportunity to make clear to Mrs. Dashwood that it is expected that Edward will marry well.

Mrs. Dashwood's relative Sir John Middleton offers Barton Cottage as a home and so off they go, with a "set of breakfast china" which in Fanny Dashwood's selfish eyes, is "twice as handsome as what belongs to this house." Arriving at Barton Cottage, they realize that the proximity to the great house at which Sir John and his family live has its demerits. They are expected to join them frequently for tea or dinner. At Barton Park, as well, are Lady Middleton's mother, Mrs. Jennings, and Colonel Brandon, a great friend of Sir John and owner of one of the nearby estates.

The favorite subject among this circle soon becomes Colonel Brandon's growing affection for Marianne. Marianne is not interested and from the description of Colonel Brandon, the reader is not surprised. While walking in the rain one afternoon with Margaret, Marianne takes a rather nasty fall down a hill. A dashing unknown gentleman runs to her rescue, scoops her up into his arms, and carries her home. It is a Mr. John Willoughby, Byronic hero *par excellence,* staying at nearby Allenham with a wealthy cousin. Each is immediately smitten with the other.

Marianne, Margaret, and Mrs. Dashwood soon have eyes for no one but Willoughby. Elinor resists and cautions Marianne against her too fervent feelings. On the day of a planned excursion to Whitwell, the party is halted when Colonel Brandon receives an urgent letter and rushes off. With no explanation from Brandon himself, Mrs. Jennings speculates to Elinor her suspicions about Colonel Brandon's "natural" (that is illegitimate) daughter, Miss Williams. Marianne and Willoughby disappear immediately on a carriage ride and are not heard of again until their return much later in the day. They had gone to Allenham, the estate that Willoughby is assumedly to inherit upon his cousin's death. This would be without the owner's permission, though she was in the house at the time of their touring it. This is particularly shocking. Certainly, there could be no doubt of the attachment between the two young people. Eventually, Willoughby manages to secure an audience with Marianne while her mother and sisters will be absent at Barton Park. Upon their return home, Mrs. Dashwood and Margaret expect to find Marianne engaged to Willoughby. Instead, they find both are very distressed: Marianne, in tears, rushes from the room. Willoughby has been ordered by his cousin immediately to London.

Willoughby's sudden departure plunges Marianne into deep despair and Elinor into speculation. Are they engaged or are they not? Elinor feels she cannot ask her sister and she is troubled for her. In the midst of Marianne's outpouring of grief, Edward Ferrars arrives. Edward stays a week with the family, and Elinor notes a dejected manner. Upon his departure, and unlike her sister's choice of solitude and gloom, Elinor seeks activity and society.

Throughout the book, Elinor is associated with sense, which "so well supported her," and Marianne with sensibility. But, neither can claim a perfect attitude or outlook. Scholars disagree precisely on just how much "sensibility" Elinor in the end possesses, and how much sense can be found in Marianne. As Carol Shields points out in *Jane Austen: A Life*, "We have real sisters here, not convenient contrarieties." And

How to Pluck a Goose. *Thomas Rowlandson.*
Courtesy of The Lewis Walpole Library, Yale University 802.6.10.1.

being real sisters, they do not negate each other.

Jane Austen has established several lines of tension in her story—Brandon's mysterious behavior, Edward's mysterious behavior, Willoughby's mysterious behavior. As much as the women of the novel were dispossessed of their home because of male inheritance, the women are now dispossessed of security and confidence by the equivocal behavior of the men in their lives. Now is the time for Austen to further complicate life for the Dashwoods by throwing at them several new individuals—most of them coarse, rude, and vulgar, and that's only our first thoughts about them! Uncomfortable times for Elinor and Marianne; humorous times for the readers. "What a sweet woman Lady Middleton is!"—this surprising comment about a woman most readers would not call sweet. And how did the Dashwood sisters respond to such insipidity? "Marianne was silent; it was impossible for her to say what she did not feel, however trivial the occasion, and upon Elinor therefore the whole task of telling lies when politeness required it, always fell."

The coarse and the vulgar, the rude and the impolite, seem to know how to find their way to Barton Park. First it is Mrs. Jennings's other daughter, Mrs. Palmer, and her husband. Then, when Mrs. Jennings encounters her relatives the Misses Steele by chance in Exeter, she invites them to stay. The result? Insipidity abounds in conversation.

Miss Anne Steele is vulgar and artless. Lucy tries to cover for her sister's more blatant signs of social coarseness, but alas, her lack of education limits her

greatly. But then, horrors!, and despite such short an acquaintance, Lucy takes Elinor aside and tells her in whispered conversation of a secret engagement. Now as we move into the heart of the story, things heat up. (Marianne's fever, later in the novel, is a reminder of just how hot things have gotten.) A stay in London will offer opportunities to be further snubbed by their sister-in-law Fanny, among others, to be bombarded with questions about money by their brother, to experience distress at an engagement, and to register stories about elopements and abandonment.

But even yet, the sisters' tribulations in London are not quite at an end. They must still endure the arrival of the Misses Steele. And they meet Mr. Robert Ferrars, Edward's brother.

Robert Ferrars has got to be one of our favorite secondary characters. One critic gamely tries to find in him whispers of Austen's interest in style for style's sake examining at length his ordering of a toothpick holder (selecting the "size, shape, and ornaments" with "the ivory, the gold, and the pearls" takes a quarter of an hour). But this is not why we are thankful for Robert Ferrars. It is because he is the person that Elinor does not wish to pay "the compliment of rational opposition."

By the end of the novel, much is sorted out. Luckily for Mrs. Jennings and the Middletons, the great gossips at Barton Hall, Mrs. Dashwood and Margaret stay at Barton. Margaret fortunately is old enough by the end of our story to fall prey to all the teasing and winkling that any Jennings or Middleton could desire.

Willoughby v. Brandon

Honorable William Galperin for the prosecution:

Ladies and Gentlemen of the Jury. In this courtroom you have heard testimony regarding the actions of Colonel Brandon, that sometime in the year 1797, he willfully plotted and executed a plan to separate Marianne Dashwood and John Willoughby from each other and to acquire Marianne for himself. Let me review for you what you have heard:

That on the evening of Monday, November 6, 1797, Willoughby's behavior "declared at once his affection and happiness." But the next morning he left Marianned in haste. He had been accosted by Mrs. Smith of Allenham, who had learned of his affair with Eliza Williams. As Willoughby was to call it: "a discovery took place." Yes, as Willoughby has testified, "Mrs. Smith had somehow or other been informed, I imagine by some distant relation, whose interest it was to deprive me of her favour, of an affair, a connection—but I need not explain myself farther." What a discovery! Mrs. Smith, from whom he would inherit her estate, had

learned that he had gotten a young woman pregnant and she offered to forgive the past if he would marry that young woman. This is what caused Willoughby's change of plans. But notice, even Willoughby, at that time, could not imagine how Mrs. Smith learned of this. Some "distant relation" whose interest it was to deprive him of her favor? Ah, he should have looked much closer. Wasn't there someone who lived nearby who had all the desire to deprive Willoughby of Mrs. Smith's favor? And wasn't there someone much closer who had the information to give?

We know that Colonel Brandon acquired information on his ward Eliza, pregnant and abandoned, on Monday, October 30. Though he immediately dashed away to follow up on this report, he had one week's time to inform Mrs. Smith of Willoughby's responsibilities in the matter. He had plenty of time to write a letter or even to visit her without returning to Barton Park.

Consider again. We have heard Willoughby testify that his fiancée Miss Sophia Grey had heard "some vague report" as Willoughby called it, "of my attachment to some young lady in Devonshire."

Willoughby has testified that "information leaked out" to his aunt; again, information leaked out to his fiancée.

Who possessed this information, ladies and gentlemen, and had an interest in it being released? Who had the means to do it, being in London at the same time as Sophia herself?

A crime requires four things only: motive, the ability to do it, the will to do it, and the opportunity to do it.

First, who had the motive? Colonel Brandon: he had both the anger that had caused him to fight a duel with Willoughby and the love for Marianne, someone whom he knew, back in October, did not love him and had declared she could not love him. He had a double motive for revealing the information and breaking up Willoughby and Marianne.

Second, who had the ability to do it? Who possessed this damaging information? Colonel Brandon. Not some "distant relation," but Colonel Brandon.

Third, who had the will to do it? Colonel Brandon. He, of all the people, has the experience from his years in the military of doing things that courteous people would never consider. He was willing to violate the law and fight a duel. How much easier it would be to slip some information at the appropriate moment to the appropriate person.

Finally, who had the opportunity? The opportunity to write a letter or visit a neighbor? To encounter another person in London?

To all of these the answer, the only answer is: COLONEL BRANDON!

Who was the source of information to Mrs. Smith?

Who was the source of the information to Sophia?

It is none other than Colonel Brandon.

Of all the possible individuals present, he had the information that could accomplish this goal. And, of all the possible individuals, he had the ability to get around, to travel, to depart hastily (as we all know he had done).

Willoughby even recognized that Colonel Brandon was spreading the information, and that he was biased. Recall that he warned Elinor, "Remember from whom you received the account."

But that is not all that we place at Colonel Brandon's feet. Why did he withhold from Marianne this information before Marianne became emotionally involved with Willoughby, this very important information he was so ready to dispense to Mrs. Smith and Sophia? Why was Brandon not direct with her? Brandon desired Marianne practically from the moment he met her. Wouldn't he have wanted what was best for her, and if protecting her from Willoughby was what he believed to be best, why didn't he do that in a way that would have succeeded earlier? By talking with her, or Elinor, or her mother?

Maybe, just maybe, he wanted, he needed, to prove to her that second attachments succeed. Did he withhold the information knowing, hoping, that he would eventually get her on the rebound? That he would be *her* second attachment?

When he could have done something, he did not. Then, he comes to London and observes the results of his manipulation.

He wasn't patient, he was calculated!

He wasn't generous, he was manipulative.

It is Colonel Brandon who manipulated the events. His actions later in the novel prove this. Why wouldn't Brandon communicate directly to Edward Ferrars his offer of a living? When he offers the living at Delaford to Edward on the condition that Edward not marry, why was that? Insisting that Edward remain a bachelor ensures that Elinor has access to the rectory, and where Elinor is, so too is Marianne, since Elinor cannot go there unaccompanied. Why does he cause Elinor to make the offer rather than doing so himself? Again, to strengthen Elinor's ties with Edward, which, again, ensures Marianne will be nearby. Why was that living so spartan? To make sure that Edward stayed unmarried. And there was the implicit promise, or shall we call it really a threat? If I "think very differently of him from what I do now" . . . Edward needed to perform in a certain way to gain Brandon's approval. Brandon may help in the future depending on if Elinor is able to get Edward to end his engagement. . . . Consider, Brandon is promising Elinor much.

Some people suspect him. At times, Mrs. Jennings is offended by Brandon. And so too Mr. John Dashwood. We have heard how he inquired about Brandon's motive, and that he doubted it was disinterested.

Colonel Brandon—troublemaker. Disrupter of the course of the true love. Using his authority and information behind the scenes to manipulate information, to manipulate lives.

Now, Ladies and Gentlemen, what say ye, innocent or guilty?

Honorable Joan Klingel Ray for the defense:

Beware, jury, of convicting someone on appearance alone. Yes, you have heard of flannel coats, of how he is neither "young nor very gay." We have heard that he is "so grave and so dull." Is that a reason to convict an honorable man? It is Mrs. Jennings who believes Colonel Brandon to fall in love quickly, attributing him with it when he first met Marianne in September. But we know that she is "remarkably quick in the discovery of attachments."

In his life, Colonel Brandon has been treated cruelly by many men, starting with his father and his brother. The woman he loved was given to his brother. He has seen the result of cads who love and dump women, not just with his beloved Eliza, but also with her illegitimate daughter, whom he has cared for as she has grown. Indeed, back when Eliza was forced to marry his elder brother, the younger Brandon, ever honorable, even "procured an exchange," meaning he transferred his military regiment, so that he could leave England with the intention of "promo[ting] the happiness of both [Eliza and his brother] by removing from her for years." Even as a young man, then, Brandon displayed generosity and unselfish love for Eliza, hoping for the best for her and her new husband.

How is it that Willoughby, the scoundrel, deceiver, the man who would sacrifice love for money, who would bend to what he supposed to be his aunt's wishes, how is it this Willoughby has become the victim, when instead he left victims in his wake? Yes, we are all touched by Elinor Dashwood's report of his speech at Cleveland. But what in it can be verified? Are we really to conclude that Colonel Brandon wrote a letter to himself that called him suddenly from the Middleton house on the day of the planned visit to Whitwell, as Willoughby charged that day?

Think of how Willoughby talked of him with Marianne. Is it a crime to be seen by others as dull, when in reality he was worried sick about his ward? After all, his ward, Eliza Williams, had been missing eight months. How this Eliza has been ignored in this recitation is shocking. Was she not seduced, betrayed, abandoned by Willoughby? We must believe that they had equal footing in the relationship to believe anything else that Willoughby claims. How can this be granted? Moreover, why did Willoughby succumb to pressure from his aunt?

As for Edward remaining single when offered the living at Delaford. Did not Colonel Brandon provide this stipulation because he understood Elinor's love for Edward? Did he not comprehend that postponing Edward's misguided marriage to another increased the chances that such an undesirable entanglement might be ended, thus freeing Edward for Elinor?

Let's call Willoughby what he should be called: a sociopath. We have heard the medical testimony concerning sociopathy. If Willoughby does not exhibit these traits, who does?

Let us review the testimony:

First, "sociopaths tend to be outgoing, glib, even charming"—all of which Willoughby is (just ask the Dashwood ladies about when they met him!).

Second, "they exhibit selfish and unemotional sexual behavior." Recall his cavalier attitude about the pregnant seventeen-year-old Eliza. He claimed that she could have found out where he was and communicated with him: "common sense might have told her how to find it." Is "common sense" to be found in a frightened, pregnant, abandoned teen-ager?

Third, "sociopaths are irresponsible." Is there any mention of him supporting his child by Eliza? None that I have heard. With his own money and his wife's, what is to keep him from acting charitably? Nothing but his own sociopathic self-interested, selfish behavior.

Fourth, "sociopaths are keenly sensitive to their own pain": He claims "thunderbolts and daggers" assailed his heart when he read Marianne's letters.

Fifth, "sociopaths are also selfish and lack empathy." Even though he claimed that Marianne "was dearer to me than any other woman in the world," Willoughby matter-of-factly says, "But everything was just then settled between Miss Grey and me." He later notes matter-of-factly and without a hint of apology, Miss Grey's "money was necessary to me." A parasitic lifestyle is another sociopathic trait.

Sixth, "sociopaths seek attention by claiming themselves to be victims." Willoughby holds his benefactor's way of life against her, and sees it as a cause of his frustration, of his victimization: "The purity of her life, the formality of her notions, her ignorance of the world—everything was against me. . . . In the height of her morality, good woman! She offered to forgive the past if I would marry Eliza. That could not be—. . ."

Finally, "sociopaths desire self-gratification through self-pity": Willoughby "directly asks Elinor for pity three times . . . , he presents himself as a victim of others."

I could go on and on about these sociopathic tendencies, citing example after example. But his actions illustrate best: We have heard Elinor's testimony that at the most crucial moment Colonel Brandon offered his assistance; he would go and fetch her mother. Willoughby, on the other hand, facing the fact of Marianne's illness and perhaps being near death, is thinking of what Elinor can do *for him.*

Please, jurors, do not be led astray by Emma Thompson's interpretation, which depicted Willoughby's sorrow as some long-lasting affair. Remember that Jane Austen, herself, our most reliable witness, tells us that Willoughby "lived to exert, and frequently to enjoy himself."

We are told of how Brandon, in an emergency, "made every necessary arrangement with the utmost dispatch, and calculated with exactness the time in which she might look for his return." Is this the Machiavelli who separates lovers, or the lover who seeks to serve?

Ladies and Gentlemen of the jury, if Colonel Brandon is guilty of anything it is of his choice of clothing. Yes, he wears a flannel vest; some would call him a fuddy-duddy for this. But a flannel vest was part of the Army uniform! And if we were to discriminate guilt and innocence on clothing alone, who then is perfect? Have you yourselves never been discovered by friends to be guilty of wardrobe malfunction? Remove that flannel vest and discover Colonel Brandon to be who many of us know him to be: someone who works to mend the world; someone who cared for a ward, someone who fosters happiness, not destroys it. Brandon, according to Mrs. Dashwood, "is not as handsome as Willoughby," but doesn't that mean he is handsome to one degree or another?

It was Willoughby and Willoughby alone who ruined his own chances. Don't let him prevail in the end by ruining the good name of a good man. Ladies and Gentlemen of the jury, convict Brandon? Jury, convict Willoughby.

Authors' disclaimer: We have taken some liberties with the arguments made by two scholars, and have reimagined them as on opposing sides of a legal case. See William Galperin's case against Colonel Brandon in The Historical Austen, *pp. 113-119, and Joan Klingel Ray, "'Amiable Prejudices of a Young [Writer's] Mind': The Problems of Sense and Sensibility."* Persuasions On-Line, *vol. 26 no.1.*

The Clergy in Austen's Fiction

It is surprising to realize how little Jane Austen speaks of religion in her novels. Though clergy are certainly present in a majority of her works, it is rare that Christianity actually makes its way into any conversation, except when the clergy become enforcers of traditional views about women. The almost complete ineptitude of Mr. Elton and Mr. Collins make it seem that Austen held some sort of grudge against her father, a minister himself, or else had shared with him many laughs about his colleagues in the cloth!

As the child of a clergyman, Austen had the perfect opportunity to understand the ins and outs of the responsibilities of a clergyman, as well as what distinguishes a good congregational leader from a poor one.

The perfect mouthpiece for her observations is Edmund in *Mansfield Park*. "What is to be done in the church?" he is asked, "Men love to distinguish themselves. A clergyman is nothing." Edmund responds: "the nothing has gradations in conversation. He must not head mobs, but not set tones in dress . . . [the charge] is the most important to mankind, which has the guardianship of religion." He claims that, despite only giving two sermons a week, a fine preacher is followed and admired, ending that "where the clergy are or are not what they ought to be, so is the rest of the nation."

Indeed, this proves very much to be the case. It is hard to imagine how the Reverends Elton and Collins kept their parishes under control. After traveling to Bath and finding a wife, whatever kindliness Elton had developed is soon left on the wayside. With his wife's constant comments influencing much, those with whom he keeps company begin to seem socially inferior to him. His refusal to dance with Miss Smith is a pronounced example. The servile Mr. Collins is equally as worldly in his continuous obeisance and acquiescence to Lady Catherine de Bourgh. These two clergymen do little to serve their community, and much to serve themselves. One benefits from the presence of Knightley in deciding parish matters; the other is obedient to his patroness.

Contrarily, there are the sometimes mixed-up but well-meaning younger brothers who are preparing to "take orders," or become ordained: Edmund Bertram and Edward Ferrars. It was more common for younger sons to become clergy than their elder brothers. The majority of the fortune would often be set aside for the older male, while the younger would have to obtain other means of income, most commonly a profession such as the law, the military, or the church. But Edmund and Edward disappoint in many instances; and it is only because of the patience and forbearance of the heroine that we find them redeemed.

So far there are two types of pastors—those who make things worse and those who, in their own bumbling way, make things better. The novels that take place in Bath both include clergy who are important to the plot, though Henry Tilney in *Northanger Abbey* is certainly more important than Charles Hayter is in *Persuasion*. Yet Tilney enjoys the opportunity to tease, lecture, and, at times, deprecate Catherine Morland. Charles Hayter, "a very amiable, pleasing young man," is that unusual creature—an elder son who becomes a clergyman. However his inability to jump into action when the situation requires it does suggest a certain ineffectualness.

By her portrayal of the clergy, Austen reveals the humanity even in those who are supposed to transcend it. Those clergy who are to be the bastions of goodness are subject to the same flaws as the rest of the world. Austen is very careful to not make any of her characters—even the impeccable Mr. Knightley—omniscient. That is left for herself.

The Lives of Jane Austen

Once upon a time, the fairy godmothers of fiction got together. "We are well pleased by the novel," they agreed. "How much has it developed!" They talked of their gifts to novelists, and again agreed, the gifts had been well used. But, wait, the fairy godmother who granted the gift of originality interrupted, as they were congratulating themselves. "What if we joined our gifts? What if the next novelist were not only granted my gift, the gift of originality, but your gift?" And here she turned to the fairy godmother of comedy. For a moment, the room was silent. But then they all laughed and talked together. "Why not?" they replied. And when news arrived that on December 16, 1775, Jane Austen, future novelist, had been born, both the fairy godmothers of originality and comedy attended her christening. And then they sat back to see what would happen with the doubling of the gifts. But a bitter fairy godmother—the godmother of drudges and cads and rakes and selfish, bitter people themselves—was not sure this was a good idea. She could not stop the fairy godmothers from uniting their gifts, but at the christening of Jane Austen, she quickly stepped forward and added her gift, "you will not live to accomplish all you could."

Given how little we actually know about Jane Austen, this scenario is almost as plausible as some of the others that have been created for her. People would like to believe they know a lot about her, but we actually don't. People desire to know more. Indeed, Jane Austen awakens in us what many of her heroes awaken in modern-day readers (perhaps because of the movie versions)—projection, imagination, desire. We want to fill in the picture, connect the dots, imagine her interior world. How could she not have one, since she gives Emma and Elizabeth and Elinor and Anne such rich ones! Elizabeth observes to Bingley at Netherfield that "a deep, intricate character" is more interesting to study. Complicated people are much more interesting to Elizabeth than simple people. Bingley does the predictable thing; his is not a deep, intricate character, but a simple, uncomplicated one.

Certainly Jane Austen joins the list of people with a deep, intricate character. How she would fascinate Lizzy Bennet! How she fascinates us! Biography upon biography pours forth, drawing on much the same information but often coming to completely different conclusions. Her family, her earliest biographers, seemed to want to present her as uncomplicated, as simple. Her brother Henry, then a clergyman, wrote the first biographical notice, appended to the posthumously published *Northanger Abbey* and *Persuasion*. It begins, practically, with her death notice: "Her manners were gentle, her affections ardent, her candour was not to be surpassed, and she lived and died as became a humble Christian." He emphasized, "One trait only remains to be touched on. It makes all others unimportant. She was thoroughly religious and devout: fearful of giving offence to God, and incapable of feeling it towards any fellow creature." Austen's nephew, the Reverend James Edward Austen-Leigh, layered on top of that his own *Memoir of Jane Austen,* published during the height of the Victorian era. Jane Austen the devout and dutiful family member is lifted up; Jane Austen the novelist is misunderstood. The simple explanation substitutes for the complicated personality.

Kathryn Sutherland describes the partiality of the family record as "a mix of careful policing, rivalry, and absence of information." She points out how long it was that the family itself controlled what was said and thus what was known about Jane Austen. They weren't hesitant to re-write some letters, omit references to her "wild" writings as a young person, and otherwise create a sainted individual. They were subject to forgetfulness, family rivalry, and the pressure of the times. They were the first not only to layer over one Jane Austen with another, more palatable, one but also to generate conflicting tales and descriptions, depending upon which one of Jane's siblings they descended from.

We suggested above that Jane Austen awakens in us what many of her heroes awaken in modern-day readers—projection, imagination, desire. As for desire, what a fervent desire many faithful readers cultivate: the desire to understand the mind of the writer, the desire to find in her life the stories she created. Any biography of Austen contends with this and several practical considerations influence this desire: she died when she was only forty-one and her sister Cassandra destroyed many of her letters. One hundred and sixty remain. Did Cassandra destroy them because the letters said too much or did they not really say anything at all? Did she destroy them because they revealed Austen's interest in the larger world—plays seen, books read, people encountered? We don't know. Were they written to bare her innermost feelings? No. To entertain with her wit? Yes. We are accustomed to thinking that an expurgated text had something radical, pornographic, or in other ways unsettling in it. We then impose this belief on that time. But historians of that time suggest such a notion could be wrong and that the letters that were destroyed might not have revealed a "different" Austen than the letters that survive.

Perhaps Cassandra did not only destroy letters. Perhaps she also destroyed a diary that Austen kept. Claire Tomalin proposes this idea in her biography of Jane Austen. A diary, after all, would explain how it is that Cassandra is able to pinpoint the beginning and completion of the novels, which you can find in the chronology below.

Still, from the letters and other sources, we do know she traveled to London and back several times, visited her brother at his great house in Godmersham, traveled, and visited friends and family. We know she had close female friends who were extremely important to her and helped support her as she became a novelist. We also know that the social network that made up the scope of Austen's life and her work is vast. The experience of this immediate group of people spans numerous continents and adventures, many times providing fodder for her imaginative writing. However, do not confuse her life and her writings. This very idea is the other major factor with which biographers must contend. Austen's identity as the successful author of some of the most widely read and beloved books of all time provides a constant temptation for writers to make a novel of her life. And the novel often made of her life appears to be written by Charlotte or Emily Brontë, not Jane Austen!

In the following annotated chronology of her life, remember this: we really don't even know for sure when she started writing some of her books. Ah, yes, she was a deep, intricate person.

April 26, 1764. Austen's parents, Rev. George Austen and Cassandra Leigh, marry in St. Swithin's Church in Bath and depart for their new home at the parsonage at Deane.

1765. James, the Austen's first child, is born.

1766. George, the second son, is born. The younger George Austen figures little in the family history, as he is troubled by some form of mental illness and is sent away to be cared for by the Cullum family. George's only support from his family after this time seems to be financial. There is little record of any family visits to George, and he is even left out of his mother's will.

1767. Edward, the third son, is born.

1768. Steventon Rectory becomes the Austens' home.

1771. Henry-Thomas born.

1773. Cassandra born.

1774. Francis Austen born.

December 16, 1775. Jane Austen born. Her birth was attended by her mother's sister, Philadelphia Hancock and daughter Eliza.

1779. Charles Austen born.

Seven children is a large brood for the inhabitants of a country rectory. (Recall that George was living with the Cullums.) Add to this the lodging students of Rev. George Austen as well as an almost constant presence of visiting relatives and friends, and the rectory soon becomes even more crowded. Many of the Austen

St. Nicholas Church, Steventon. The photographer Allan Soedring points out that the spire was added in the middle of the nineteenth century, thus, "for Jane Austen's view of the church, mentally remove the spire."
©Allan Soedring www.astoft.co.uk. Used with permission.

children were sent away to other families in the parish to be nursed in their very young years, but all, in turn, returned to Steventon Rectory. Because of the Victorian biography, we think of Jane Austen as living in rural simplicity, and when away from it, longing to return. But, as Kathryn Sutherland points out, both Steventon, where Austen grew up, and Chawton, where she lived the last eight years of her life, were on important roads, and Chawton "was on the major stagecoach route from Southampton to Winchester."

1783-1786. Jane, Cassandra, and cousin Jane Cooper are sent to attend Mrs. Cawley's school in Oxford; soon after the school moved to Southampton. An outbreak of typhoid fever at the school's new location forces the girls' immediate removal to and enrollment in the Abbey School in Reading. But the Rev. George Austen withdraws his daughters under the suspicion that the curriculum is not advanced enough for the tuition. When Jane is eleven, her formal education is at an end. At home, her parents and siblings constitute an important part of her identity as constant companions, correspondents, and early audiences for her literary works.

1782. Steventon's amateur productions begin with *Matilda*.

1783. Edward is adopted by Mr. and Mrs. Thomas Knight II, who have no heirs of their own. (This had been in the works since the time he was twelve.)

1787-1788. Jane Austen begins what will be called the juvenilia. She reads her work aloud to her sisters. (Her brothers were out and about in the world: James at Oxford, Edward on a Grand Tour, Frank at the Naval Academy in Portsmouth.)

1789. Martha Lloyd and family move into the neighborhood. She becomes a beloved friend of Austen's, and one of the items of the juvenilia is dedicated to her:

> *To Miss Lloyd*
> *My dear Martha*
> *As a small testimony of the grati-*
> *tude I feel for your late generosity to*
> *me in finishing my muslin Cloak, I*
> *beg leave to offer you this little pro-*
> *duction of your Sincere Freind*

1791: "The History of England," a parody of histories of that time, probably written this year. Austen also probably started the early novel *Lady Susan* around this time.

1792. *Catharine, or The Bower* written. Though usually linked with the juvenilia, new scholarship suggests that it is actually an unfinished novel. Mary Waldron sees this novel as a turning point for Austen, as it is a much more complex fiction than what Austen had previously been writing.

1792. The Lloyds move to Ibthorpe. Austen with her sister Cassandra visits later that year.

1792. *Maybe*: Cassandra becomes engaged to the Reverend Tom Fowle, a former pupil of her father's.

1793-1794. Austen working on *Lady Susan.*

1795: *Maybe*: Jane Austen most probably begins work on "Elinor and Mari-anne," which will eventually become *Sense and Sensibility.*

January 9-10, 1796. The letter she wrote this day to Cassandra is the first letter, chronologically, that survives. Cassandra is away from Steventon to see her fiancée safely off to the West Indies as a chaplain. While she is absent, Austen writes to her entertainingly of her activities. These first letters that survive also include her references to Tom Lefroy, "a very gentlemanlike, good-looking, pleasant young man." Whether we can reconstruct what actually happened in their relationship from the letters is one thing. What Tom Lefroy remembered as an elderly man is another. This is what we know:

Tom Lefroy is staying with some relatives who live near Steventon and are great friends of the Austens. The history of the relationship is a short one: Austen writes two letters to Cassandra including various accounts of him over the course of one week. They meet at several balls, and Tom calls at Steventon Rectory with his cousin George. Austen describes all this in an arch and light-hearted way: "Imagine to yourself every-thing most profligate and shocking in the way of dancing and sitting down together." Lefroy's visit to the country is to be a short one, though she says in her second surviving letter, "I rather expect to receive an offer from my friend in the course of the evening." Is this serious? For she follows up immediately with "I shall refuse him, however, unless he promises to give away his white Coat."

Here we have the source for what becomes great speculation and then morphs into story, as in *Becoming Jane*: that she and Tom Lefroy were in love, but his family had different plans for their promising young nephew. Tom's departure, therefore, is hastened, and he is away to London before the 18th of January. Jane receives no proposal. Though Jane had not been devoid of other admirers at the start of her flirtation with Tom Lefroy, we are told she was clearly disappointed at not having received an offer. She talks of him still two years later, writing of Mrs. Lefroy's visit to Steventon, saying "of her nephew she said nothing at all . . . She did not once mention the name of [Tom] to *me,* and I was too proud to make any enquiries." She continues, "There seems no likelihood of his coming into Hampshire this Christmas, and it is therefore most probable that our indifference will soon be mutual, unless his regard, which appeared to spring from knowing nothing of me at first, is best supported by never seeing me."

Was it anything more than a flirtation? Did she model Elizabeth's flirtation with Wickham on this, at least a little? Can an elderly man who knows of Jane Austen's fame be trusted in his recollections of love?

Recent scholarship conducted by Deborah Kaplan proposes an alternative reading of these two potent letters. Kaplan's *Jane Austen Among Women* sees a connection between Austen's playfulness in her letters and her creation of characters such as *Lady Susan,* who is able to manipulate the feelings of men. "Although Austen wrote *Lady Susan* before 1796, when her surviving letters commence, it is worth noting that many of the letters she wrote to Cassandra contain short, comic sex-reversal fantasies." Kaplan finds these fantasies in many letters that span many years. "Austen likes to predict or direct, with all the confidence of a Lady Susan or a Catherine Vernon, the desires and behavior of men. Moreover, she enjoys inventing women desirable to men and men vulnerable to rejection"—as Austen playfully predicted she would reject Tom Lefroy unless he "give away his white coat."

October 1796. According to Cassandra, Austen begins *First Impressions.* Austen finished it the following August. Though Austen will return to it and revise it into *Pride and Prejudice,* we don't know much about this manuscript at all. We do know that Austen, famously "lop't it and crop't it" in transforming it.

1797. Tom Fowle, Cassandra's betrothed, dies of yellow fever on the voyage back from the West Indies. He leaves Cassandra £1,000.

1797. *First Impressions* receives an enthusiastic response from Austen's family. Her father offers a manuscript to a publisher, but it is rejected sight unseen. It is supposed that the manuscript was *First Impressions.* Austen begins revising "Elinor and Marianne."

Godmersham Park, *1785, by William Watts/Private Collection/The Bridgeman Art Library.*

1798. Austen joins a subscription library. 18-19 December, says in a letter to Cassandra that they are "great Novel-readers & not ashamed of being so."

Around this time, she maybe begins "Susan," which becomes *Northanger Abbey.* She also visits Edward Austen Knight's new home at Godmersham Park, the handsome estate of his adoptive parents, the Knights. There will be several visits to it during her lifetime, the last in 1813.

1799. Austen visits Bath with her mother and Edward, his wife, and his children, Fanny and Edward Jr. She has a few positive things to say, if not about the weather, at least about the house they will be staying in. She sends accounts of Bath fashions and shopping trips in Bath Street to Cassandra.

December 1800. Austen returns with Martha Lloyd from a visit to the Lloyds at Ibthorpe in early December to learn that her parents have decided to give up Steventon rectory in favor of Bath. Why did her parents decide this? Perhaps because of Mrs. Austen's poor health (though she is often seen as a hypochondriac); Bath is known for its restorative characteristics. Perhaps it is because of Rev. Austen's age (seventy years old) and possible inability to discharge parish duties any longer. The Austen finances may also have been in distress, and settling in Bath would have been cheaper than maintaining an independent country home. Rev. Austen might have wanted to settle his son into the house and the living that had been promised him. Whatever the reason for this decision, much

The French Connection. Jane's cousin Eliza, a vibrant woman, married Jean-Francois Capo de Feuillide and became the Comtess de Feuillide. Returning to England, she brought along with her tales of her life in the French aristocracy. She could describe Marie Antoinette's hairstyles and fashions. While France was in the throes of revolution, Eliza de Feuillide was forced to flee her home in Paris. Her husband was imprisoned and guillotined in 1794. By the late eighteenth century, however, the lively Eliza de Feuillide had become a happy and independent widow in the bustle of city life. For some time, Eliza had been receiving attentions from two of the Austen brothers, James, now a widower, and Henry. In 1797 she turned a few heads by accepting a proposal from Henry, ten years her junior, after having rejected James. She took with her into the marriage her son, Hastings, from her first marriage. Henry, eager to cater to his new wife's metropolitan sensibilities, turned to banking instead of pursuing his naval career to its conclusion.

lore surrounds Jane Austen's reaction to the news. According to one family member (reporting what she had heard), Austen fainted after hearing the plan. The myth corresponds to the favorite image of Jane Austen as a lover of the peaceful countryside. It also may have arisen from the side of the family that soon occupied the manse that the Austens were vacating, and they felt a little guilty. Perhaps, too, Austen's faint acts symbolically within family tradition. Kathryn Sutherland suggests that Austen's loss of consciousness becomes the physical representation of what people also believe happened when she moved away—she lost consciousness of her art and abandoned writing. Thus the faint represents her future until she is reunited with the country eight years down the road when she moves to Chawton.

Perhaps people want to believe the fainting episode occurred because it corresponds to the myth of Jane Austen,

the almost hermit. In each successive repetition, it becomes burnished as though it is true. (Are we, then, guilty too?) Maybe Jane Austen found much to object to in Bath, but she always was prone to being caught up in the excitement of the city: she went to concerts and other entertainments; she met people and enjoyed meeting them. She even writes, "I get more and more reconciled to the idea of our removal." Whatever may have been her feelings on the subject, however, to Bath they were to go. Importantly, we now know that she did not stop writing during the interstitial years between Steventon and Chawton.

We know that Austen worked on *The Watsons* during this time, though at some point she abandons it. (She might have stopped working on it as late as 1807.) She might have been redrafting *Northanger Abbey*, and either revising or completing *Lady Susan*—for that manuscript exists on paper from 1805. She might also have been writing other things as well. Whether or not Austen fainted on that day, it did not set the stage for her to abandon her writing.

May 1801. The Austens go to Bath and live at 4 Sydney Place.

1801-1804. Sometime between these dates, Jane Austen supposedly has a romance.

December 2, 1802. Harris Bigg-Wither proposes to Austen while she is visiting her brother James and his family. (James had succeeded his father as rector at Steventon.) She accepts Bigg-Wither's proposal.

December 3, 1802. Austen declines the proposal, and she and Cassandra set off for Bath. We do not know why, and when biographers explain her reasons for changing her mind, they really do not know why, either.

1803. Richard Crosby, the publisher, buys *Susan*. He never publishes it and it only appears after Austen's death as *Northanger Abbey*.

1803-1805. During the summer Jane and her family visit Lyme Regis. When they return to Bath, they move to 3 Green Park Buildings East.

January 21, 1805. Austen's father dies in Bath. A short time later, mother and daughters move to 25 Gay Street. When

Sydney Place, Bath. No. 4 is the fourth door. ©Allan Soedring www.astoft.co.uk. Used with permission.

Chawton Cottage. ©Allan Soedring www.astoft.co.uk. Used with permission.

Martha Lloyd's mother dies in April, she joins the Austen women.

1806. The Austen women move to Adlestrop.

1807. The Austen women move to Southhampton.

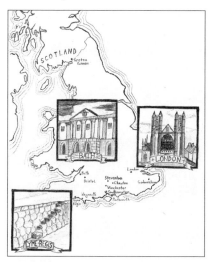

April 5, 1809. Under a pseudonym, Austen writes Crosby & Co., inquiring about their plans for *Susan*. They write back offering that it could be bought back for the price they paid for it (£10), but saying they had never stipulated when it would be published.

July 7, 1809. The Austen women move to Chawton Cottage.

1810. *Sense and Sensibility* accepted for publication.

February 1811. Austen begins plans for *Mansfield Park*.

October 30, 1811. *Sense and Sensibility* published.

1811 (Maybe wintertime). Austen begins revising *First Impressions*. It will become *Pride and Prejudice*.

1812. Jane Austen sells copyright to *Pride and Prejudice.*

January 28, 1813. *Pride and Prejudice* published. Austen continues to work on *Mansfield Park.*

1813. (Probably.) Austen finishes *Mansfield Park* sometime in the summer and by the end of the year, it has been accepted for publication.

January 21, 1814. Austen begins *Emma.*

May 9, 1814. *Mansfield Park* published.

March 29, 1815. *Emma* finished.

August 8, 1815. Austen starts *Persuasion.*

December 1815. *Emma* published.

1816. Austen's brother, Henry, goes bankrupt. David Spring has called the people in trade, the clergymen, and the lawyers in Austen's novels "pseudo-gentry." Kathryn Sutherland believes the term applies to Austen's family, too. Some were upwardly mobile, like her brother Edward, who came to live in great houses; and some were downwardly mobile, like Henry Austen. But they share this: "They aspire to the lifestyle of the traditional rural gentry." Henry's bankruptcy is disruptive for Austen, as he had been acting as Austen's literary agent. Did this contribute to her final illness?

Spring 1816 and forward. Austen is ill. She finishes the first draft of *Persuasion* that summer, and completes it in August. In September she writes her sister that "my back has given me scarcely any pain for many days." She turns down an invitation to dinner on her birthday, because "the walk is beyond my strength (though I am otherwise very well)." In a letter in early 1817, she believes that "*bile* is at the bottom of all I have suffered."

January 27, 1817. Austen begins work on *Sanditon.* In February, she has pain in a knee, and it is wrapped in flannel. In March, she writes that she has had "a good deal of fever." She also reports that she is "recovering my looks a little, which have been bad enough, black and white and every wrong colour." She stops working on *Sanditon* in March.

In early April, she reports to her brother than she has been "really too unwell the last fortnight to write anything." She also makes her will, leaving everything to her executor Cassandra (except for £50 to Henry and £50 to Madam Bigeon, a housekeeper, who had attended her sister-in-law Eliza.)

On May 22, she described her symptoms as "feverish nights, weakness, and languor." In May Cassandra takes her to Winchester for medical care.

July 18, 1817. Jane Austen dies at 4:30 A.M. Cassandra writes to Fanny Knight, their niece: "I *have* lost a treasure, such a Sister, such a friend as never can have been surpassed,—She was the sun of my life, the gilder of every pleasure, the soother of every sorrow, I had not a thought concealed from her, & it is as if I had lost a part of myself. I loved her only too well, not better than she deserved."

Did she die of Addison's disease, as Sir Zachary Cope proposed in 1964? (This disease was not identified until 1860.) Cope identified several symptoms including skin discoloration and

Jane Austen's tomb, Winchester Cathedral. Courtesy Geoff and Mercia Chapman of the Jane Austen Society of Melbourne, Australia.

Tomalin suggests it might have been a lymphoma, like Hodgkin's Disease, whose symptoms match Austen's more closely. Or was it breast cancer, as Carol Shields suggests? After all, breast cancer had probably killed an aunt and a cousin.

Even in death, Austen leaves us wondering.

End of December, 1817. *Northanger Abbey* and *Persuasion* published, along with a "Biographical Notice" by Henry Austen.

bilious attacks, as well as her response to stressful situations. But Addison's does not cause recurrent fevers. Claire

The marble gravestone commissioned for her grave never acknowledges Jane Austen as an author.

In Memory of
JANE AUSTEN,
youngest daughter of the late
Revd GEORGE AUSTEN,
formerly Rector of Steventon in this County
she departed this life on the 18ᵗʰ July 1817,
aged 41, after a long illness supported with
the patience and the hopes of a Christian.

The benevolence of her heart,
the sweetness of her temper, and
the extraordinary endowments of her mind
obtained the regard of all who knew her and
the warmest love of her intimate connections.

Their grief is in proportion to their affection
they know their loss to be irreparable,
but in their deepest affliction they are consoled
by a firm though humble hope that her charity,
devotion, faith and purity have rendered
her soul acceptable in the sight of her
REDEEMER.

CAPSULE

Mansfield Park

Tom: *"Mansfield Park, you've got to be kidding!"*
Audrey: *"No."*
Tom: *"But it's a notoriously bad book. Even Lionel Trilling, one of her greatest admirers, thought that."*
Audrey: *"Well, if Lionel Trilling thought that, he's an idiot."*
Tom (scoffing): *"The whole story revolves around, what? the immorality of a group of young people putting on a play."*
Audrey: *"In the context of the novel, it makes perfect sense."*
Tom: *"But the context of the novel, and nearly everything else Jane Austen wrote is near ridiculous from today's perspective."*
Audrey: *"Has it ever occurred to you that today, looked at from Jane Austen's perspective, would look even worse?"*

—Whit Stillman's

Metropolitan, 1990

Mansfield Park is alternately loved and hated; admired for its success as a novel or reviled for making Fanny Price the heroine. To some it is a moral story, for others a boring story. It's an achievement; it's a failure. To one Fanny Price is a "Romantic monster," to another she is "a helpless and muddled girl." For some, it is the religious feeling that

pervades the novel that is disturbing: all this talk of crosses and clergy, ordination and sermons, seems to act as a killjoy to the novel—or at least to what we expect from a Jane Austen novel. Where has her lightness and brightness of tone gone? We expect Lizzy Bennet, who talks back to the world, and we get a Fanny Price, who struggles with what to say and how to say it. With Fanny, it is her thoughts, more than her speech, to which we must learn to attend. She will not tease us, as Lizzy does Darcy.

In *Mansfield Park* there are so many characters to dislike, or at least be made uneasy by, and few to really like. The residents of Mansfield Park rival each other for the title "most selfish." There is Lady Bertram, who seems to suffer from narcolepsy (perhaps drug-induced). There is Sir Thomas, whose children are happier when he is absent; then they can laugh. There is at least one rake. And of course there is the wicked, nasty, abusive Mrs. Norris, Lady Bertram's sister. (That Filch's patrolling cat in the Harry Potter series is named Mrs. Norris tells us that J. K. Rowling read her Austen.)

Mansfield Park begins not, as is commonly thought, with Fanny Price's being brought to her rich relatives. Instead, we are led through a tale of three sisters. One marries wealthily and becomes Lady Bertram. One's match is saved from being contemptible through

Portsmouth Point, *Thomas Rowlandson, 1811. Fanny Price begins her life in Portsmouth. Courtesy of The Lewis Walpole Library, Yale University 814.0.2.1.*

the kindness of her sister's husband, Sir Thomas Bertram. Rev. and Mrs. Norris are given a living and a home in the parsonage at Mansfield. The third sister, however, marries perhaps only for affection. A Lieutenant Price of the Marines is her choice, and fixes her in irrevocable poverty. This rupture of sisterly promise launches us into the heart of the story that Jane Austen herself prized, even if it has been not as kindly received by some of her readers (and nonreaders, too!). How are we to reconcile with the mousy Fanny Price, who is to become the heroine of this work? Not being disposed, as a modern audience, to cling faithfully to her morality, is there anything left to admire here?

To speak of Fanny Price, the unlikely heroine of the novel, and daughter of the third sister confined ever after to a household of noise, is to speak, at first, of the dirt and poverty in Portsmouth. This, however, is not to be Fanny's fate.

The wealthy family at Mansfield has agreed to take on her education (as suggested by Mrs. Norris) and she is sent thither, away from her family, at the tender age of ten. (No other heroine of an Austen novel is introduced to us so young.) She arrives at Mansfield Park to the cool welcome of her relatives' satisfaction only in that she has "nothing to disgust" them and the explanation, which will follow her through the next many years, that she is by no means "a *Miss Bertram*" and will not be treated as such. The proper hierarchy must be maintained. The Misses Bertram themselves are paraded before Fanny shortly after her arrival. Maria at thirteen and Julia at twelve seem worlds older than ten-year-old Fanny because of the degree of difference in their circumstances and experience. Tom and Edmund, at seventeen and sixteen respectively, have "all the grandeur of men in the eyes of their little cousin."

Fanny tries to become accustomed to life in the large house, causing wonder everywhere she goes for her ignorance and lack of manners. She finds comfort only in Edmund, whose "good sense" and "uprightness of mind" separate him from his sisters' cool treatment of Fanny. He listens to her stories of her favorite brother William and furnishes her with paper to write to him. Mr. Norris dies. There is some talk of Fanny's going to live with Mrs. Norris at the "White house" in the village, now that there would be a spare room. Mrs. Norris, horrid as ever, provides relief for both Fanny and herself by refusing the possibility of such a thing. The empty parsonage, which will eventually be Edmund's living once he has taken orders, falls to a Dr. and Mrs. Grant. Aside from some offenses in lifestyle to Mrs. Norris's ideas of thriftiness, the Grants seem to promise no trouble for the inhabitants of the Park.

A year after the settling of the Grants, Sir Thomas and Tom are called away from Mansfield to deal with business affairs in Antigua. The affairs promise to keep them occupied for some time. Time has also elevated the Misses Bertram in importance and beauty, and Maria soon has the good fortune of capturing the attentions of the wealthy Mr. Rushworth, a heavy and silly gentleman who seems to possess little to object to but stupidity and little to recommend him but wealth. Maria soon finds herself engaged to Mr. Rushworth and his £12,000 a year. Tom returns from Antigua, followed soon after by his father's consent to Maria's engagement to Mr. Rushworth. Only Edmund seems to remember to find fault with Mr. Rushworth's overbearing silliness.

Into these circumstances, and into Fanny's eighteenth year, are introduced two newcomers to Mansfield Park. Mrs. Grant's half-siblings, Mary and Henry Crawford, come as guests to the parsonage. Mary is beautiful, and, though Henry is not so, the air of liveliness and modernity brought about by much time in London is enough to strongly recommend the pair to the party at Mansfield Park. Today's reader might be far more entertained and delighted by the bright and energetic Mary Crawford than by Fanny Price. Mary is sociable; and even Fanny will find Mary's sparkling personality irresistible at times. Yet Fanny needs Mary to be a bad girl (even if she is unaware of these feelings), because, unfortunately for Fanny, they both are interested in the same man.

With the arrival of the two strangers, jealousies and entanglements abound. Fanny is not above being jealous; but never to the degree that the two Bertram sisters exhibit. Indeed, acting out occurs as they rehearse the scandalous *Lovers' Vows;* the play provides a platform for much overt flirtation. The play also reveals how much dissembling is at the heart of Mansfield Park all the time.

Fanny Price seems to occupy negative space. She lives in a cold, unheated room at Mansfield Park. Later, when she returns to Portsmouth, she does not exactly receive a hero's welcome. Her opinions during most of the novel are not heeded. She might object to something (theatrical), but no matter, the show must go on. Edward, unthinkingly, hands over the horse he offered to Fanny to Mary Crawford. Displaced in many ways, she, however, cannot be replaced. She holds the moral center of Mansfield Park. Fanny's negative space, as we are calling it, contrasts starkly with place, with Mansfield Park itself, and Sotherton, Mr. Rushworth's large estate.

Whether Sotherton should be improved becomes a subject of discussion at Mansfield Park. Henry Crawford is offered as an expert; Mrs. Norris believes that it is worth the money to hire Humphry Repton. Fanny is not equally enthusiastic. She knows Rushworth has already cut down "two or three fine old trees." Fanny, possessor of no estate, only has imaginary places to console her: transparencies of Tintern Abbey, a cave in Italy, and a lake in

"Miss Crawford's attractions did not lessen. The harp arrived, and rather added to her beauty, wit, and good-humour; for she played with the greatest obligingness, with an expression and taste which were peculiarly becoming, and there was something clever to be said at the close of every air. Edmund was at the Parsonage every day, to be indulged with his favourite instrument: one morning secured an invitation for the next; for the lady could not be unwilling to have a listener, and every thing was soon in a fair train."
Harmony before Matrimony, *James Gillray, 1805.*
Courtesy of The Lewis Walpole Library, Yale University 805.10.25.2.

Cumberland. If it were in her power, she would not create the negative space that comes from tree removal.

Mansfield Park is taken up for some time with the rehearsal of *Lovers' Vows* and undergoes "improvements" as scene painters are busy in what is usually Sir Thomas's part of the house. Mr. Yates may be heard thundering about in the midst of his speeches, and Henry and Maria find time to rehearse their scenes together much more often than there can be much need for. Everything seems to be gathering momentum toward a final performance, until, quite unexpectedly, Sir Thomas returns to Mansfield and puts an abrupt end to all of these pursuits.

At times Sir Thomas calls to mind another father, General Tilney, and the comparison is not kind to him. His children are more relaxed and happier when he is absent. He is concerned with appearances. He is often the one who agrees with Mrs. Norris or gets Mrs. Norris to do his bidding. He is the one who enforces Fanny's second-class status in the home. He could put a stop to a wedding that clearly is not based on love, but he does not. And, then, when his guilt slowly dawns on us, we find that Austen gives us something surprisingly unusual in her novels: a father who can learn from his mistakes.

is an illness and recovery; there is an elopement and adultery. Though all this, Austen does something original: we are given the interior life of Fanny Price, a rendering of consciousness to a depth and a degree that is as innovative as Shakespeare's soliloquies. She is not an unbending prig, as some would have it, but someone who is struggling with her own competing emotions in the light of a strong moral call to do the right things in her life. It is not so much that she isn't wrong; there are times when she is. It is that she sets herself the task of moral goodness and struggles to enact it.

Many people try to explain the mood of *Mansfield Park* by looking at Jane Austen's life. In doing so, they cheat themselves (and Austen) of the genius of the novel. Here is an artist at work: she has set herself a difficult task and she is testing herself to see if she can accomplish it. And she did: she created a masterpiece. She experiments with symbolism (see "What happened at the Ha-Ha?"). She invents a very unusual type of heroine. The "boy gets girl" or "girl gets boy" part of the story actually takes up very little space. Austen is interested in the significance of place in a very particular way. She explicitly draws upon another text (*Lovers' Vows*). She deploys irony from the first paragraph: "'But there certainly are not so

"The real crisis of the novel has to do with an interior failure—the failure of the human spirit to renew itself."—Julia Brown

From a surprising corner, Fanny becomes someone's love interest. Can Sir Thomas leave her alone on this? No. There are conversations and a ball; there is banishment and there is regret; there

many men of large fortune in the world, as there are pretty women to deserve them." The same might be said of masterpieces and readers.

What Does Lady Bertram Do?

One thing Lady Bertram might seek credit for is that it had "really occurred to her, unprompted, that Fanny, preparing for a ball might be glad of better help than the upper housemaid's, and when dressed herself, she actually sent her own maid to assist her." The maid was, however, "too late of course to be of any use." Progress of the Toilet—Dress Completed, *James Gillray, 1810. Courtesy of The Lewis Walpole Library, Yale University 810.2.26.3.*

Lady Bertram deservedly comes under much criticism by readers; she is inattentive (at best) to her children's waywardness; she allows her sister to cruelly dole out assignments to Fanny; she is passive, often unresponsive, and is overall quite a laughingstock: sitting there on her couch with her pug, dozing as the house is thrown topsy-turvy by the play, sending her maid (too late) to help Fanny dress the night of the ball. The Lady Bertram of the novel would never exhibit the sharpness of perception or active intervention as the 2007 televised *Mansfield Park* credits her with, especially in arranging an opportunity for a proposal. But perhaps we share with the 2007 screenwriter Maggie Wadey a desire to find the good in Lady Bertram. Martha Bowden, answering the question "What Does Lady Bertram Do?" reminds us that

1. She invited Fanny, when she arrived at Mansfield Park from Portsmouth, to sit on the couch with her and the pug. (A common practice of easing children's fear by introducing them to a gentle dog.)

2. By not giving advice for eight and a half years, she provided a "peaceful" contrast to her hectoring sister.

3. She sent money and baby-linens to accompany letters her sister writes.

4. "We have been all alive with acting," she proclaims to her husband; yes, she felt the electricity, too.

5. She writes letters to Fanny when she is in Portsmouth.

6. She is truly touched/shocked when her very sick son Tom arrives home.

7. When Fanny is absent, she talks of Fanny "almost every hour."

8. She does needlework and when Fanny untangles her needlework, we see she really does care for her aunt.

9. She is correct that her husband will settle things more quickly than had been thought and will return from the West Indies before expected.

10. She knows how to embarrass her sister, and she does:

> "I am glad you gave him [William] something considerable," said Lady Bertram, "for I gave him only £10."
>
> "Indeed! cried Mrs. Norris, reddening. "Upon my word, he must have gone off with his pockets well lined, and at no expense for his journey to London either!"

Clearly, Mrs. Norris had given him much less, and perhaps Lady Bertram is shrewder than we think.

What Happened at the Ha-ha?

"The sun shines and the park looks very cheerful. But unluckily that iron gate, that ha-ha, give me a feeling of restraint and hardship. I cannot get out, as the starling said." As she spoke, and it was with expression, she walked to the gate; he followed her. "Mr Rushworth is so long fetching this key!"
—**Maria Bertram in** Mansfield Park

For Fanny Price, many things at Mansfield Park are constantly out of reach: respect, friends, family, and sometimes even the park itself. When Maria Bertram and Mr. Crawford encounter a locked iron gate at Sotherton, Fanny begs them to refrain from their endeavors to squeeze through it. Unwilling to follow, Fanny warns "You will hurt yourself, Miss Bertram," she cried; "you will certainly hurt yourself against those spikes; you will tear your gown; you will be in danger of slipping into the ha-ha. You had better not go." Is this a puritanical Fanny warning against the licentious dangers of laughing fits? Far from it, though there are certainly sexual connotations in *Mansfield Park* and throughout all of Jane Austen's work.

The ha-ha was a special device used in landscaping that protected gardens from wildlife while still preserving the ever-important picturesque ideal of an estate's grounds: rolling, uninterrupted "natural" beauty. Instead of gating the entire garden and thus interrupting the view, the landscaper would separate garden and grounds by raising up the former, creating a four- to six-foot "step" in the land. The step was often reinforced by a simple stone wall. In this manner, when looking out from the house, one would see only the illusion of a hillock and the sweep of the land continuing. The name "Ha-Ha"—or "Ah-Ah" in France, where the technique began—originated from guests' reactions of surprise and amusement upon walking up to the edge of the step without realizing it was there.

There are subtle variations on the idea of the ha-ha. One basic ha-ha concept consists of surrounding the gardened area with a small moatlike ditch portioned off by a stone wall; a packed-earth walkway allows egress from the gardens, while a gate protects this walkway from wandering quadruped garden-munchers.

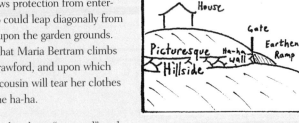

Cross-section of a ditch ha-ha.

Another construction utilizes a steppe-like idea, in which the house and gardens lie atop a hillside that rolls down to a drop-off made similarly of a stone wall. A gate opening upon an earthen ramp at one point allows one to enter and exit the area. Thus, upon looking out a household window, one would only see the garden and hillsides, with the briefest of interruptions in the form of the gate. A small extension to either side of the gate allows protection from enterprising animals who could leap diagonally from the ramp and land upon the garden grounds. It is this extension that Maria Bertram climbs around with Mr. Crawford, and upon which Fanny is afraid her cousin will tear her clothes and then fall into the ha-ha.

Diagram of a ha-ha.

Julia discovers that they have "escaped" and she "scrambles across the fence" as well. Their escapades later in the novel suggests that both women are willing to "escape" from family expectations. That Mr. Crawford will again lead one of them astray is foreshadowed here. Crawford refers to "Mr. Rushworth's authority and protection" which matter a great deal more when one is married than when one is trying to slip through a ha-ha. But in both cases, while Mr. Rushworth is likened to being a jailer who has it within his power to release Maria, it is Henry whom she wants, and Henry has already proven that day in Sotherton that he is a big tease, flirting both with Julia and Maria, and arousing each's jealousy of the other. Will he let the starling out? And what is the starling's fate if let out? Fanny knows.

Fanny's warnings, then, against the threat of the iron bars catching and tearing Miss Bertram's dress are more than just surface worries—she is truly afraid that Miss Bertram will be "slipping into" a life of ill repute and that it is Henry Crawford leading her astray.

Aha! Miss Austen invites us to slip into this implied world of impropriety alongside her, and then into a good laugh.

Raiders of the Early Works:
The Juvenilia

As fondly as we might wish to consider the body of Jane Austen's work, to calculate exactly how many times we have read *Pride and Prejudice,* to emphasize that we have read Austen's canon backward and forward all the way past *Persuasion* to *Sanditon,* there still remains that one nagging problem for the "Janeite" who wishes to go above and beyond the call of duty. What about all of those persistent references in our favorite biographies to such unfamiliar titles as "Frederic and through. Sure, some of the more charming early works, the *History of England,* for instance, sit on the shelf, charmingly bound in charming individual volumes, collected from trips to Bath or just to an especially charming bookstore. Really, who could expect more? Despite these reassurances, however, the references continue.

What do we do, then, with Jane Austen's early works, or "juvenilia"? This is certainly not the Austen of *Persuasion, Emma,* and the mature works that we

"The girl of fifteen is laughing, in her corner,
at the world."—Virginia Woolf

Elfrida" or "Lesley Castle"? A look of consternation furrows the brow of the dedicated reader, now well into this respectably heavy history of Austen's life. Annoyed but persistent, the Janeite forges on, certain that an established knowledge of the six novels, well-meaning intention to read *The Watsons,* and consideration of *Sanditon*'s unfinished status will be enough to carry her or him have come to love; however, what was eventually to be called *Pride and Prejudice* found its beginning during an earlier part of Austen's life. This Jane Austen is excitable and sharp, if perhaps a bit unpolished (if any such qualification may be permitted). Sudden deaths, imprisonment, mysterious fevers, and secret marriages are nothing out of the ordinary here. Whole worlds are traversed in less than ten pages. While some of Austen's later finesse in plot development may be absent here, her satirical sense and wit are certainly not. While attempting a daring prison escape, Eliza of "Henry and Eliza" is found throwing her two children out of the high cell window onto a pile of clothes, only to find them "in perfect Health and fast asleep" at the bottom once she has climbed down the ladder unhindered by having babes in her arms.

R. W. Chapman, an important editor of Austen's works in the early twentieth century, called the juvenilia "immature or fragmentary fictions" that were worth "hardly any comment," but Austen's sense of comic timing and consideration of the current trends in English thought resembles Monty Python skits. For example, in "Edgar and Emma" Austen plays with the popular eighteenth-century notion of sentimentalism, which emphasized emotions over reason and glorified "sentimental," rather than basely physical, love. This included the pain of true love. Austen satirizes this when Emma, distressed that the object of her affections is away at college and does not come to visit with the rest of his family, "when having no check to the overflowings of her greif [sic], she gave free vent to them, and retiring to her own room, continued in tears the remainder of her Life." Perhaps more importantly, this scene contains some key similarities to the "sensibilities" that will direct Marianne Dashwood's actions in the later *Sense and Sensibility*. If this is the case, then Jane Austen's juvenilia

is far from unimportant, even for someone claiming only to be concerned with the six completed novels.

Jane Austen probably began these writings when she was eleven years old. The early works themselves survive in three volumes copied out in Austen's own handwriting. Twenty-seven items (about ninety thousand words) were transcribed into notebooks. Novels were often published in three volumes at this time (as would be Austen's own novels years later). Thus, Austen gave her notebooks the titles "Volume the First," "Volume the Second," and "Volume the Third." In form and content, she was experimenting with and spoofing the writing of her time, including histories of England. John Halperin refers to the Austen who wrote the juvenilia as a "literary demolition expert." Juliet McMaster says in the juvenilia we can see Austen "writing with her hair down and breaking every rule."

There are no surviving rough drafts of these works, but there is ample evidence that Jane Austen often came back to her early stories and worked on improving them. Apparently, she too thought that they were worthy of notice. This is contrary to the opinions of her nephew James Edward Austen-Leigh, who wrote *A Memoir of Jane Austen*. Austen-Leigh writes that "it would be as unfair to expose this preliminary process to the world, as it would be to display all that goes on behind the curtain of the theatre before it is drawn up."

Allison Sulloway points outs that "Austen's juvenilia is both violent and mournful in ways that anticipate her mature fiction. She learned to modify the violence so that it is almost unrecognizable in her novels, but in 'volume the First' there are numerous descriptions of executions, amputations, female starvation, suicides, and attempted and successful murders of all kinds: matricide, fratricide, sororicide, and the attempted infanticide of an unwelcome newborn girl, who takes her revenge far more violently than indulging in some 'bantering.' She grows up to raise and command an army with which she slaughters her enemies."

The three tattered notebooks that survive are each dedicated to members of Austen's family, and the final volume still bears the inscription from Jane Austen's father Rev. George Austen, "Effusions of Fancy by a very Young Lady consisting of Tales in a Style entirely new." This appealing headline is appropriated in the film version of *Mansfield Park,* as are lines from much of the juvenilia. The director of this film recognized also the potential in Austen's early effusive, comic writing and, wisely or not, used it as an addition to Fanny Price's character to counter her marked silence throughout most of the novel itself.

As is evidenced by its use in the *Mansfield Park* film, the juvenilia *sounds* wonderful when spoken. Many scholars suggest that Austen would have read them aloud to her family members in their house at Steventon. Austen herself pokes fun at the idea of her stories ever really appealing to a large audience by suggesting, in her dedication of *Catharine, or the Bower,* that "The beautiful Cassandra, and The History of England . . . have obtained a place in every library in the Kingdom, and run through threescore Editions." What would she say if she knew the juvenilia has now run through at least four editions and many, many readers, suggesting once again its wanting to be read and considered.

CAPSULE

Love and Freindship: "Beware My Laura"

"Beware my Laura (she would often say) Beware of the insipid Vanities and idle Dissipations of the Metropolis of England; Beware of the unmeaning Luxuries of Bath and of the Stinking fish of Southampton"

—Love and Freindship

Laura, writing of the wisdom gained from her fifty-five years to her friend Isabel's daughter, Marianne, tells the story of her youth. It begins in a "romantic" cottage in the Vale of Uske in Wales. Laura has returned to her "paternal roof" here after having been educated in a convent in France. Now in her eighteenth year, she sees what she believes to be her destiny in a handsome stranger who begs shelter for himself and his servant at the door of Laura's home. He has refused to marry the woman his father has chosen for him, though he loves her, simply because he hates his father. He vows "Never shall it be said that I obliged my father." He immediately is wedded to Laura by her father, "who tho' he had never taken orders had been bred to the Church."

The couple then removes to the house of Edward's (for that is the stranger's name) kind aunt Phillipa and his sister Augusta, who is found to be entirely

disagreeable and wretched. The subsequent appearances of Edward's former suggested fiancée and Edward's father provoke further discomfort. The couple therefore makes away with Edward's father's carriage to retreat to the home of Edward's friend Augustus and his wife Sophia. The two women become instant confidants and, so affected by the reunion of their two husbands, "fainted Alternately on a Sofa."

Having determined, after most insistent invitations, to remain forever with Augustus and Sophia, Edward and Laura's felicity is interrupted by the arrest of Augustus as a result of his mounting debts. His execution is the determined solution of the court, and, having nothing else to do, the party all "sighed and fainted on the Sofa" again.

After the party recovers from the bout of fainting fits, Edward gathers his wits and sets off to London to be with his friend. His benevolence, however, is seen to be lacking when he does not return to our poor Laura and Sophia, cowering in a country house soon to be claimed by creditors. His desertion is "too unexpected a Blow to [their] Gentle Sensibility—. we could not support it—we could only faint." The women finally determine to pursue the wayward Edward to London, but to no avail. He is nowhere to be found. As the fragile

Sophia is entirely a victim of sensibility, she is in no state to see her husband in prison: "my feelings are sufficiently shocked by the *recital*, of his Distress, but to behold it will overpower my Sensibility."

They then determine to hasten to Sophia's relatives in Scotland. They are not far along on their journey when another stranger encounters them. Laura has a different sort of revelation about this elderly man—"an instinctive Sympathy whispered to my Heart, that he was my Grandfather." She is not mistaken, but the elderly man, Lord St Clair, is in for more surprises, as he recognizes not only Sophia as one of his other grandchildren, but Philander and Gustavus as well, who have happened to enter the exact same inn as the other two unfortunate young women. Overjoyed for a moment, then recollecting himself, Lord St Clair thrusts banknotes at the young people and immediately leaves the inn.

Confused but not defeated, Sophia and Laura proceed to the house of Sophia's cousin Macdonald and his daughter Janetta. Here Sophia and Laura are instrumental in saving Janetta from what they consider to be a horrifying match to a man who "had no soul, that he had never read the Sorrows of Werter, and that his Hair bore not the least resemblance to auburn" to whom they "were certain that Janetta could feel no affection . . . or at least that she ought to feel none. The very circumstance of his being her father's choice too, was so much in his disfavour." They convince her instead that she is desperately in love with one Captain M'Kenzie who appears to have no real affection

for her, though Laura and Sophia think differently about his real feelings toward Janetta. The captain is informed of his love for Janetta, agrees that it must be so, and marries her immediately.

Sophia and Laura's stay at Macdonald's house is to be limited, however, as they are caught in the act of stealing banknotes from his study to punish him for his unforgivable practicality and rational behavior in wishing his daughter to marry a reasonable man. Worse things are in store for our easily swayed pair, as they witness the overturning of the phaeton that was to have brought their husbands back to them. Upon seeing their husbands "weltering in their blood," Sophia "shrieked and fainted on the Ground—[Laura] screamed and instantly ran mad . . . For an Hour and a Quarter did we continue in this unfortunate Situation—Sophia fainting every moment and I running Mad as often." In the midst of this, both husbands die, and Sophia and Laura retire to the cottage of an old woman.

The next day, graver events occur. Sophia has taken sick from her continued exposure to the cold, and soon dies. Before doing so, however, she gives Laura some prudent advice: "Beware of fainting fits . . . One fatal swoon has cost me my Life . . . Beware of swoons Dear Laura . . . A frenzy fit is not one quarter so pernicious; it is an exercise to the Body and if not too violent, is I dare say conducive to Health in its consequences—Run mad as often as you chuse; but do not faint."

Leaving the cottage after her friend's death, Laura finds herself in a coach with nearly all of the previous characters in the story, including Isabel, the mother of Marianne, who is the recipient of all of the letters telling this story. Laura learns of what has befallen Edward's family in their absence, and deems all of his father's goings-on to be as expected "from a Man who possessed not the smallest atom of Sensibility, who scarcely knew the meaning of Simpathy [sic], and who actually snored."

The rest of Laura's journey is spent learning the fates of Philander and Gustavus, the other grandchildren of Lord St Clair, who have been employing themselves as traveling players. All is brought to a close with Laura's removal to a "romantic Village in the Highlands of Scotland," Augusta's marriage to the reasonable man intended for Janetta, Edward's father's marriage to his own choice for his son, and Laura's gaining of her solitude where she may "uninterrupted by unmeaning Visits, indulge in . . . unceasing Lamentations for the Death of my Father, my Mother, my Husband and my Freind [sic]."

Excerpt from the Juvenilia:
"The Adventures of Mr. Harley"

a short, but interesting Tale, is with all imaginable Respect inscribed to Mr Francis William Austen Midshipman on board his Majestys [sic] Ship the Perseverance by his Obedient Servant

The Author

Mr Harley was one of many Children. Destined by his father for the Church and by his Mother for the Sea, desirous of pleasing both, he prevailed on Sir John to obtain for him a Chaplaincy on board a Man of War. He accordingly, cut his Hair and sailed.

In half a year he returned and sat-off in the Stage Coach for Hogsworth Green, the seat of Emma. His fellow travelers were, A man without a Hat, Another with two, An old maid and a young Wife.

This last appeared about 17 with fine dark Eyes and an elegant Shape; inshort Mr Harley soon found out, that she was his Emma and recollected that he had married her a few weeks before he left England.

FINIS.

If She Could See Them Now:
Austen's Relationship with Her Publishers

Jane Austen suffered every author's nightmare: a book that lay unpublished for years (*Northanger Abbey*) and books that were remaindered (but only after her death). She miscalculated and sold the copyright to her most popular novel. She saw her own book titles ("First Impressions," which became *Pride and Prejudice* and "Susan," which became *Northanger Abbey*) published on someone else's books before she could have her own books published.

Was Austen reluctant to publish, as some family myths claim? No way. She knew what she was doing—she was involved in the negotiations with publishers and tracked her earnings very closely. Kathryn Sutherland, who has studied the early texts of the novels, the manuscripts, the corrected editions, and everything one possibly can study about the printed history of Jane Austen, concludes that Austen "shows from the outset a twin determination to enter the market as writer at the elite end and to garner as much prestige and money from the business as she can."

Jane Austen was a reader; she knew what publishers were publishing because she read their authors: Maria Edgeworth, Mrs. Radcliffe, Charlotte Lennox, Fanny Burney.

In Regency England, besides buying the book outright, other opportunities for reading existed: there were circulating libraries, subscription libraries, and reading clubs. Because England was almost constantly at war during Austen's lifetime, the price of books went from expensive to prohibitively expensive. Publishers often aimed their books toward the circulating library. The library was to publishers what the novel was to libraries—the mainstay.

Austen's family encouraged her to write and were eager listeners, beginning in her teens, to what she wrote. George Austen encouraged his daughter to publish her work and acted as her first agent, writing to publisher Thomas Cadell in London in 1797. The offer of the manuscript was rejected, however, by return of post. Family tradition reports that the manuscript rejected was *First Impressions*.

Four publishing possibilities existed at this time. You could publish by subscription. Jane Austen was a subscriber, herself, to Fanny Burney's *Camilla,* but for herself as an author, Jane Austen did not choose this avenue. A second option was to arrange the publication of the novel on commission, in which the book is published at the author's risk. This was Austen's method of choice for her novels, and it is how *Sense and Sensibility,* her first published novel, was published. Her publisher was Thomas Egerton (see title page of the book on p. 25). Egerton printed and distributed the book, and for this, received a commission of 10 percent. The revenue the book earned would be used to cover the costs the publisher incurred. Waiting for its publication, she wrote, "I am never too busy to think of Sense and Sensibility. I can no more forget it, than a mother can forget her suckling child." The first edition of one thousand copies was published in November 1811. It sold out by July 1813, and Austen earned £140. By September, she knew there would be a second edition. When the second edition came out she wrote to Cassandra, "I cannot help hoping that *many* will feel themselves obliged to buy it."

Austen's third option was to sell the copyright of the book. The copyright lasted for twenty-eight years. Jane Austen chose this method for *Pride and Prejudice,* which she sold for £110. In a letter of 29 November 1812, she wrote about the price "I would rather have had £150, but we could not both be pleased, & I am not at all surprised that he should not chuse to hazard so much." *Pride and Prejudice* went through three editions in her lifetime. Because she had sold the copyright, she made no further money on it. (As she gained more experience, she was able to make wiser decisions.) Austen's letter about the selling of *Pride and Prejudice* continues, "Its' being sold will I hope be a great saving of Trouble to Henry, & therefore must be welcome to me.—The Money is to be paid at the end of the twelvemonth." The reference to Henry is to her brother, who had been acting as her literary representative. It was expected that male relatives would negotiate with the publishers on behalf of a woman author. Soon, however, Austen will take over more and more herself.

Her letter indicates how closely she was involved in the entire business of publishing. We see that Jane wanted more for the copyright. She knew *Sense and Sensibility* had been successful, and she knows when to expect the money. When Austen gets her first copy, she refers to it as "my own darling Child," and notes the price. She and her family take an early opportunity to read it out loud to a neighbor (though not revealing who the author of the book is). Austen was concerned with how the book is presented, how it is responded to, how much it costs, and how it will be advertised. Later she will note in a letter the misprints she finds in one of her books. She was intimately involved and interested in all aspects of her books' publication.

Praise and Pewter

The success of *Pride and Prejudice* meant that Austen was alert to several things: First, she noticed Egerton charged more for the *Pride and Prejudice* than he did for *Sense and Sensibility* (he had more to make from the former than the latter). Second, that selling the copyright was not as profitable to her as publishing the book on commission. So, with her third book, *Mansfield Park,* a small first edition was published on commission.

"Tho' I like praise as well as anybody, I like what Edward calls Pewter *too."*
—*Jane Austen*
Regency coins courtesy Baronda Ellen Bradley.

That edition sold out faster than *Pride and Prejudice* did. Considering a second edition, she wrote, "it is not settled yet whether I *do* hazard a second edition. We are to see Egerton today, when it will be determined.—People are more ready to borrow & praise than to buy . . . but tho' I like praise as well as anybody, I like what Edward calls *Pewter* too."

When Egerton decided not to bring out a second edition, she changed publishers.

Henry did the negotiation with John Murray about *Emma.* Austen writes, "Mr Murray's letter is come. He is a rogue, of course, but a civil one. He offers £450 but wants to have the copyright of *Mansfield Park* and *Sense and Sensibility* included. It will end in my publishing for myself I daresay. He sends more praise however than I expected."

Instead, she agreed to publishing on commission. Jan Fergus, who has studied Austen's publishing history closely, says that "Austen would have done well to accept" Murray's offer. She would have received that money, £450, within a year. Murray, with little stake in *Emma* (only a 10 percent interest), printed two thousand copies. *Emma* sold 1,200 copies in 1816. But the second edition of *Mansfield Park,* published in February 1816, lost money. When Murray subtracted the losses from *Mansfield Park* against the profits of *Emma,* Austen had made about £39.

Kathryn Sutherland reports that during the time that Austen was seeking publication of her novels, about sixty to eighty new titles were published a year in England. Generally, a first run of a new work would be modest—500 to 750 copies. When *Emma* was published with two thousand copies, this was indeed a very encouraging sign! Besides this, the publisher of *Emma,* Murray, was a step up from her earlier novels. He published poets like Byron, but not many novels. Moving to Murray, Austen got a larger print run and the book was handsomer. And it garnered Austen her first review, from Walter Scott. Sutherland tells us "When she moved to Murray only four years after her début as a published author, Jane Austen had arrived."

M.A.D.?

Austen's first novel accepted for publication was not the first novel *published,* and this understandably rankled Austen. She had sold "Susan" to Benjamin Crosby for £10 in 1803. But he did not publish it. It sat on the shelf for many years.

Why didn't Crosby publish "Susan"? In 1932, the novelist Rebecca West imagined what had happened: the publisher, at first, had taken but a casual glance at Austen's manuscript, and thought it "a pleasant tale about pleasant people, written in simple English; and it had the further advantage, from the point of view of the circulating libraries, that it was plainly written by a lady who wrote from her own knowledge of life as it was lived in country seats and at Bath." So he paid £10. But then he looked again. Wasn't it mocking the other books he published? This was a predicament! And then he put it aside. If much later, as it sat there in his office, Crosby had realized he had in his office a work by the author of *Pride and Prejudice,* perhaps Austen would have found this novel finally published. But we get ahead of ourselves; instead it languished at the publisher's office. She wrote to him on April 5, 1809, as "Mrs. Ashton Dennis," a name which allowed herself to sign the letter "M.A.D.", to remind him that they had bought the book six years earlier, and that if they needed a second manuscript copy (because the first was presumably lost), she could send them one. (Note: she made second copies of her work!)

On behalf of his father, Richard Crosby wrote to Mrs. Dennis telling her that they would take legal action if she were to publish the manuscript elsewhere. But she could buy it back for the £10 they had paid for it. She must not have had the money to do this, and so it remained until 1816 when Henry Austen took over the negotiation. Again they offered to resign their right to publish it if they were reimbursed the £10. Once Henry had paid them, and only then, did Henry inform Crosby who the author was.

Because another book called *Susan* had appeared in 1809, Austen changed the heroine's name to *Catherine.* She wrote an introduction to explain that the book was originally meant to appear much earlier. But then her brother Henry went bankrupt and her health began to fail. On 13 March 1817, she wrote "Miss Catherine is put upon the Shelve for the present, and I do not know that she will ever come out." Austen died that July, and shortly thereafter Henry and Cassandra approached John Murray about the publication of what they had now entitled *Northanger Abbey* and *Persuasion.* Murray agreed, and in December 1817, wrote to Lady Abercorn, "I am printing two short but very clever novels by poor Miss Austen, the author of 'Pride and Prejudice.'" A "Biographical Notice of the Author" by Henry accompanied those short, clever novels.

And with this, Austen's name appeared, for the first time, as author of her own books.

"Jane Austen Had Arrived"

Kathryn Sutherland says that with the publication of *Emma* and the switch to John Murray, Jane Austen had arrived. But, there were still bumpy times ahead. In 1817, Austen calculated how much pewter she had earned: about £600:

£140 for the first edition of *Sense and Sensibility*

£110 for the copyright of *Pride and Prejudice*

£350 for the first edition of *Mansfield Park* and the second of *Sense and Sensibility.*

Murray remaindered Austen's books in 1821, four years after her death. Cassandra and Henry sold the copyright of the books, other than *Pride and Prejudice,* for £250 to Richard Bentley, who brought them out in 1833. By the end of the twentieth century, Austen's novels were marketed as "chick lit." Now, in the twenty-first century, the romance field has discovered Austen, trying to reach the teen market. Jane Austen gets the praise, but her publishers get the pewter.

1818-1976 Individual Reprints of Jane Austen Novels

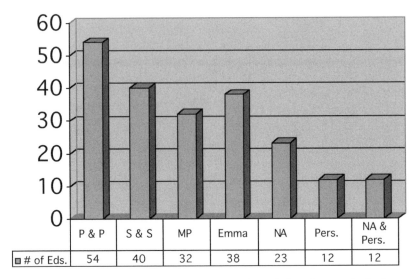

	P & P	S & S	MP	Emma	NA	Pers.	NA & Pers.
▣ # of Eds.	54	40	32	38	23	12	12

1818-1976 Individual reprints of Jane Austen novels, excluding foreign, abridged, or school editions. Information from Barbara M. Benedict and Deirdre Le Faye's "Introduction" to Northanger Abbey *in* The Cambridge Edition of the Works of Jane Austen.

CAPSULE

Emma

Besides Anne Elliot, whose situation is very different, Emma Woodhouse—"handsome, clever, and rich, with a comfortable home and happy disposition"—is the only heroine not under pressure to marry. She is also, as many critics have pointed out, the only character in Austen's six major published novels to successfully achieve book-title status. (Other characters in other novels *almost* put their names to book titles, *Sense and Sensibility* was at first to be "Elinor and Marianne," and *Northanger Abbey* was known to Austen as "Catherine.") That Emma is the title character seems both fitting and odd for the novel itself, as Emma's consciousness does indeed direct most of the narrative. However, the involvement of so-called "minor" characters takes a comparatively large degree of importance. Indeed in the earlier *Pride and Prejudice* and *Sense and Sensibility* we meet a variety of important characters and settings, but the town of Meryton and its inhabitants in *Pride and Prejudice* have nothing like the weight of Highbury society in all its variants in *Emma*.

The close-knit and eagerly protected sets of people in Highbury are especially important because of the novel's fixed nature. There are no London seasons here; nor are there extended visits to other parts of the countryside like Lizzy's visits to Hunsford and Devonshire in *Pride and Prejudice*. Because the narrative is linked so closely to Emma's consciousness, living alone at Hartfield with her father (who is either truly ill, a nervous mess, or a hypochondriac), the narrative is also limited in terms of space and scope. Aside from the excursion to Box Hill, *Emma* is concerned only with Highbury and the surrounding estates of Hartfield and Donwell Abbey.

The closeness of the parameters here brings some predictable results. Primarily, of course, everyone knows everyone, as is to be expected in any small town. As a result of this, everyone is also aware of the advantages and disadvantages of acquaintances with different groups of people. So, with a limited

The anonymous gift of a pianoforte to Jane Fairfax introduces mystery into the lives of Highbury, and a reminder to Emma that Miss Fairfax's "performance, both vocal and instrumental, she never could attempt to conceal from herself, was infinitely superior to her own." From a set of Rowlandson's Etchings. 1790. Courtesy of The Lewis Walpole Library, Yale University. 790.6.27.1.

number of acceptable acquaintances, boredom must set in for someone as clever and wealthy as Emma. Given this, the introduction of unknown or mysterious factors may cause quite a stir.

Emma most adequately deals with all of these factors, including the mysterious. The novel opens by registering a change in the town life that will also afford opportunities for introduction to a large ensemble cast. Miss Taylor, Emma's former governess, has married, now becoming Mrs. Weston. The post-ceremony opening scene at Hartfield introduces the reader to Emma and her father, whose incessant repetition of "poor Miss Taylor" marks him as an opponent to change for the novel to come. Emma mourns the disruption of the deep friendship that had grown up between her and the serenely ladylike Mrs. Weston.

She finds Mr. Weston honorable and delightful, and then her thoughts flit to the visibly lonely Mr. Elton, the parish clergyman. Emma considers the ceremony itself to be the successful fruits of her "matchmaking."

Mr. Knightley, owner of nearby Donwell Abbey, stops by to inquire about the wedding. As it is a mild night, he needs to draw back from the fire, prompting Mr. Woodhouse to worry about his catching cold. Besides introducing us to Mr. Woodhouse's ongoing health worries, this is also the first of [71] many sessions of bandying of words between Knightley and Emma. This close relationship is to be a constant throughout the novel.

There are at least four eligible bachelors in *Emma*: Mr. George Knightley, squire, a magistrate, administrator of justice for the community, generous friend; Rev. Elton, Frank Churchill, and Robert Martin. There are three motherless daughters in *Emma*: Emma, Harriet Smith (the daughter of a somebody), and Jane Fairfax. Into their lives some romance must come, but they are confused and confusing romances to be sure.

Convinced that the successful union of Miss Taylor and Mr. Weston owes itself entirely to her own ingenuity, Emma decides that her considerable talent as a matchmaker should not go to waste. Instead, she determines that the effusive Mr. Elton will be her next target. His match, in Emma's estimation, is thrown into her path by her father's acquaintance with the schoolmistress Mrs. Goddard. Harriet Smith, a former pupil at the school, is a simple girl of uncertain parentage whose claims of beauty and sweetness cause Emma to like her instantly.

The notion of Harriet and Mr. Elton's perfection for one another throws Emma into a flurry of schemes to bring them together: painting Harriet's portrait while Mr. Elton looks on, pretending to lace up her boot so that Harriet and Mr. Elton may walk alone together,

wheedling compliments out of Mr. Elton on Harriet's manners, and so on. All of Emma's efforts receive enthusiastic praise from Mr. Elton, whose fervor, Emma assumes, is for Harriet. So confident is Emma of Harriet's success in gaining Mr. Elton that she, in one of her more unforgivable moments, persuades Harriet to reject a marriage proposal from Robert Martin, a respectable farmer for whom it is clear Harriet harbors a genuine affection. To this, Mr. Knightley says "Better be without sense than misapply it as you do."

Soon the news is known about town that someone new—two or three someones "new"—are to be expected. As new information is precious in a town whose usual great concern is whether or not it will rain, the anticipation of the addition of two new young people at once is enough to busy the people of Highbury with talking for hours. Jane Fairfax is the first to arrive.

Highbury has not long to chatter about its new addition and her superiority at singing and playing the pianoforte before it receives another shocking bit of news. Mr. Elton, who has been away in Bath for no great amount of time, has already found himself a fiancée in a Miss Hawkins with £10,000 to her name. Now the number of expected arrivals in town rises once again to two: Mr. Frank Churchill and the new Mrs. Elton.

Emma speaks with Mrs. Elton first at Hartfield and is instantly put off by Mrs. Elton's snobbishness and vulgar familiarity with the people of Highbury, whom she has only just met. Particularly offensive is her praise of "Knightley" and her surprise at finding Mrs. Weston's manners to be genteel. Mrs. Elton's disagreeable qualities continue to manifest themselves in her subsequent ill treatment of Harriet and her adoption of Jane Fairfax as her pet project.

And before we know it we are caught up with the lives of the Highbury residents ourselves. It is as good a situation as if we had Miss Bates herself, a garrulous, friendly, and kind woman who lives with her mother, the widow of a rector, keeping us informed of all that happens. But whereas Miss Bates cannot keep a secret, the story of *Emma* is concerned with secrets and the secret-keepers. The puzzles, conundrums, and word games that fill the pages of the novel hint that this is so. *Emma* abounds in word games, from the collection of Harriet's charades (including Mr. Elton's) to the Scrabble-like anagram game played by Emma, Frank Churchill, and Miss Smith. The book is a riddle that is filled with riddles; even the letters are "crossed." (That is, once the page of a letter was filled, the letter was rotated 90° and written upon the other words.)

Reginald Ferrars called *Emma* Austen's "Book of Books." It is also a book with a book within. It is said that there is a second novel hidden within *Emma*. Some see it as like a detective story. As the riddles and letters suggest, decipherment is the theme. We reread the novel to see the red herrings, the missed clues. Like Emma, we discover that we have been clueless. By the end, secrets become known, and some change does come to the town.

Knightley in Bath.
Sketch by Douglas Buchanan.

Many call Emma a snob, but when the real snob—Augusta Elton—comes to town, august in her manner, we see what snobbery actually consists of: Dropping references to "barouche-landaus" and being officious, overfamiliar, petty, and cruel. When Richard Jenkins lists the villains in Austen's novels (individuals like Lucy Steele and Willoughby, for instance), he suggests that in *Emma*, the Eltons are not villains, though *he* is mean and *she* is vulgarly self-centered, because "they have no power over the heroine's life." Who are the villains then? Ah, the clues are there.

By the end of the book, Emma has discovered a great deal about herself, as well as something important about others: "essentially the autonomy of other people." She has learned to handle a great deal of change, but, then, there are some things that will never change, and her father's fire will probably still cause most other people to draw further away from it.

Mr. Knightley, Detective

*Was Mrs. Churchill's death merely convenient or something more sinister? In the
following letter, we imagine what the possible speculations of Mr. Knightley might
be—if he had a mind to do a little detecting. After all, he is a man for whom suspicions of Mr. Churchill's behavior is nothing new.*

My Dearest Emma,

I am writing to you with the utmost need for secrecy. While in London this day
on the business we discussed, I have discovered something quite dire indeed.
This afternoon I met with Mr. Frank Churchill's bookkeeper. As you may remember, Mr. Churchill had applied to me for a small loan to assist in purchasing a
Broadwood pianoforte for the now-Mrs. Churchill—a new instrument without the
duplicitous connotations of its predecessor.

As I glanced over Mr. Churchill's books and recent receipts of purchase in order
to obtain that everything was in order and to assuage my doubts as to his character, I happened upon the section of the ledger for June 25, the day before the
unfortunate death of Mr. Churchill's aunt. Marked in those lines were two small
trivial purchases and another larger, unidentified purchase. Only the place of purchase was marked—Chichester & Sons.

Upon quitting the meeting I quickly found the location of the store, my curiosity
piqued. Once finding the shop, I entered and saw it to be a supplier of various and
sundry alchemical instruments and supplies. Searching for goods that approximat-
ed the price tallied in the ledger, I soon came upon a small aisle filled with brown
bottles containing medicines and chemical concoctions. Three or four bottles
matched the price I had seen.

I questioned the old storekeeper upon this matter and asked him as to whether he
had sold any of those products recently to a man of Mr. Churchill's description.
The vendor conceded that he had, and identified the liquid that had been purchased. I thanked him and dashed out of the store, intent on finding a physician
friend of mine whom I had met during my school years.

Emma, I pray you are sitting while you read this, for what I am about to tell you is chilling indeed. The kind physician informed me as to the effects of the liquid. It is a dangerous substance often used in chemical experimentations. I risked asking what would occur to the unfortunate individual who imbibed such a liquid. The answer—complications of the heart and sudden seizures.

I recall the letter which Mr. Churchill wrote to you, concerning, I believe, the "confusion of his mind" and the "multiplicity of his business" following his aunt's death. I am all but convinced that this was not just the distress of a nephew—it was the guilt of a murderer. It seemed odd to me that Mrs. Jane Churchill had not accepted any post prior to her confrontation with Mr. Churchill at our outing at Box Hill. On further consideration, it seems as if she knew all along she would not be needing any outside source of income. I fear that they were contriving this plan together, and, afraid that Jane had lost patience and would leave him, *and* astonished that his once-sickly relative had suddenly improved in health, I believe Mr. Churchill decided to speed along the course of nature in his unsuspecting aunt.

I entreat you to speak of this to no one, and to keep a close eye on Miss Bates. I fear Mr. Churchill's short patience with this talkative relative will make her next in his plans. I will hurry back to you with all due haste.

With greatest love, and fear,

Mr. Knightley

Emma's Dream:
Austen and Shakespeare Meet
on a Midsummer Night

Lysander:
Ay me! for aught that I could ever read,
Could ever hear by tale or history,
The course of true love never did run smooth;
But either it was different in blood—

Hermia:
O cross! too high to be enthrall'd to low.

Lysander:
Or else misgraffèd in respect of years—

Hermia:
O spite! too old to be engag'd to young.

Lysander:
Or else it stood upon the choice of friends—

Hermia:
O hell! to choose love by another's eyes.

A Midsummer Night's Dream Act 1,
scene 1, 132-140

"There does seem to be something in the air of Hartfield which give love exactly the right direction and sends it into the very channel where it ought to flow.

The course of true love never did run smooth.

A Hartfield edition of Shakespeare would have a long note on that passage."

—Emma to Harriet Smith

The Love Letter. *Courtesy of The Lewis Walpole Library, Yale University 785.10.11.1.*

Was Shakespeare's *A Midsummer Night's Dream* the inspiration for *Emma*? Let us ask, rather, "Can the course of true love run smooth?" In *Emma*, Austen says with Shakespeare, not very likely.

Midsummer begins, like *Emma*, with tangled affections and social strictures: Lysander and Hermia are in love, but Demetrius *also* loves Hermia, who does not return his affections in the least. Demetrius, meanwhile, is being pursued by the fair Helena. Unfortunately for Lysander and Hermia, Theseus—the Duke of Athens, engaged to Hippolyta,

queen of the Amazons—rules that so long as Demetrius loves Hermia, she must either marry him, or forfeit her life to the sacrificial altar or to a nunnery. So says the ancient law of Athens.

Things look bleak for Lysander and Hermia, who decide that the best tactic is to run off into the nearby woods, which turn out to be the haunt of the fairies. Among these are Oberon and Titania, King and Queen of the wood, and "that shrewd and knavish sprite" Robin Goodfellow, also known as Puck.

Demetrius, learning of his love's escape, chases after her; Helena follows in turn. During the course of the night, Puck deposits a love potion on the eyes of the sleeping humans, first turning Lysander's, and then Demetrius', affections to Helena. Fortunately, Oberon intervenes ere long to straighten out the lovers' ties: at last, Lysander and Hermia are back together, and Demetrius and Helena are in love.

Before he does this, Oberon has one trick of his own to play: Titania is duped, via the same love potion, into loving the unlucky Bottom the Weaver, an erstwhile actor whose troop was rehearsing in the fairy-filled forest. Titania—and Bottom—are further humiliated when Bottom's features are transformed to those of a donkey!

By dawn, all is made right, and not only are all four couples happy (Lysander and Hermia, Demetrius and Helena, Theseus and Hippolyta, Titania and Oberon), but Bottom's troupe survives the local acting competition, presenting "The most lamentable comedy, and most cruel death of Pyramus and Thisby." This play-within-a-play's characters, Pyramus and Thisby, are the only unhappy couple in *Midsummer,* dispatched respectively by a lion and by suicide.

Though virginal suicides and death by lion factor little into Austen's schemes (to say nothing of Emma's), the complexities of *Midsummer's* relationships certainly smack of Austenian machinations. It is impossible to overlay the relationships exactly. Yet, there are patterns common to the two plots. For instance, ample evidence is provided that Demetrius led Helena on before the play be-gins, just as Frank Churchill establishes a relationship (engagement) with Jane Fairfax before they enter Emma's circle. While the females in each story remain constant throughout their respective plots, the males tend toward being cads. Demetrius loves Hermia through most of *Midsummer,* and Mr. Churchill allows his affections to wander in order to disguise his engagement with Jane. Helena is described as "All fancy-sick she is, and pale of cheer." Jane has "wan, sick looks."

Mr. Churchill, along with Mr. Elton, is on the receiving end of "false" and "coerced" crushes, much like Bottom. Emma convinces herself, albeit briefly, that she likes Mr. Churchill, and also convinces Miss Smith that she is in love with Mr. Elton. Once Miss Smith sees past the asinine Elton and Emma disperses her affections for Churchill—who makes Jane the "butt" of his actions— the women find their true matches, the Oberons to their Titanias. Like Bottom, who "must to the barbers," Frank claims to go to London for a haircut.

If this parallel is continued further, it makes Mr. Martin and Mr. Knightley equivalent to Oberon himself, which is strangely fitting. Knightley is Oberon's lordly aspect while Martin the farmer resonates with the fairies' connection with earth and nature. Oberon's character is somewhere between the two, as the fairies exist "in between." In Shakespeare, they exist between the waking and the dreaming world; in Christianized folklore, they exist between Heaven and Hell, and cannot enter either.

But wait: wouldn't the final lordly marriage of Emma and Knightley more befit a parallel to Theseus and Hippolyta, whose wedding brings the political stability to their country as Knightley's brings stability to his tenants? Or wouldn't a better match to Theseus and Hippolyta be Mr. and Mrs. Weston, whose love has remained a constant from the beginning? Ay, there's the rub, that in these parallels Austen must give us pause.

The problem is that there are just too many couples in *Emma* for it to fit in with *Midsummer*. There are five couples in Austen's work, four in Shakespeare's, unless the ill-fated Pyramus and Thisby are included, and, as fictional characters, do they or don't they count? Austen seems to have taken the patterns in *Midsummer* and broken and refracted them in *Emma* as in a kaleidoscope. Certain characters parallel others, while some parallel none at all, and others overlap—just as Emma and Knightley and the Westons overlap with Theseus and Hippolyta.

Moonlit nights begin both works. The Crown is described by Miss Bates as "meeting quite in fairy-land!" And the dance is prelude to some of the key events that occur around midsummer; the visit to Donwell Abbey, "under a bright mid-day sun, at almost midsummer." The excursion to Box Hill occurs on an even hotter day. Some say Knightley proposes on Old Midsummer's Day

(July 26). And what causes the course of true love not to run smooth? Hermia says "too high to be enthrall'd to low"—isn't that what Elton says, scoffingly, when he hears Emma intended him for Miss Smith. "*Miss* Smith?—Message to Miss *Smith*?" Hermia also identifies another problem, "too old to be engag'd to young." Knightley and Emma are able to overcome this!

Emma herself is a confusing blend of characters: receiver of love, giver of love, and manipulator of love. The last suggests that she retains some of the trickster characteristics of Puck. Her attempts at concocting love meet with the same ill fortune as the fairy's do. Oberon's plans for easing the troubled hearts in the complicated love square of Hermia, Lysander, Helena, and Demetrius are continually botched by the trickster spirit. It is finally Oberon who must mend the rifts—just as it is Knightley who keeps Emma in check and encourages Mr. Martin to renew his wooing of Miss Smith.

Something other than exactitude is gained by viewing *Emma* through *Midsummer*. A sort of illumination is achieved: the relationships in *Emma* begin to resonate with the love plots of another comedic work. There is a calm achieved, knowing that all is right with the world, that both Puck—and Austen—shall make amends.

Initial Impressions, or,
"I'm Missing Your Letters":
The Austen Crossword Puzzle

1	2	3			4			5	6	7	8	9	
10					11			12					13
14			15	16	17		18	19		20			21
22		23					24		25		26		
	27				28		29		30				
31			32				33					34	35
36			37								38		
39		40								41			
42			43	44	45	46	47	48	49	50	51	52	
53			54				55				56		
		57					58			59			
60	61			62		63		64				65	
66			67		68			69			70		
71		72		73			74			75			
	76						77						

ACROSS

1.   Gambling debts of 77 across
5.   Passion
10. Gardening implement
11. "__ say can you see"
12. Nancy Steele's clothing worry at Kensington Gardens
13. Canadian interjection
14. Article, for Bingley or Wentworth
15. The five vowels, without those in 56 across
18. NA heroine
20. Quick
22. "by __ Lady"
23. Not yours
24. It disappears when you stand up
26. Subterranean vein of metal
27. Characteristic of Austen's countryside
29. Gettin' fou' stars?
31. "__ or __ not, there is no try"
32. In place of
33. Greek deity who certainly watches over Austen's heroines
34. E, P, PP, SS, NA, and ___
36. "The Great ël __'"
37. 37 Across's 43 Across inflames 31 Down's 35 Down
38. This __ that.
39. "King," to Britain's Caesarian conquerors
41. "King," to Eliza de Feuillide's husband
42. Business title addendum, "& __"
43. 37 Across's 43 Across inflames 31 Down's 35 Down
52. LP replacement
53. Lost city of British myth
54. Egyptian cheer for the sun god?

55. "___ and alack!" (popular Romantic cry)
56. Ancient predecessor of Jane Austen and Geoffrey Chaucer's language (abbr.)
57. This type of person understood 39 Across
58. Mister W's daughter, before her marriage to Mister GK
60. Dregs
62. Admiral and Mrs. Croft's home?
64. Tools like pocketknives have many ___
65. Pirate syllable?
66. Many 58 Acrosses
68. Sister to 63 Down (abbr.)
69. ___ and match
70. "___ be, or not ___ be"
71. Afternoon drink
72. Slang "isn't"
73. Blue__? (as in bird)
75. Singular 45 Down
76. Mr. Gardiner's relation to 37 across
77. Dastard and holder of 1 Across

DOWN

1.   "Eureka!"
2.   Fish eggs
3.   In e-mail, concerning a FWD
4.   Jazz standard "__ What?"
5.   Young daughter of the foppish family thwarting CM in NA
6.   In law, a thing
7.   Lucy Steele and Robert Ferrar's honeymoon locale
8.   Star-belted celestial design
9.   Pirate syllable

13. Mrs. Norris's action, toward food she stole
15. Austen's heroines walk down this in the end, though their author never did
16. Up to
17. Two of the vowel's; "a.k.a, a.k.a., me"
18. PP victim of a simpering clergyman
19. Kitt-E B's sister?
21. 3,000 pounds to nothing convincer (abbr.)
23. In Zen, this was Joshu's
25. Cut down
27. Loverboys
28. Shakespearean cousin
30. Tiny or tater
31. 37 Across's 43 Across inflames 31 Down's 35 Down
34. Milk provider, in childspeak?
35. 37 Across's 43 Across inflames 31 Down's 35 Down
40. Unknown
41. Question word?
43. Commonplace writing, not Austen's

44. Male sheep
45. Many epochs
46. Charlotte B. title character
47. Female companion to 44 Down
48. Water blocker
49. Odysseus conquered its topless towers
50. Austen's sister's nickname?
51. British county, not Sus or Wes
57. Stock with new personnel, perhaps to Wentworth
59. Latin, "sum, __, est; summus, estis, sunt"
60. To rent a room
61. 58 Across nickname?
63. This heroine's husband's profession lies on 62 across (abbr.)
65. Travel aimlessly
67. "The Not-Ready-for-Prime-Time Players" show
70. "The Flowers that Bloom in the Spring, ___ la"
73. Latin plural for 76 Down
74. SS dastard
75. Canadian interjection
76. Not me

Solutions to the crossword puzzle may be found on pp. 211-212.

CAPSULE

Northanger Abbey

It is perhaps appropriate that Jane Austen's *Northanger Abbey* finds its heroine, Catherine Morland, poking about in dark, antique closets in search of long-forgotten manuscripts, for Austen's novel, originally titled *Susan,* met with this very fate for many years. It was purchased by a publisher "by the spring of the year 1803," after having been drafted beginning around 1798. Richard Crosby of London, the publisher, advertised the work. For some reason, however, the manuscript languished, locked away in a London publishing house. Jane Austen wrote angrily to the publisher after a six-year delay and was offered the opportunity to buy her manuscript back. The helpless manuscript, then, in true Gothic fashion, was being held hostage. Austen finally accepts this opportunity in 1816, but the book is not published until after her death. In 1817, Jane Austen's brother Henry oversaw the joint publication of *Persuasion* and *Northanger Abbey,* almost twenty years after Jane Austen had begun her manuscript of the latter.

There are in Austen's text some aspects that may have been challenging for the publisher. In many respects, this work differs from Austen's five other major published novels. In essence, this work is a novel about reading novels. In making her heroine an avid novel-reader, and emphasizing this fact, Austen gives herself a canvas on which to display her

views on her own art form. This she does with an emphatic authorial voice, chiding those high-standing persons who would deride novels as simply unintelligent sources of pleasure for women. She makes her case in this text for novels as significant forms of expression, with "genius, wit, and taste to recommend them," works in which "the greatest powers of mind are displayed, in which the most thorough knowledge of human nature, the happiest delineation of its varieties, the liveliest effusions of wit and humour, are conveyed to the world in the best chosen language."

Such authorial interjections are brought about through the actions of the spirited Catherine Morland, who is by no means an idealized heroine. She is somewhat plain and fond of boyish pastimes (including rolling down hills and "base ball" in its earliest reference in literature). One critic, Richard Jenkyns, says that "If this were Jane Austen's only novel, Catherine would be celebrated as one of the most charming heroines in English fiction." Yes, she is quite a heroine! In fact, we learn from another critic, Emily Auerbach, that "Austen uses *heroine, hero, heroism, heroic, heroines* more times in *Northanger Abbey* than double that of the five other novels combined."

Catherine, her parents, and her nine siblings reside in Fullerton. So, too, fortuitously for our heroine, do Mr. and Mrs. Allen, a wealthy, property-owning older couple. Mrs. Allen has been called by one writer "the apotheosis of the negative." G. B. Stern finds in her character "the complete proof of that extraordinary phenomenon which makes genius able to present us with a bore in whose actual company we would not willingly endure five minutes were she suddenly introduced to us outside the frame of fiction, and yet hang with ecstasy on every word she utters, longing for more, when created by Jane Austen."

When Mr. Allen is ordered to Bath, a spa with hot springs, for his health, Catherine is invited along to experience a new part of the world. And so begins her education. In the introduction to the new Cambridge edition of *Northanger Abbey,* we are told, "Although almost all critics agree that Catherine needs to learn something, they differ on what and how." *Where* is less in debate. She will

The Pump Room—a favorite venue for seeing and being seen in Bath, as Catherine Morland quickly finds out: "Every morning now brought its regular duties—shops were to be visited; some new part of the town to be looked at; and the pump-room to be attended, where they paraded up and down for an hour, looking at everybody and speaking to no one."

The Pump Room, *Bath, the Bridgeman Art Library*

Henry Tilney, sketch © Anne Timmons. Courtesy of the artist.

Catherine Morland and Isabella Thorpe, sketch © Anne Timmons. Courtesy of the artist.

learn many things during the eighteen chapters she spends in Bath.

Unfortunately the country party is not blessed with a large acquaintance in Bath, so the first few appearances at balls and at the Pump Room pass without event. Very soon after their arrival, however, in the Lower Assembly Rooms, Catherine is introduced to one Henry Tilney, a clergyman. He seems to be everything that is agreeable and charming and talks to Catherine, condescendingly, of writing and muslins, of the journal he is sure she keeps and what she should write in it.

Catherine's attentions are diverted by her introduction to the daughters of one of Mrs. Allen's old schoolfellows, Mrs. Thorpe. Isabella Thorpe, the eldest daughter, is four years older than Catherine, and the two begin immedi-

ately to embark upon an intimate friendship. Isabella's brother John is a friend of Catherine's brother James. What really binds the two friends together is their shared love of novels. The frequency of Bath's rainy days pose no great threat to the contentment of these two friends, as Maria Edgeworth's, Fanny Burney's, or Anne Radcliffe's novels are always ready to while away the hours. Foremost of these works is Mrs. Radcliffe's Gothic tale, *The Mysteries of Udolpho,* an exotic story of foreign castles with intrigue and danger at every turn.

The two girls are involved in a discussion of this very work on the morning in which they chance to run into both John Thorpe and James Morland. Two things become evident in this encounter. The first is John Thorpe's undeniable silliness and triviality. He talks only of carriages and horses and makes himself still more disagreeable by voicing his impatience with novels and novelists. He is ill-bred and coarse. The second of these two things is the evidence of some affection, or at least shyness, existent between Isabella Thorpe and James Morland.

Catherine's dangers sometimes seem small: Thorpe has forgotten his promise to dance with her and she is left without a partner; his sister, Isabella Thorpe is like him, shallow, vulgar, self-centered, self-absorbed. Catherine remarks at one point, "I cannot speak well enough to be unintelligible." She is blunt, and therefore honest; around her is artifice and falsehood.

The young Thorpes build fictions about Catherine. They lie *to* her and they lie *about* her. Catherine must defeat their fictions; what the Tilneys are doing; who Catherine chooses to be with; misinformation they give the Tilneys; whether Catherine is an heiress or not; what Isabella believes; *who* Isabella loves. With reality constantly contradicting the Thorpes (that he has a dangerous horse, Not!; that Isabella sits near the door because it is "out of the way," Ha!) they seem the only ones not to notice. And as Catherine compares what they say to what she can see, her education is under way. She learns how to read past artifice, how to see under superficial manners.

Finally, Catherine is able to free herself, for a morning, from the clutches of the Thorpes, and she walks happily about the surrounding countryside in the company of Henry and Eleanor Tilney. Their ramblings lead them into discus-

"As soon as divine service was over, the Thorpes and Allens eagerly joined each other; and after staying long enough in the pump-room to discover that the crowd was insupportable, and that there was not a genteel face to be seen, which everybody discovers every Sunday throughout the season, they hastened away to the Crescent, to breathe the fresh air of better company. Here Catherine and Isabella, arm in arm, again tasted the sweets of friendship in an unreserved conversation."
Lansdown Crescent, *Bath, 1820* The Bridgeman Art Library

sions of novels and of drawing, a subject in which Catherine is less versed than in the former. This offers Henry an opportunity to instruct her. "Listening" to Henry Tilney teach and tease Catherine, one begins to wonder: is he the one to trust for her education? Certainly, his lecture on the picturesque leaves her less, not more, assured.

The fact that they are not vulgar does not signal that the Tilney men are trustworthy. Though well mannered they, too, may be unscrupulous, and, in the end, reveal themselves to be bullies in one form or another. Henry deprecates women and convinces Catherine not to trust her own instincts. As for his brother and father, their behavior turns out to be less than scrupulous.

James and Isabella become engaged and Catherine's brother rides home to ask for their father's consent. A letter arrives the next day, assuring Isabella that Mr. Morland will do nothing to hinder the match. Matters of money, inheritance, and so forth remain to be sorted out later, but Isabella is happy with the assurance of approval. Yet, when she attends a ball with Isabella, Catherine is surprised when Henry Tilney's older brother, Captain Frederick Tilney, seeks an introduction to Isabella and soon is seen leading the formerly aloof Isabella to the floor to dance.

Isabella learns that her marriage to James must wait two or three years. Can Isabella, who had been expecting more money and the promise of a more luxurious style of living, settle for this?

Catherine is invited to accompany the Tilneys to their country home, Northanger Abbey, but not before she and her brother, become uncomfortable with Captain Tilney's behavior with Isabella. Henry assures her that Captain Tilney is perfectly aware of the state of affairs and that it is Isabella and not Frederick Tilney that is at fault. Henry convinces her that it will all amount to nothing, and Catherine bids farewell to Isabella with much affection in preparation for her departure to Northanger Abbey.

The Bath chapters are meant to show up the conduct novel, in which the heroine must fight off fortune hunters and false friends and win the heart of a suitor. As she rides with Henry Tilney to Northanger Abbey, the novel becomes more fully Gothic in its references. For Henry, who has condescended to her at times, now fuels her fantasies. Henry hopes that Catherine has "a stout heart" and "Nerves fit for sliding panels and tapestry" that "a building such as 'what one reads about' may produce." Henry spins a tale of secret passageways, drops of blood, hidden manuscripts, and other horrors, and Catherine, in spite of herself, begins to be really drawn in, wondering if she could indeed brave such things in pursuit of undiscovered truth.

So much greater, then, is her disappointment when the party arrives at Northanger Abbey. The approach offers no unseen obstacles, nor blinding rainstorm. The abbey is wonderful, but—horror of horrors!—"The furniture was in all the profusion and elegance of modern taste." The windows, though Gothic in shape, are large, clear, and bright, leaving barely any room for dark, damp corners. And with her arrival, we see that Austen is going to do something different with the Gothic, not parody it, or not only, but transform it, incorporate it, turn it inside out, and show us the ordinary—and legitimate—terrors that lay within.

Catherine on a very genuine dark and stormy night explores a large dark Japanese cabinet, complete with a lock and a key in the door. In the morning she learns the paper she has found within is a laundry list. She becomes convinced General Tilney killed his wife or is keeping her a prisoner. She tries to determine whether this is true. Our heroine then undergoes several apprehensive moments; she is discovered. Tension, disappointments, and height-

Gothic clichés	*Gothic tradition politicized in Northanger Abbey*
mysterious lineage	who is Catherine's father?
retirement to rural life	her father moves to Fullerton
fortune hunters	how many fortune hunters can you find in the novel?
a ruined castle	updated Northanger Abbey
male tyrant	General Tilney
deserted heroine	Catherine
abduction	Thorpe takes a protesting Catherine for a ride
chests that hold terrible secrets	washing bill (symbol of domestic demands?)
mysterious disappearances	relief at General Tilney's absence
imprisonment in a castle	forced from Northanger Abbey
radiant, beautiful heroine	plain Catherine

ened feelings ensue. Are Catherine's Gothic apprehensions foolish or is she also noticing aspects of the Tilney household that merit deep concern—such as the inhibition of the grown children when the father is present. Why, too, is General Tilney taking such interest in her? She learns from James that Isabella has broken the engagement; Isabella writes hoping for news of Captain Tilney; it becomes clear he has dropped her.

Frontispiece to the 1833 edition of Northanger Abbey, *published by Richard Bentley. Courtesy of the Burke Jane Austen Collection, Goucher College Library.*

The plots with its turns and twists, and earnest Catherine with her thwarted plans, is heightened by its references to *Mysteries of Udolpho* and other Gothic tales, the kind at which Henry Tilney had scoffed. With a sure hand, Austen guides us through Catherine's small—but to her seemingly large—disappointments and challenges, reminding us of the terrors of the Gothic novels she loves to read. And then a true terror occurs.

One author says that the job of the fiction writer is to put a girl in a tree, throw stones at her, throw some more stones at her, and then get her down. At home, Catherine Morland, former tomboy, could have been found, truly, in a tree. Perhaps reading in a tree (as with the 1987 BBC *Northanger Abbey*). But take her out of her environment, throw her into the world of Bath society and the stones start coming—the Thorpes misuse her. Then take her from her "guardian" and throw her into the world of Northanger Abbey with the tyrannical General Tilney. Meanwhile, Jane Austen enjoys reminding us she is the author who has put her heroine in the tree, and she really must throw a few more stones before she will let her get safely down.

Why has General Tilney taken such a keen interest in Catherine? What does he learn when he goes to London? What famous carriage ride makes him infamous? Catherine suspects General Tilney of murdering his wife. She is wrong, but how far wrong? Austen implies that the oppression of a patriarchal tyrant is subtler than murder. Certainly, his children's fear of him, their silences and lack of joviality in front of him, indicate a tyrannical presence. When his behavior earns our belief of him as a Gothic villain, we may conclude with Catherine "that in suspecting General Tilney of either murdering or shutting up his wife, she had scarcely sinned against his character, or magnified his cruelty."

Then there is Henry Tilney, with his tongue-in-cheek antiwoman comments, "a taste for flowers is always desirable in your sex," and "a teachableness of disposition in a young lady is a great blessing." Why did Jane Austen make him so? To do *her* bidding. Between them, Austen and her fictional creation, he may be the Oxford-educated one, but she shows him up. His comments may also be a reminder that he may not be a trustworthy man, either. Catherine may be the first heroine in Austen's six completed novels to consider settling for a less than ideal man, but she won't be the last.

By the time Jane Austen wrote *Northanger Abbey,* the French Revolution had changed the Gothic novel. One could no longer naïvely contemplate talk of imprisonment, castles, and tyrants. Even young heroines would know something more is going on. Some critics see *Northanger Abbey* as the most political of Austen's novels, as it contains a critique of a patriarchal tyrant; Catherine's complaint about male-dominated history ("the men all so good for nothing, and hardly any women at all"); and highlights the consequences of the miseducation of women and women's financial dependency.

Northanger Abbey, in one sense, is about the education of a naïve reader—both the reader in the book, Catherine Morland, and the reader holding the book. It's an entertaining book about books, book reading, book writing, parental authority, and patriarchal tyranny. We are led to conclude, as one critic observes, that "Horror, like charity, begins at home."

Say Cheese!:
Picturesque Beauty and Jane Austen

Jane Austen's relationship to the English landscape must take into account her own understanding of the term "picturesque." Though common even today in moderately intelligent conversation, taken to mean something like "quaint," this word enjoyed a much more specific meaning and even procured its very own "cult" of followers during Jane Austen's time, thanks to the writings of William Gilpin. Today's "picturesque" implies, among other things, something like a Kodak moment. The scene in question may even be spontaneously framed within the confines of the speaker's fingers. In many ways, this is not so distant from some understandings of the term in the late eighteenth century.

A popular invention called the Claude glass, named after landscape designer Claude Lorrian, allowed the imaginative (or unimaginative, as the case may be) traveler a more complete experience of the great outdoors by allowing him or her to instantly capture it in a frame, leaving the undesirable attributes outside the edges. Then, instead of enduring the painfully rambling and unruly sight of the landscape untamed, the eye of the viewer is substantially relieved to find the scene before them transformed into a charming *landscape,* as in painting.

This simple device, consisting of a mirror and glass, is actually very useful in thinking about the important concept of the picturesque. Many sources talk about the term as referring to the type of beauty seen in painting. There is some debate as to exactly how "natural" landscapes that met this criterion would be. As the formal, symmetrical, French-influenced style of the earlier eighteenth century began to go out of fashion, there was a push to create "natural" looking surroundings even where such surroundings did not really exist. Thinking about this in reference to the Claude glass is useful because of the sense of artificiality that both supply. Objects that upset the viewer's idea of beauty in "nature" may be left out of the frame, even if they are occurring naturally. This is also a way of creating controllable boundaries.

View of the River Dee, c. 1761 (oil on canvas) by Richard Wilson (1714-82), National Gallery, London, UK/The Bridgeman Art Library.

If the entire overwhelming landscape is considered, it is much more difficult to create smaller, picturesque scenes.

Indeed, boundaries of various kinds were becoming important at this time. The enclosure acts that were passed after 1750 initiated the formation of the hedgerows that are now so familiar a part of the English countryside. Seemingly in contrast to this very phenomenon, the "picturesque" grated against symmetrical imagery. In order to be as far from the antique, French ideal of the previous century, the "picturesque" sought beauty in uneven numbers. Groups of three were infinitely preferred to groups of four or five, as is evidenced in *Pride and Prejudice* by Lizzy Bennet's excuse when she declines to accompany Caroline Bingley, Mrs. Hurst, and Mr. Darcy on a walk. She jokingly refers to this particular principle of the picturesque:

But Elizabeth, who had not the least inclination to remain with them, laughingly answered:

"No, no; stay where you are. You are charmingly grouped, and appear to uncommon advantage. The picturesque would be spoilt by admitting a fourth. Goodbye."

In this instance, Lizzy seems to be mocking this concept, but there are other Jane Austen characters who view this subject with the utmost seriousness. Marianne Dashwood, for instance, is convinced of the sanctity of these ideas, no matter how much they may be made fun of by the amiable Edward Ferrars, who warns her that regarding the picturesque he will disappoint: "I shall call hills steep, which ought to be bold! surfaces strange and uncouth, which ought to be irregular and rugged; and distant objects out of sight, which ought only to be indistinct through the soft medium of a hazy atmosphere. . . . I can easily believe it to be full of rocks and promontories, grey moss and brush wood, but these are all lost on me. I know nothing of the picturesque."

Eleanor and Henry Tilney, in *Northanger Abbey,* accept Catherine Morland's ignorance of theories of the picturesque eagerly, as it affords an opportunity to educate her on the subject. Austen tells us that the Tilneys "were viewing the country with the eyes of persons accustomed to drawing, and decided on its capability of being formed into pictures, with all the eagerness of real taste." After hearing Henry's "lecture on the picturesque" ("He talked of foregrounds, distances, and second distances—side-screens and perspectives—lights and shades"), Catherine declares the entire city of Bath to be an unfit subject of a landscape. This, too, is consistent with the wish for natural features encouraged by the picturesque. But, tellingly, Henry Tilney's lecture creates an irony that his pupil might miss, but Austen's readers do not: Catherine is now afraid to take a walk on her own because "she should not know what was picturesque when she saw it."

Northanger Abbey:
The Graphic Novel

A discussion with Anne Timmons, graphic artist

In 2007, Eureka Productions published *Gothic Classics* (Volume Fourteen), with stories from Joseph Sheridan Le Fanu (*Camilla*), Ann Radcliffe (*The Mysteries of Udolpho*), Edgar Allan Poe ("The Oval Portrait"), Myla Jo Closser ("At the Gate"), and Jane Austen. Trina Robbins adapted *Northanger Abbey* and Anne Timmons illustrated it. Robbins herself had adapted *Emma* into a graphic novel for schoolkids for Scholastic. We interviewed Anne Timmons to discover more about the process of visualizing the novel that filmmakers rarely choose to visualize.

Q: How did you prepare to illustrate *Northanger Abbey*?

A: When working on a period piece like this I usually start with the characters first. I did quite a bit of research by Google-ing a lot of the costume websites. I was amazed how many sites have such concise and detailed information. Everything down to the color and fabrics. I watched a lot of Jane Austen films to get an idea of how the characters moved in the costume of the Regency Period. Then I also studied the architecture of this period.

When it was time to draw, I laid out the entire story in small roughed-out panels, also known as thumbnails. They gave me an idea of what the page would look like. Then I drew the story in pencil. I e-mailed the files to Trina (who wrote the adaptation) and she gave me suggestions and advice. Then I inked over the pencils and scanned the finished art. Once the art was a digital file, I could e-mail it to the publisher, who did the lettering.

I also listened to music that may have been played in the time period. I made playlists from soundtracks of *Pride and Prejudice* and *Barry Lyndon*.

Q: In the process of working on the graphic novel, what insights to *Northanger Abbey* did you discover?

A: Drawing a story set in the past can be very challenging. I thoroughly enjoyed the experience. I like to do research. And while I'm working on a project that is set in the past, I have to realize that what may be very easy for us to do now would take longer to do in the past. Something as simple as lighting a room. What may seem perfectly obvious to us in 2008 may not be so available in the early 1800s. For example, you are ready for bed. That process in a dark castlelike building, as Northanger Abbey is, could be a challenge all by itself. You need to be able to see to get to your bed and sometimes all you have is one candle. And if you are inquisitive, as Catherine is, you are going to make sure your candle is close by. I thought about that carefully when I drew the scene of her looking at the rolled-up paper in the cabinet. We take things like electric lights and central heating for granted.

Q: Say I am an Austen devotee, and new to graphic novels. What would I be surprised to learn about graphic novels and Austen?

A: One thing I noticed about Austen readers is they love everything Austen. Books, movies, television, if it's Austen, they're ready for it! And I was delighted to discover the enthusiasm for this project through the Internet. Readers who enjoyed Austen were posting at an Austen blog months before *Gothic Classics* Vol. 14 was out! This website has a message board devoted to all about Jane. New books, films, etc. Check out: http://www. austenblog.com/2006/06/27/northanger-abbey-and-udolpho-to-be-a-graphic-classic/. They were thrilled to hear about it and extremely supportive to hear this was going to be a graphic novel.

Q: *Northanger Abbey* is about books, book reading, and book writing, about how one responds to what one reads. Did you find these issues applied to the graphic novel as well?

A: Yes. Many of the readers knew the book very well and they were delighted to see that *Gothic Classics* included *Mystery of Udolpho,* too. We've had some incredibly positive reviews.

Q: Not only is the book about reading books, Austen reminds us that she controls the story. In the graphic novel, did Austen cede control to you as illustrator? Can you give us an example?

A: I would certainly hope she would've liked what we did. I feel the language kept me grounded so that I got the feel of not only the story but also the time of day, seasons, etcetera.

Q: The greater part of the novel (eighteen out of thirty-one chapters) takes place in Bath, rather than a fictional place. How did that influence you?

Anne Timmon's illustration for Northanger Abbey: the Graphic Novel *showing the scene of Catherine Morland investigating a cabinet at night at Northanger Abbey. From* Gothic Classics, *Vol. 14. © 2007 Eureka Productions.*

A: I was delighted to draw a place I've never been to before. I had plenty of reference and had an idea of how the area was laid out from street maps. I enjoyed drawing the circular buildings and the wrought-iron stair railings.

Q: Some critics see *Northanger Abbey* as the most political of Austen's novels, containing as it does a critique of patriarchal tyrant (General Tilney), Catherine's complaint about male-dominated history, and an implicit criticism of the miseducation of girls and of women's financial dependency. Were these issues ones that you were able to portray?

A: I was limited in the aspects of *Northanger Abbey* that I could convey because we had to compress the story in forty pages. But we did touch upon some of these things with Catherine's reaction to General Tilney's personality and I certainly tried to convey that conflict at the Abbey.

Q: *Northanger Abbey* is one of the least filmed of Austen's novels; did this make your task easier or was it immaterial? If you were going to do a film version, besides the Abbey, Bath, and the carriage rides, is there something in the novel that really benefits from our ability to see it?

A: One of my favorite scenes to draw was the walk at Beechen Cliff. There is a lot of excitement leading up to this moment. The fact that Catherine had to wait for more favorable weather so it would be easy on her clothes and shoes. To finally to be able to walk on a dry spring day (and not be confined indoors), would have been a wonderful experience.

Q: I liked the way the panel sizes change according to the demands of the story; can you describe the process of deciding when the story required a larger canvas than the usual sized frame?

A: A lot of that is attributed to Trina's delightful pacing. She and I have worked together for many years and I admire her ability to take a story and break it down to scenes. She makes suggestions on some of the panel sizes. Sometimes I follow it and sometimes I change things around a little.

Q: I have seen discussions of how hard it is to convey Austen's irony through the medium of film. Did you find this a problem for the graphic novel? Does the graphic novel provide an opportunity to show irony that a movie has more difficulty doing? Unlike film, graphic novels can show thoughts; unlike novels, graphic novels can show expressions and actions. Is this place "between" film and novels a good place for someone to discover Austen?

A: I really feel if you can experience any of the above you listed then you have an open mind and would probably enjoy a lot of graphic novels. Graphic novels give the reader a chance to take a breath, look at the panel, and see where the character is, what they are reacting to, and see the expression on the characters' faces. It's an artist's interpretation of what the scene might have been like.

Q: If you could work on another graphic novelization of Austen's work, which novel would you chose and why?

A: *Emma.* I think it's because I like the characters so much. I mean, who hasn't had a friend try to set you up with someone?

Q: Traditionally, critics have seen *Northanger Abbey* as a parody of Gothic fiction, but recent criticism has proposed that it is actually an homage to the Gothic, and to women reading. Did these debates or considerations enter into your work as an illustrator?

A: Certainly not consciously. I didn't really pay much attention to very many points of view on that subject while I was drawing. I wanted to focus my attention on conveying the story through the drawings. Taking time with facial expression, body movement, etc.

Q: In working so closely with one of Jane Austen's novels, did you discover something about yourself, a sort of Austen-mediated self-revelation?

A: I'm kind of a daydreamer and I do like to imagine myself being somewhere and thinking, "What would it be like to visit a place I could've only imagined?"

For more information on *Gothic Classics,* go to www.graphicclassics.com. For more information on Anne Timmons, visit her website at http://homepage. mac.com/tafrin/Menu4.html.

The Ideal Jane Austen Tour
by Mary Lou White

We talked with Mary Lou White, who, before retiring, was Professor of Education at Wright State University in Dayton, Ohio, specializing in children's literature. While teaching, she organized International Literary Study Tours. In 1995, she retired and started her own business (Book Adventures), which included providing Jane Austen tours. She has since retired from Book Adventures, but continues, at times, assisting the Jane Austen Tour.

The ideal Jane Austen tour is to see the places where she lived and the places where she visited, the authentic places. You look at the views and then are able to create your own stage for visualizing the books. She had a marvelous sense of place and it comes through in her writing. Home and church and countryside were always very significant to Austen. That is part of place. To know you are walking in the places where Jane Austen walked is perhaps the most thrilling to the Jane Austen aficionado who realizes, *this is the place where she got ideas; this is the road she walked.*

The ideal tour would take you to see some of the surroundings where she lived. To see things from Austen's time that you can still see and that you understand from her writings. Place was important to Austen. To the devotee, place is important as well. Because then you, the reader, get the sense of what Austen is talking about. Though automobiles and buses may be running by, you can still picture the scene with a dusty road. You get an idea of the tranquillity of life. Any reader has to have imagination; the ideal tour feeds the imagination.

Jane Austen was very conscious of place, the smallness of the village. She wrote about what things looked like. She talked about the hills and the breezes. When you are in the places where Jane Austen lived and visited, even though it is two hundred years later, the breeze still blows in the same way, and the trees still grow in the same way. The large estates that she visited are still elegant. You get the sense of the great houses and the smaller homes. The imagination is fueled when you see the reality of what it was even though it was two hundred years before.

It's almost like hallowed ground for the purists among Jane Austen readers.

Steventon

Steventon is a lovely place to begin. It's still a small area; it hasn't been built up. The house where she was born isn't there, but the site remains. The church is still there. You can look in the thirteenth-century church and see

Site of Steventon Rectory.
©Allan Soedring www.astoft.co.uk.
Used with permission.

The entrance to St. Nicholas Church.
© Elaine Maylen.

Ibthorpe House. © Elaine Maylen.

some of the pages where she wrote a few things when she was a child and she shouldn't have been writing! You can see the plaques to the family and the graves. You realize this was a family of church people, of ministers, of people who had a strong faith.

Near Steventon are places she visited. There are some grand houses there that are still elegant. One site is the handsome sixteenth-century family home, The Vyne, near Basingstoke, where Jane Austen attended at least one party. It is open to the public for a fee. The grand staircase and handsome paneling allow you to visualize people going up the stairs in beautiful dresses. People two hundred years ago found lovely settings for homes and the sites are still attractive.

Ibthorpe—where the Lloyds lived—is a beautiful place. It's lovely to see the English countryside and imagine that it is somewhat as she would have seen it. You can still look from the house and see the sheep grazing. This sort of warms you, because you can think it was probably like that at the time. Even though there is electricity, there are also creaky stairs.

The churches near Steventon are quite nice. Some of them have been rebuilt. You wander in the graveyard and see some of those names that she probably picked and chose for her characters.

Deane is the neighboring village. Austen's father held that living as well. James Austen lived in that parsonage before becoming rector at Steventon.

Two miles farther is Ashe. The rec-

tory Isaac and Anne Lefroy lived in is there. (She was Austen's good friend, but fell from a horse and died in 1804.) In Ashe House, there is a living room and a dining room with an arch between them. Seeing it, you realize that if you rolled up the carpet, there would be room to dance; and that is just what the Lefroys did when they had their parties.

Winchester

Next on the tour would be to go to Winchester and see Winchester Cathedral, where Austen is buried under an absolutely beautiful engraved stone in the floor of the nave of the cathedral. (The north aisle.) It has a beautiful

> "Our Lodgings are very comfortable. We have a neat little Draw-room with a Bow-window overlooking Dr. Gabell's Garden."
> —**Jane Austen to her brother James,** May 27, 1817

memorial window and a brass plaque.

8 College Street, where Austen died, is a touching site. It is now part of Winchester College, but it is a private home. There is an upstairs room where there is a bay window; she was able to lay there during the day and look at the garden and Winchester Cathedral. You don't go there without crying. It is a very touching thing.

It is another example of where place is very important. You come to the feeling of death and the end of things.

8 College Street, Winchester. Courtesy Geoff and Mercia Chapman of the Jane Austen Society of Melbourne, Australia.

Chawton Cottage. Courtesy Geoff and Mercia Chapman of the Jane Austen Society of Melbourne, Australia.

Winchester Cathedral. ©Allan Soedring www.astoft.co.uk. Used with permission.

Chawton

Chawton Cottage is the house where Jane Austen lived during the last eight years of her life. Chawton Cottage is not really a cottage by American standards . . . it has two stories, and outbuildings. Chawton Cottage is now called "Jane Austen's House Museum." You can see many mementos of Jane Austen there: some of her clothing, a quilt, articles of jewelry, and other items.

"There are six Bedchambers at Chawton; Henry wrote to my Mother the other day, & luckily mentioned the number—which is just what we wanted to be assured of. He speaks also of Garrets for Storeplaces, one of which she immediately planned fitting up for Edward's Manservant—& now perhaps it must be for our own—for she is already quite reconciled to our keeping one." —**Jane Austen to Cassandra**, November 20, 1808

When you are in Chawton, the place where she wrote most of her books, you can see her writing desk, you can see where she sat. There was a door that creaked. She didn't want to have it fixed. She wanted to know if she would be interrupted. It still creaks.

> "She was careful that her occupation should not be suspected by servants, or visitors, or any persons beyond her own family party. She wrote upon small sheets of paper which could easily be put away, or covered with a piece of blotting paper. There was, between the front door and the offices, a swing door which creaked when it was opened; but she objected to having this little inconvenience remedied, because it gave her notice when anyone was coming." —**The Reverend James Edward Austen-Leigh**, *Memoir of Jane Austen*

Chawton House Library is just down the road from this cottage. It is the great house that Austen's wealthy brother Edward owned. An American, Sandy Lerner, leased the house and restored it as the Chawton House Library, a library that focuses on women's writings from 1600 to 1830. The great house itself, which is very imposing, has been completely refurbished.

We have to realize that Jane, by the time she was living in Chawton Cottage herself, didn't have much money, because women at that time didn't inherit. She lived with her mother and her sister and friend Mary Lloyd and her brother Edward provided this house. She had these two different aspects of her life: she had lived in some humble surroundings and yet her brother had this huge stately manor. It is interesting to see the contrast between the two styles of homes.

St. Nicholas Church is where the Austens worshipped when living at Chawton. Mrs. Austen and Jane's beloved sister Cassandra are both buried there.

Godmersham

Godmersham. © Elaine Maylen.

View of St. Nicholas Church and Chawton Great House. ©Allan Soedring www.astoft.co.uk. Used with permission.

Her brother Edward lived in another stately manor, Godmersham, eight miles from Canterbury. Austen went to visit it several times. She'd go there frequently and her sister Cassandra would go, too, to help out there. Of course, there was a housekeeper at Godmersham, but an unwed aunt was always welcome. It is still a gorgeous place. The land is still there—lots and lots of acreage—and the vistas from the site are wonderful. Visiting it reminds you again that she knew grand houses and she knew cottages.

> "Apples are scarce in this Country."—**Jane Austen to Cassandra**, Godmersham Park, September 23-24, 1813
>
> "In this House there is a constant succession of small events, somebody is always going or coming; this morning we had Edwd Bridges unexpectedly to breakfast with us, in his way from Ramsgate where is his wife, to Lenham where is his Church—& tomorrow he dines & sleeps here on his return."—**Jane Austen to her brother Francis**, Godmersham Park, September 25, 1813
>
> "Edward is much concerned about his pond; he cannot now doubt the fact of its running out, which he was resolved to do as long as possible."—**Jane Austen to Cassandra**, Godmersham Park, October 21, 1813

Goodnestone

Edward Austen Knight married Elizabeth Bridges, a girl who lived at Goodnestone, east of Canterbury in Kent. Her family still has that home, which Jane Austen visited. There is a lovely living room, dining room, and hall that would be opened up for dancing. And beautiful grounds! You can just picture from looking at that site, some of the walks her characters would take.

Goodnestone is still a lived-in home. Thus you see not only the architecture but also figurines, furniture, and lovely musical instruments. You feel the spirit of the place and your own imagination can take it from there.

> "As you have been here so lately, I need not particularly describe the house or style of living, in which all seems for use and comfort; nor need I be diffuse on the state of Lady Bridges's bookcase and corner-shelves upstairs. What a treat to my mother to arrange them!"—**Jane Austen to Cassandra**, Goodnestone Farm, August 27, 1805

Bath

Upper Assembly Rooms, Bath. Courtesy Geoff and Mercia Chapman of the Jane Austen Society of Melbourne, Australia.

People love Bath. Going there after seeing Steventon, you experience the contrast between the small country village and the city. Bath is wonderful because the Assembly Rooms, so beautiful, are still there and open to the public. You can also go to 4 Sydney Place, where the Austens lived for three years when they first went to Bath. It is a town house. The owner has kept the downstairs apartment unrented so Jane Austen devotees can come and see it. (And there is a plaque on the house.) Austen's uncle James Leigh Perrot rented a house at No. 1, The Paragon. St. Swithin's, Walcott, where Austen's parents were married, is still there. Her father is buried in the churchyard.

Across from 4 Sydney Place is Sydney Gardens, which are very nice. But then the father died, and the money stopped, and they had to move (first to 27 Green Park Buildings, and 25 Gay Street). Also in Bath is the Jane Austen Center. They have mannequins with dresses from the films. They have a wonderful series of pictures of Bath homes, and many quite interesting things about Jane Austen. They also publish an informative newsletter and magazine. The Centre is right at Green Park, which is close to another residence where Austen lived.

London

Jane Austen went to London to visit her brother, Henry, a banker, whose office was at 10 Henrietta Street, Covent Garden. You can go to Westminster Abbey, where there is a plaque to Austen. You can also go to the National Portrait Gallery and see Cassandra's portrait of her sister. Jane Austen liked walking in Kensington Garden. Jane Austen's writing desk is at the British Library. (The British Library also possesses manuscript pages from *Persuasion*.)

It is wonderful to travel in Jane Austen country with Jane Austen devotees

The Royal Crescent, Bath. ©Allan Soedring www.astoft.co.uk. Used with permission.

because they add their own takes on the stories and the geography and the movies. They can quote verbatim from the books and they can tell you precisely what was in the movies and tell you what was wrong and what was right about the film.

The sense of the lack of the speed that they had in Austen's day is something that you sense when you travel. When you travel by car or by motor coach and you realize that it takes half a day to get from one place to another you think of how long it took for them to travel during the Ausen era. Also, they didn't have the kinds of shoes now available. They didn't have stout shoes at all when they walked in the country lanes. She was a wonderful walker, but she had no sneakers or sturdy shoes, and. . . . lots of mud.

> "Three of the Miss Debaries called here the morning after my arrival, but I have not yet been able to return their civility;—You know it is not an uncommon circumstance in this parish to have the road from Ibthrop to the Parsonage much dirtier & more impracticable for walking than the road from the Parsonage to Ibthrop."—**Jane Austen to her sister Cassandra**, Ibthrop November 30 – December 1, 1800

One of the reasons the films are so popular and effective is that they bring to your eyes the sites you have been visualizing. Filmmakers try to get nice houses that are of that era and do reflect that sense of place that Jane Austen described. But visiting Austen-related sites yourself adds reality to the imagination. Walking on the ground that Jane Austen walked creates the aura of place and brings the story to you so much more vividly.

Chawton Cottage: http://www.jane-austens-house-museum.org.uk/

Chawton Great House, now Chawton Library: http://www.chawton.org/library/library.html

Jane Austen Centre, Bath: http://www.janeausten.co.uk/

Photographs and information on places associated with Jane Austen:

http://www.astoft.co.uk/austen

Jane Austen's Locations:

http://www.pemberly.com/jasites/jasites.html

SIDEBAR

More than a Constitutional: Heroines Who Favor Walking

"To walk three miles, or four miles, or five miles, or whatever it is, above her ankles in dirt, and alone, quite alone! what could she mean by it? It seems to me to shew an abominable sort of conceited independence, a most country town indifference to decorum."
—*Caroline Bingley*

So what's the big deal about Elizabeth hoofing it to visit her sickly sister? Doesn't everyone walk around a little bit?

Walking actually happened to be a chief form of exercise for the gentry. Even the hypochondriacally inclined Mr. Woodhouse would take a turn about his garden. Perambulation through specially made walkways in Bath was a draw for tourists, and for those without personal carriages walking was the chief mode of transportation.

There is something daring—perhaps even a little Gothic—about the walking in which some of Austen's heroines engage. There is, of course, the ill-fated ramble through the hills that causes Marianne Dashwood's fall, and the famous three-mile walk by Elizabeth to the Bingleys'. The reason Miss Bingley and Elizabeth's mother look down on this action

Walking Dress, 1814. *The Bridgeman Art Library.*

is that there is simply no need to walk all of three miles when one has a carriage. It is unfashionable and lowly. Commoners and tradespeople may walk such a distance, but for Elizabeth to do so threatens how others view her station, not to mention the fact that she would engage in such a long walk alone. Thus, this "excessive" walking by heroines can be viewed as an instance of their fiery spirit and zeal, which, though they might suffer social castigation, are the aspects of an independent personality that will win them their hero.

Most of the important things that happen to Lizzy Bennet happen outdoors, while she is walking. Around Rosings, Elizabeth's "favourite walk, and where she frequently went while the others were calling on Lady Catherine, was along the open grove which edged that side of the park, where there was a nice sheltered path, which no one seemed to value but herself." On one such walk, she learns shocking news. She walks at Pemberly. It is at a "prettyish kind of little wilderness" that she withstands Lady Catherine's rage. Darcy and she walk and work out their entire past (and future).

One aspect of Fanny Price's frailty is that walking easily tires her. The fact that Mary Crawford is more robust gets her more time with Edmund; she can walk for longer and ride horses for longer and leave Fanny Price in the dust. That Mrs. Norris sends Fanny twice in one day to Mrs. Norris's house shows Mrs. Norris's abusiveness, because everyone knows of Fanny's enervation.

Mrs. Hurst might have complained of Elizabeth Bennet, "She has nothing, in short, to recommend her, but being an excellent walker." In Austen novel's, except for Fanny Price, *not* being an excellent walker confirms to us that the character has little to recommend her. Mary Musgrove comes to mind.

Our heroines walk for exercise (like Lizzy to Netherfield), they walk to accomplish errands (like Fanny to Mrs. Norris's), they walk to enjoy scenery (the walk around Pemberly, the walk to the Cobb at Lyme Regis, the walk to Kensington Gardens in *Sense and Sensibility*), they walk to escape companionship (Lizzy, when she leaves the Bingley sisters and Darcy), they walk *for* companionship (Lizzy and Jane), they walk for solace or to enhance their melancholy (Marianne at Cleveland).

Jane Austen loved walks as well, and would indulge in rambling over country whenever she could. In her letter of 21 May 1801 to her sister Cassandra, Austen wrote of her walk with a friend, Mrs. Chamberlayne:

> Our grand walk to Weston was again fixed for Yesterday, & was accomplished in a very striking manner; Every one of the party declined it under some pretence or other except our two selves, & we had therefore a tete a tete; but that we should equally have had after the first two yards, had half the Inhabitants of Bath set off with us.—It would have amused you to see our progress;—we went up by Sion Hill, & returned across the fields;—in climbing a hill Mrs. Chamberlayne is very capital; I could with difficulty keep pace with her—yet would not flinch for the World.—on plain ground I was quite her equal—and so we posted away under a fine hot sun, She without any parasol or any shade to her hat, stopping for nothing, & crossing the Church Yard at Weston with as much expedition as if we were afraid of being buried alive.—After seeing what she is equal to, I cannot help feeling a regard for her.

Miss Bingley certainly would not have approved.

The Watsons and Lady Susan

The Watsons and *Lady Susan* occupy unique positions in the Austen canon. Not part of the juvenilia, nor numbered among the six published novels, neither is quite short enough nor insignificant enough to be disregarded entirely. Austen devotees may well exclaim that no work, nay, not one word confirmed to have been written by beloved Jane should ever bear the shame of being simply "disregarded." While we quite agree, it does seem that these two works are vulnerable to just such a passing over. Perhaps this is because both of these are, in fact, difficult texts in their own right. *The Watsons,* of course, is unfinished, and the central character of *Lady Susan* is largely despicable, not to mention the fact that epistolary novels (novels written in the form of letters) may not hold as much appeal for a modern audience as they did for inhabitants of the late eighteenth century.

In 1805, the date of the completed manuscript of *Lady Susan,* the epistolary style was beginning to feel outdated. 1805, however, is considered to be when Austen recopied a work that she began, and probably completed, ten or maybe twelve years earlier. This was a very youthful venture, but its form denies Austen the power of one of her greatest strengths—dialogue. Some conversations are related in the letters, but they do not have the same feel as some good banter

between Elizabeth and Lady Catherine De Bourgh or Marianne and Willoughby.

If all of this is so, then what does *Lady Susan* have to recommend it? Answer: It has Lady Susan herself. This creation, practically a villainess, is an odd central figure for Austen. She is at least thirty-five, according to the characters in the story, but her beauty is marked. Her cruelty is also repeatedly emphasized. However, compared to her rather drab companions in the work, Lady Susan seems to sparkle. The short work opens with some of Austen's more shocking material. Lady Susan is essentially being expelled from the house in which she has been staying, having captured the attentions of two men, one of whom happens to be married and the other a devoted suitor to another woman.

Lady Susan writes of her two conquests, Mr. Manwaring and Sir James Martin respectively, to her friend Mrs. Johnson. The other main correspondent is Lady Susan's sister-in-law, Mrs. Catherine Vernon, who dreads, but must welcome, a visit from Lady Susan to her home. She writes to her mother.

Lady Susan's arrival includes her efforts at capturing the heart of Mrs. Vernon's brother, Reginald De Courcy, a puppy of a man. Mrs. Vernon frets, he falls, Lady Susan seems near triumph. But then her daughter Frederica and, shortly thereafter, Sir James Martin

From a set of Rowlandson's Etchings. *1790. Courtesy of The Lewis Walpole Library, Yale University. 790.6.27.1*

arrive at Churchill. Letters continue to fly detailing Lady Susan's plans and Mrs. Vernon's hopes to defeat them. Even when Lady Susan appears defeated, she is not; she rises to plan again. Lady Susan is one clever woman.

Forty-one letters and a conclusion provide the story of Lady Susan's machinations. How deliciously evil she is! One never senses anxiety or disappointment, even when her plans go much awry, even when the man she is plotting after confronts her about her dastardly plans for her daughter, even when she is confronted for having a lover, even when . . . well, you get the idea. This woman is unbeatable. She is cruel, selfish, manipulative, charming, energetic in pursuing her self-interest, cynical, and vain. We might have left out something in this catalog of her sins (which she might have listed as her strengths). She is the evil stepmother to the innocent Snow White, the mother willing to sacrifice her daughter's happiness.

Whenever her sister-in-law, Catherine Vernon, believes she has finally gained the upper hand, Lady Susan proves her wrong. Lady Susan's beliefs include: "There is exquisite pleasure in subduing an insolent spirit, in making a person predetermined to dislike, acknowledge one's superiority." Or "Where there is a disposition to dislike, a motive will never be wanting." Or "There is something agreeable in feelings so easily worked on."

One of Austen's biographers, Claire Tomalin, finds Lady Susan's spark in Mary Crawford. So what happened? Why do we encounter Mary Crawford in Austen's fiction, but Lady Susan languishing in manuscript? Some believe Lady Susan, clever heroine, frightened Austen, clever writer. Tomalin says, "The exercise [that is, *Lady Susan*] is brilliant. So brilliant, that Austen may have frightened herself, and felt she had written herself into a dangerous corner, and been too clever, too bold, too black." Fifteen years before Tomalin, Gilbert and Gubar say of Lady Susan, "She is the first of a series of heroines, of varying degrees of attractiveness, whose lively wit and energetic imagination make them both fascinating and frightening to their creator." In the novel, Lady Susan's own relatives could neither silence nor defeat her. But the world was more successful. Though the manuscript was clearly important to Austen (and probably the reason she copied it out in 1805), it was not published until 1871. This left Lady Susan in an unfamiliar situation for this heroine: ignored and unheeded.

* * *

Deborah Kaplan, who has researched both *The Watsons* and *Lady Susan,* calls these works "The 'Middle Fictions.'" Representing talent that has matured from the juvenilia, they are daring and present an Austen who has decided to write for the public rather than only for her family. Kaplan finds both works celebrate female friendships and because of this become "bold, innovative critiques of male power." These critiques are so strong (as are the female friendships) that "they challenge the comic courtship plot."

The paper on which the manuscript for *The Watsons* is written is marked with "1803," but memoirs from Austen's family date the beginning of this composition around 1804. The fragment is also unique as it deals with a family in a lower social position than that of most

of the characters in Austen's other texts. The beginning is somewhat reminiscent of *Sense and Sensibility,* as an ailing father is becoming more and more sickly, accompanied only by daughters. The possibility of being literally homeless looms largely over the four unmarried daughters of Mr. Watson. His two sons, Robert and Sam, are already leading independent lives.

The story begins with an invitation for Miss Emma Watson, lately returned to her father and sisters from her prolonged stay with an aunt. Her sisters are practically strangers to her, and Elizabeth, the eldest of the sisters, chatters on about what Emma will encounter during her stay with the Edwards family. Emma is to attend a ball in the company of Mary Edwards, an honor that Elizabeth had enjoyed on the previous occasion. Emma, on Elizabeth's orders, is to be on the lookout for Tom Musgrave, an unabashed flirt and a dangerous partner for either dancing or conversation. The Osbornes are to be the other people of note, as their wealth and status beg recognition. In this conversation we also learn of the two absent sisters, Penelope and Margaret, both older than Emma.

Emma is safely deposited at the Edwards' home and begins her preparation for the ball. Much of the rest of the text is concerned with this event. Emma's prettiness causes comment among the guests, but she is to distinguish herself even further later in the evening. The much-anticipated Osbornes arrive with their party accompanied by the socially ambitious Tom Musgrave. The Dowager Lady Osborne appears with her son, Lord Osborne, her daughter Miss Osborne, and Miss Osborne's friend Miss Carr. Reverend Mr. Howard, Lord Osborne's former tutor, also accompanies them, along with his widowed sister, Mrs. Blake, and her ten-year-old son, Charles. The last and youngest of these guests arrives in the utmost excitement, as he is to dance his first two dances with Miss Osborne.

When the same Miss Osborne is engaged for these dances by a handsome officer, however, the boy is crestfallen. Emma, feeling the little boy's distress, offers to dance with him herself. This moment is truly effective, and the comical picture of a grown woman dancing with a little boy is counteracted by the mother's gratitude for her son. Indeed this unselfish act calls Emma to everyone's attention; even the rest of the important Osborne party must take notice of her.

The next day Emma returns home to her sister and her father. Soon Lord Osborne and Tom Musgrave make a surprise call at the house. Emma is flattered by this attention to herself, but does not enjoy the visit overall. It does not bring her Mr. Howard, whose attentions are the only ones she is interested in. The house is peaceful for a few days after the departure of the two men, until Margaret returns, in the company of Robert and his wife Jane, with whom she has been staying. Margaret appears to have picked up some of the silliness and haughty manners of her brother and sister-in-law. Robert Watson is an attorney and is accustomed to some luxury and a generous helping of self-satisfaction. His wife is only too happy to indulge the latter habit and adds her own pride to it.

For the remainder of Robert and Jane's visit, Emma chooses to sit with her father as an alternative to being among the party. When, on Robert and Jane's impending departure, Emma is invited to come and stay with them, she has some difficulty with her eventual refusal. Eventually, Robert and Jane do leave without her, and Austen's manuscript ends here.

One main theme that appears in *The Watsons* is the friendship between Elizabeth and Emma. The friendship they achieve often goes unnoticed because the ending, which conforms *The Watsons* to the traditional "heroine/courtship/marriage to a deserving man" plot, was introduced simultaneously with the printing of the manuscript. James Austen-Leigh's *Memoir of Jane Austen* reports what Cassandra remembered that Jane had told her of the imagined end of *The Watsons*:

Mr Watson was soon to die; and Emma to become dependent for a home on her narrow-minded sister-in-law and brother. She was to decline an offer of marriage from Lord Osborne, and much of the interest of the tale was to arise from Lady Osborne's love for Mr. Howard, and his counter affection for Emma, whom he was finally to marry.

There is much speculation as to why Jane Austen chose to abandon this manuscript. A major reason is offered in the fact that her own father died in 1805, soon after the beginning of this composition. Perhaps she felt the similarities between her own situation and Emma's. Perhaps she thought the prospects for the Watson daughters to be too grim, "a bitter re-run of *Pride and Prejudice*," as Deirdre Le Faye suggests. Certainly, there are similarities in the first assembly at Meryton and the ball Emma attends; between a haughty Mr. Darcy and a snooty Lord Osborne, whom we first meet at their respective dances. And, too, we meet a plentitude of sisters who must look for husbands or face poverty.

Perhaps the depiction of Elizabeth and Emma's friendship, of a women's culture that was complete in and of itself, contributed to its unfinished state, as Deborah Kaplan proposes. "Austen may have seen that her representation of female friendship would ultimately be incompatible with the courtship plot and, if allowed to reshape that plot, would be not altogether appropriate for either her own community or a general audience."

In any case, we are left to forever wonder about Emma and her sisters. And because she neither destroyed the manuscript, nor finished it, that was Austen's choice.

Cinderella and Evil Witches: Myth-Placed Affections

Jane Austen came before Freud, Jung, Joseph Campbell, and the hosts of psychoanalysts who could point out archetypal usages in her books. What Jane Austen would have said about mythic influence, we do not know. While she may not have been out to tell a grand allegorical tale of archetypes, symbols, and Classical deities—her mentioning of these last is scant indeed—we will take the liberty of "myth"-interpreting a few of her themes.

Triple Hecate/Mother-Maiden-Crone: Perhaps the archetype most widely spread across Austen's work. The Mother-Maiden-Crone figures appear throughout almost all mythologies, and quite often embody the hand of fate. Indeed, they actually are the Fates in the Classical world, the three witches in Shakespeare's *Macbeth,* the three aspects of the Celtic war-goddess the Morr'gan, the dark goddess Hecate's triple aspect, and the three Fate-like Norns of Norse myth. Interactions among women make up the majority of Austen's work, and so of course

this threefold female figure is bound to crop up: Mrs. Bates, Miss Bates, and Jane Fairfax, for example. Mrs. Bates represents the Crone, and, while Miss Bates is not physically a mother, she does certainly embody the caretaking aspects usually associated with the role. This leaves Jane Fairfax as the Maiden, whose mythic virginal purity and good graces are being strained to the limit by the insensitivities of Mr. Frank Churchill. At Rosings, we find Lady Catherine/Mrs. Jenkinson/ Miss Anne de Bourgh, in a similar lineup (crone/mother figure/maiden). *Mansfield Park* opens with the tale of three sisters with three drastically different fates: the rich Lady Bertram, the hateful Mrs. Norris, and Fanny's poor mother Mrs. Price. What about *Sense and Sensibility*? There are three sisters and a mother. Surely this does not fit in. Perhaps, in a situation such as this, it is the *threat* of crone-hood that lingers over the Mother and Maidens. With so little money left to them, the daughters live with the threat of poor spinsterhood, of becoming the Crone, if they do not attract a husband.

The Betrayer/The Trickster: Often likeable and pleasant at first, the Betrayer/Trickster character will eventually threaten domestic safety in Austen's works. Not all tricksters are evil, of course—the Classical Prometheus simply encountered some bad luck after stealing fire from the gods, and the African spider-trickster Anansi is actually the hero of many stories—but in the world of Jane Austen, the Trickster figure usually leads to no good. Though on a much lesser scale than the Norse god Loki, whose tricks ultimately lead to the world-ending battle of Ragnarok, Frank Churchill's tricks and machinations almost end Jane Fairfax's world. Likewise, Mr. Thorpe's lying gossip almost ends Catherine Morland's hopes in *Northanger Abbey,* and William Elliot's role as "false suitor" almost ends the relations between Anne Elliot and Captain Wentworth.

The Betrayer, though, is the one to watch for. The Serpent of Judeo-Christian tradition, this is, among others, the dastardly Wickham. Not only does he lie and misrepresent to discredit Darcy, but he then steals off with the youngest daughter. The Betrayer not only disrupts the peace but also causes suffering among the people.

The Hero and Heroine: Perhaps too obvious to mention, but worth doing so because of the twists that Austen includes. Mrs. Norris, evil stepmother to Fanny's Sleeping Beauty; Lady Susan, evil queen to her daughter's Snow White, and Cinderellas galore. Though it is often up to the Prince Charming of each novel to sweep the Austenian Snow Whites and Cinderellas off their feet, it is often up to the Snow Whites and Cinderellas to teach their respective heroes a little sense—or, in the case of Colonel Brandon and his all-but-impassioned Shakespeare reading, a little sensibility.

The Quest: Entwined within the fate of the Hero and Heroine is the Hero's quest. Though these are often far cries from dragon slaying, they are still crucial aspects to the story and to the Hero's character. While Marianne is ill, Colonel Brandon, needing to be of use, is directed to fetch Mrs. Dashwood. Henry Tilney rides off in search of Catherine Morland. Darcy must fulfill three tasks in his hero's journey to undo the three hurts of putting down Lizzy's family, separating her sister and Bingley, and keeping silent about Wickham's wickedness. So in reverse order he repairs what Wickham has done, he restores Bingley and sister, and finally he endures the family (he comes to dinner with Mrs. Bennet). (Perhaps, too, this is why the 1995 BBC version shows Colin Firth as Darcy diving into a pond and swimming—besides providing the wet-shirted image, it symbolizes his emotional rebirth.) If it were not for the Quest, the hero's love would not be proved, and not only would the heroine be sad, she would discover her beloved was a schmuck.

Rapunzel, or, the Imprisoned Heroine: One specific element of the Quest is the rescuing of the Imprisoned Heroine, personified in Anne Elliot. Her ideal young beauty was "imprisoned" by Lady Russell, who persuaded her to decline Captain Wentworth's initial marriage proposal. Lady Russell thereby keeps Anne "locked away" for years while the prince—read Wentworth—must muddle through the wildernesses of life, looking for his princess. Anne is finally convinced to "let down her hair," to free herself from others' bonds, and so lives happily ever after.

On Reading Jane Austen

(original composition by Douglas Buchanan)

When dining, or pining,
Or signing my name,
When walking or talking
Besides an old flame,
'Midst fallings from wallings
You'll hear me exclaim;
There's no one I'd rather be reading than Jane

She's pretty and witty
She's wondrously wise
She makes Edward talk
And then Elinor cries;
Elizabeth's love all her rantings disguise
And makes Darcy wonder: "How fine are her eyes?"

Emma's dilemmas
End when she is wed;
Catherine's passions are all in her head
Anne goes for a Bath but gets Wentworth instead
And then we all wish Fanny Dashwood were dead.

Hey now, ho now,
Austen's the queen of barouche and landau
Now it is all clear:
Fanny's the end, so this song must end here.

On Reading Jane Austen

Douglas Buchanan

What's Up with White Soup?: Understanding Food in Jane Austen

Ah, yes, that famous white soup. It is a rich soup made from veal stock and almonds and cream with additions such as rice or bread crumbs to thicken it, and sometimes leeks or egg yolks. Why would a ball depend upon having it in stock, as Bingley implies? Well, the ingredients for white soup are expensive (almonds, cream, egg yolks), and might not be in stock at Netherfield. But Sheila Kaye-Smith suggests that when Mr. Bingley promises a ball at Netherfield "as soon as Nichols has made white soup enough," it is a statement not meant to be taken literally. It is simply a reference to the association of soup with a ball. Kaye-Smith says that Austen never mentions soup, "except as an extra at balls. Indeed, it seems to have had special festive implications." We have Miss Bates's word for it, when she sees the soup at the ball at the Crown.

On the other hand, we have encountered one (and only one) supposition that white soup was the white goop that is put on butlers' hair. And it was this goop that would have to be prepared in order for the ball to go forward.

Generally, as we will see, Austen uses food to reveal something about a character; in the case of white soup she might not have revealed enough. But we know that happily the white soup was made and the cards were sent around.

Throughout her novels, we have glimpses of meals from breakfast to dinner and dinner to breakfast and all the sundry times in between.

Eating Orders

Breakfast was the first meal of the day for Jane Austen. Unlike previous eras where the table would be laden with meat and eggs—or in a working-class household, bread, ale, and cheese—breakfasts of the Regency gentry were much lighter. Varieties of bread, such as toast or cakes, with tea, coffee, or cocoa were the staple options. Fish and steak would be laid out for more substantial morning repasts. When Jane Austen's mother visited Stoneleigh Abbey in 1806, she reported a breakfast of "Chocolate, Coffee, Tea, Plumb Cake, Pound Cake, Hot Rolls, Cold Rolls, Bread, butter." The remnants of breakfast the day following the *Mansfield Park* ball included "cold pork bones and mustard" and "broken eggshells."

Breakfasts would usually begin between 9:00 and 10:00, the later hour being the most common as it allowed for early-morning walks and preparations for the day. If one were traveling, a heartier meal would be served up much earlier in the morning. Catherine Morland of *Northanger Abbey,* for example, must eat at the ungodly hour of seven o'clock before she travels back home.

Because "the morning hours of the Cottage were always later than those of the other house," Mary Musgrove and Anne Elliot are just beginning breakfast when Captain Wentworth and the others are setting off to hunt.

Luncheon did not become an acceptable term until after Austen's death, around the 1830s, taking some time to work its way into the vocabulary of the upper class. Until Jane Austen's time, dinner was served in the middle of the day, but as it became more fashionable to eat later and later, some midday repast was needed to avoid total starvation. Mr. Knightley provides food typical for "luncheon" for his strawberry-picking guests: cold meat, fruit, and a refreshing beverage. Of course, the fashionable guests at no time refer to this meal as "lunch."

Stoneleigh Abbey had been in Jane Austen's mother's family for generations, though Jane Austen only visited it once, with her mother, in 1806. © Elaine Maylen.

There was no specific time frame for luncheons, as they were not formalized meals. Often there would be food available throughout the middle of the day for family and visitors alike. By having this meal remain casual, the servants were free to focus on the most important event of the day: dinner.

Dinner. This meal officially ended the "morning," which was the period of the day preceding dinnertime. The females were obliged to change into fancier attire for this meal and would take what was known as "half-hour" to do so, though of course for the Bingley sisters this stretches into an hour and a half:

The Corporal in Good Quarters. *Thomas Rowlandson, 1808. Courtesy of The Lewis Walpole Library, Yale University 802.7.18.1.*

"At five o'clock the two ladies retired to dress, and at half past six Elizabeth was summoned to dinner."

For a fashionable household, the meal would begin around 5:00 or 6:00 in the evening, with the children being fed about 2:00 or 3:00 in the afternoon. A fancy dinner party, though, or dinner at a very great house would often begin later; Austen herself refers to the different time that they ate dinner at Steventon rectory from when Cassandra would dine at the great house Godmersham. When Lord Osborne and Tom Musgrave arrive uninvited to the Watsons' simple home around 3 P.M., Emma Watson is embarrassed because they are about to eat dinner. Her sister Elizabeth explains to them, "You know what early hours we keep."

The host would escort the lady with the highest standing into the dining room, followed by the rest of the women, and finally the gentlemen. Typically, the seating arrangements were not preassigned, save for the head and foot of the table, which were reserved for the host or honored guest.

A simple family dinner might only consist of one course, but for guests two courses would often be made. Mrs. Bennet wants to have two courses when Mr. Bingley comes to dinner. The first consisted of meat and poultry, a tureen of soup at one end and a fish at the other, a few vegetable dishes, and perhaps some breads and savory jellies. It was rude to continually ask for the passing of a dish, and, as all the food would be laid on the table at once, one often had to rely on luck or quick decision making in choosing seats to have ready access to the dishes one wanted, as Maggie Lane explains in *Jane Austen and Food*.

Once this course was finished the table would be cleared by the servants. During this time it was wise to cease any private conversation one did not want overheard, as there would be no food to distract the would-be eavesdroppers. That is why, in *Emma*, "The conversation was here interrupted. They were called on to share in the awkwardness of a rather long interval between the courses, and obliged to be as formal and as orderly as the others; but when the table was again safely covered, when every corner dish was placed exactly right, and occupation and ease were generally restored," Frank Churchill and Emma could resume their very secretive conversation.

The second course typically consisted of lighter fare, such as tarts, meat, pastries, pies, and sweet jellies.

After this course the entire table was cleared and dessert (from the French word *dessevir*, "to clear the table") was put on. As the servants were now washing up (and eating their own meal—they were allowed the leftovers from the host's table; whatever was left would then be used for luncheon the next day) the dessert was typically finger food that did not require plating or silver. Nuts, dried fruit, stuffed olives, and so forth were typical of this course, originally used to extend the time of the dinner.

Unlike the relative informality of the processional in, the exit of the ladies conformed precisely to their order of social standing. This explains Lydia's joy after her marriage in taking Jane's place, and why Elizabeth Elliot follows Lady Russell "out of all the drawing-rooms and dining-rooms in the country."

While the women retreated to the drawing room to amuse themselves (or, as was often the case, lapse into boredom), the men remained at the table to partake of drinks, cigars, and conversation. Though it was previously thought rude for a man to leave the table before his fellows, this taboo had evaporated by Jane Austen's time.

Tea would be held once the men joined the women; this marked the official end of dinnertime. Both tea and coffee were provided, along with snacks such as cakes, toast, rolls, and other breads. This is how Elizabeth finds herself trapped serving coffee after the dinner to which Darcy and Bingley have been invited. Following this was a period of general entertainment and conversation, ranging from reading aloud to card playing, dancing, and music making.

Supper, the final meal of the day, was often a necessity for the less fashionable, who held their dinner in the middle of the day. It was less of a meal and more of a hot snack. Mr. Woodhouse s habit of taking gruel before going to bed is another thing. Supper was becoming passé, as those fashionable enough to have a very late dinner had no need of the meal whatsoever. The one exception to this was at balls, where the late-night dancing and frolicking made sustenance

a necessity, and this brings us back to white soup.

Boiled Pork? When Food is Mentioned in Austen Novels

Maggie Black and Deidre Le Faye point out in their *Jane Austen Cookbook* the significance "that only her sillier or more unattractive characters talk specifically about food." It is also more frequently discussed in the juvenilia and is a "central joke" in *Lesley Castle*. But "by 1797, when Jane was working on *Sense and Sensibility,* she mentions food only where the references help either to delineate a character or to advance the plot."

Take, for example, Emma's situation. She has great hopes that during the time that she has maneuvered for Mr. Elton to be alone for Miss Smith, that a declaration of love has occurred. She discovers to her great disappointment that instead, "Mr. Elton was still talking, still engaged in some interesting detail; and Emma experienced some disappointment when she found that he was only giving his fair companion an account of the yesterday's party at his friend Cole's, and that she was come in herself for the Stilton cheese, the north Wiltshire, the butter, the cellery, the beet-root and all the dessert."

As a novel, *Emma* mentions specific items of food more frequently than many of the other novels because it illuminates both Mr. Woodhouse and Miss Bates. We recognize the deprivation under which Miss Bates and her mother live. Mr. Woodhouse's opinions about food also indicate what type of person he is. (His apples are baked three times, whereas for Miss Bates, twice is enough.) *Emma* also illustrates the generosity of food sharing: It was not uncommon for families to give to their neighbors if they had too much of one product from their grounds, be it meat or produce. Emma sends food to the Bates family. Knightley's gift of apples to the Bates household is hardly uncommon for the time, though it does certainly show his spirit of generosity, as Miss Bates makes very, very clear:

"Oh! Mr. Knightley, one moment more; something of consequence—so shocked! Jane and I are both so shocked about the apples!"

"What is the matter now?"

"To think of your sending us all your store apples. You said you had a great many, and now you have not one left. We really are so shocked! Mrs. Hodges may well be angry. William Larkins mentioned it here. You should not have done it, indeed you should not. Ah! he is off. He never can bear to be thanked. But I thought he would have staid now, and it would have been a pity not to have mentioned—"

Mansfield Park also sheds light on some of the eating habits and food preferences of its characters. Little Fanny, new to the surroundings of Mansfield, cannot eat two full bites of gooseberry tart "before tears interrupted her." Fanny's not eating in the novel will be con-trasted with the gourmand Dr. Grant.

Consider the debate about apricots between Dr. Grant and Mrs. Norris:

"It was only the spring twelvemonth before Mr. Norris's death that we put in the apricot against the stable wall, which is now grown such a noble tree, and getting to such perfection, sir," addressing herself then to Dr. Grant.

"The tree thrives well, beyond a doubt, madam," replied Dr. Grant. "The soil is good; and I never pass it without regretting that the fruit should be so little worth the trouble of gathering."

"Sir, it is a Moor Park, we bought it as a Moor Park, and it cost us—that is, it was a present from Sir Thomas, but I saw the bill—and I know it cost seven shillings, and was charged as a Moor Park."

"You were imposed on, ma'am," replied Dr. Grant: "these potatoes have as much the flavour of a Moor Park apricot as the fruit from that tree. It is an insipid fruit at the best; but a good apricot is eatable, which none from my garden are."

"The truth is, ma'am," said Mrs. Grant, pretending to whisper across the table to Mrs. Norris, "that Dr. Grant hardly knows what the natural taste of our apricot is: he is scarcely ever indulged with one, for it is so valuable a fruit; with a little assistance, and ours is such a remarkably large, fair sort, that what with early tarts and preserves, my cook contrives to get them all."

We already have little reason to like Mrs. Norris, and her protestations about a cost she did not bear are typical of her. But Dr. Grant, though he can't distinguish a potato from an apricot, does know disappointment over a green goose.

Besides the differences between Miss Bates and Mr. Woodhouse, Fanny Price and Dr. Grant, we have a glimpse of the difference between someone like Mr. Hurst and Elizabeth Bennet in a very brief mention about food preferences: "he was an indolent man, who lived only to eat, drink, and play at cards—who, when he found her prefer a plain dish to a ragout, had nothing to say to her."

Sheila Kaye-Smith and G. B. Stern derived a menu from all of the novels, noting in passing how little attention Austen actually pays to the contents of the meals that are devoured by her characters. This would be their menu:

White Soup
Boiled Salmon
Fricassee of Chicken and Asparagus
Roast Saddle of Mutton
Gooseberry Tart

They chose mutton over pork because the idea of boiling it, as Mr. Woodhouse recommends, was most unappealing.

It is in the juvenilia that appetites are given free rein, as in "Frederic and Elfirda" in which "two ladies sat down to Supper on a young Leveret [a young hare], a brace of Partridges, a leash of Pheasants and a Dozen of Pigeons." A feast made for Dr. Grant, who, of course, is one of the few people who actually dies during a Jane Austen novel. And what kills him off? Not those apricots or the green goose, but "three great institutional dinners in one week." And that was the end of him.

For a full discussion of Food during Austen's lifetime and as it is mentioned in her novels, see All Things Austen: An Encyclopedia of Austen's World *and* Cooking with Jane Austen, *both by Kristin Olsen, Maggie Lane's* Jane Austen and Food, *and Maggie Black and Deidre Le Faye's* Jane Austen Cookbook.

Jane Austen Film Chronology

Jane Austen ~ A Film Timeline

	1940 ---- 1950 ---- 1960 ---- 1970 ---- 1980 ---- 1990 ---- 2000 ---- 2008
P&P	X 1940 · X 1949 · X 1952 · X 1958 · X 1967 · X 1980 · X 1995 · X 1998 · X '01 · X '03 · X '04 · X '05 · X 2008
S&S	X 1950 · X 1971 · X 1981 · X 1995 · X 2000 · X 2003 · X '08
NA	X 1986 · X 1993 · X 1998 · X 2007
Pers.	X 1961 · X 1971 · X 1995 · X '04 · X '06 · X '07
Emma	X 1948 · X 1954 · X 1960 · X 1960 · X 1972 · X 1995 · X 1996
MP X	X 1983 · X 1990 · X 1999 · X 2007
Other Works	X 1980
Bios, Homages	X 1995 · X 1997 · X '01 · X '04 · X '07 · X '08

125

A Jane Austen film chronology including film and television adaptations, biography, fictionalized biography, and homages to Austen's work:

1940. *Pride and Prejudice*. MGM, 118 minutes.

1948. *Emma*. BBC television play, 105 minutes.

1949. *Pride and Prejudice*. NBC *Philco Television Playhouse*, 60 minutes.

1950. *Sense and Sensibility*. NBC *Philco Television Playhouse*, 60 minutes.

1952. *Pride and Prejudice*. BBC miniseries, 180 minutes.

1954. *Emma*. NBC *Kraft Television Theatre*, 60 minutes.

1958. *Pride and Prejudice*. BBC miniseries, 180 minutes.

1960. *Emma*. BBC miniseries, 180 minutes.

1960. *Emma*. CBS *Camera Three*, 60 minutes.

1961. *Persuasion*. BBC miniseries, four parts.

1967. *Pride and Prejudice*. BBC miniseries, 180 minutes.

1971. *Sense and Sensibility*. BBC miniseries, 200 minutes.

1971. *Persuasion*. ITV/Granada miniseries, 225 minutes.

1972. *Emma*. BBC miniseries, 270 minutes.

1980. *Pride and Prejudice*. BBC miniseries, 265 minutes.

1980. *Jane Austen in Manhattan*. Merchant/Ivory. 111 minutes (UK); 108 minutes (USA).

1981. *Sense and Sensibility*. BBC, 174 minutes.

1983. *Mansfield Park*. ITV/BBC/PBS miniseries, 312 minutes.

1986. *Northanger Abbey*. BBC/A & E, 90 minutes.

1990. *Metropolitan*. New Line Cinema. "Loose adaptation" of *Mansfield Park*, 98 minutes.

1993. *Ruby in Paradise*. October Films. Homage to *Northanger Abbey*, 114 minutes.

1995. *Persuasion*. BBC/Sony: TV/theatrical release., 104 minutes.

1995. *Jane Austen: The Famous Author Series*. KULTUR, 30 minutes.

1995. *Pride and Prejudice*. BBC/A&E miniseries, 300 minutes.

1995. *Wishbone*: "Furst Impressions." PBS Series. Homage to *Pride and Prejudice*, 30 minutes.

1995. *Clueless*. Adaptation of *Emma*. Paramount Pictures, 97 minutes.

1995. *Sense and Sensibility*. Columbia, 135 minutes.

1996. *Emma*. Meridian Broadcasting, ITV/A & E, 107 minutes.

1996. *Emma*. Miramax Films, 120 minutes.

1997. *Jane Austen: Life, Society & Works*. BFS Entertainment & Multimedia, 176 minutes.

1998. *You've Got Mail*. Warner Brothers. Homage to *Pride and Prejudice*, 119 minutes.

1998. *Wishbone*: "Pup Fiction." PBS Series. Homage to *Northanger Abbey*, 30 minutes.

1999. *Mansfield Park*. Miramax Films & BBC, 112 minutes.

2000. *Kandukondain Kandukondain* (I Have Found It). Adaptation of *Sense and Sensibility*, Rajiv Menon Productions Kalyani Infotech Production & "V" Creations, 150 minutes.

2000. *Crouching Tiger, Hidden Dragon*. Columbia/Sony. "Bruce Lee meets Jane Austen," 120 minutes.

2001. *Bridget Jones' Diary*. Miramax/Studio Canal/Working Title. Homage to *Pride and Prejudice*, 97 minutes.

2001. *Austen Country*. Delta Entertainment Corporation, 55 minutes.

2003. *Pride and Prejudice: A Latter Day Comedy*, LDS feature film. Excel Entertainment Group, 104 minutes.

2004. *Bride and Prejudice*. Miramax Films and Pathe Pictures. 112 minutes.

2004. *Bridget Jones: The Edge of Reason*. Universal Pictures/Studio Canal/Working Title. Homage to *Persuasion*, 108 minutes.

2004. "Jane Austen." A & E *Biography*. Working Dog Productions, 50 minutes.

2005. *Pride and Prejudice*. Focus Features, 129 minutes.

2006. *The Lake House*. Homage to *Persuasion*, Warner Brothers, 105 minutes.

2007. *The Jane Austen Book Club*. Mockingbird Pictures/Sony, 106 minutes.

2007. *Becoming Jane*. Blueprint Pictures/Miramax, 120 minutes

2007. *Northanger Abbey*. Masterpiece Theatre, ITV/Grenada with WGBH, 93 minutes.

2007. *Sense and Sensibility*. Masterpiece Theatre, BBC/WGBH, 180 minutes.

2007. *Mansfield Park*. Masterpiece Theatre, ITV/WGBH, 93 minutes.

2007. *Persuasion*. Masterpiece Theatre, ITV/Grenada with WGBH, 92 minutes.

2008. *Miss Austen Regrets*. Masterpiece Theatre, BBC/WGBH, 90 minutes.

2008. *Sense and Sensibilidad*. A Latina version of *Sense and Sensibility* set in contemporary Los Angeles.

2008. *Lost in Austen*. A TV miniseries . . . about Amanda, a Jane Austen fan, who discovers she has swapped places with Elizabeth Bennet.

For more information on films see www.jasna.org, www.IMDB.com, and Sue Parill's book, *Jane Austen on Film and Television: A Critical Study of the Adaptations*.

Jane Austen at the Movies

In 1940, although Great Britain was at war with Germany, the United States was still holding to a position of neutrality. Hollywood, fresh on the heels of its huge success with *Gone With the Wind,* looked across the pond for another book to film. At a time when life was dire, and Hitler was gaining ground across Western Europe, MGM selected a most beloved British book: *Pride and Prejudice.* In "The Janeites," Kipling describes the way a group of soldiers bonded during World War I through their shared loved of Jane Austen's novels. "There's no one to touch Jane when you're in a tight place," Kipling's character Humberstall observes. Ah, yes, the woman who lived during an era when England was practically always at war finds her new medium when her country is again at war. In fact, some scholars believe that the producers' aim to get the United States to join England in the war was part of the context that shaped the film.

And with that, *Pride and Prejudice* hit the big screen. That light and bright comedy grabs a reader from the first

Pride and Prejudice, *MGM, 1940.*

sentence so that you are holding onto your seat throughout the novel, like one of the riders in the carriage-race scene between Mrs. Bennet and Mrs. Lucas (a wonderful moment in the 1940 film). Though ten years too old, Greer Garson was cast as Elizabeth, with Laurence Olivier as Darcy. (Some report that the roles were meant for Vivien Leigh and Clark Gable.)

The first *Pride and Prejudice* film is a strange amalgam of British themes within an antebellum *Gone With the Wind* American setting. Practically the only thing missing is mint juleps! Dressed in their crinolines, the Bennet sisters become "Five Gorgeous Beauties are on a Madcap Manhunt." With Maureen O'Sullivan as Jane, and archery, a garden party, a maypole, and dancing to "Drink To Me Only," this *Pride and Prejudice* reinvents the story from the moment the film begins. Most surprisingly, the imperious Lady Catherine is a deliberate ambassador for good. (Some attribute this radical change both to the actress playing Lady Catherine, Edna May Oliver, whose role was usually to put things right, as well as to the desire to get Americans to come to the aid of Great Britain, so the upper-class Brits had to appear open to democratization.)

The screenwriter was Aldous Huxley, who recognized that "The very fact of transforming the book into a picture must necessarily alter its whole quality in a profound way." He was going to work the "odd, crossword puzzle job" trying "to do one's best for Jane Austen."

Not until 1995 did screenwriters, directors, producers, and actors again work the odd, crossword puzzle job of bringing Austen's novels to the big screen. Television, on the other hand, went for her early and has stuck with her faithfully, eventually creating an Austenian phenomenon in the 1995 BBC version of *Pride and Prejudice*.

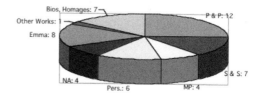

Austen just kept on coming. In the 2008, in the United States, *Masterpiece Theatre* brought all six of the novels to PBS stations around the country under the heading "The Complete Jane Austen."

THE COMPLETE Jane Austen

Courtesy of PBS/WGBH Masterpiece Theatre.

Why Film Austen?

- Well-known author whose reputation for great writing is already established.
- Her novels are copyright free. No royalties to pay!
- Well-scripted plots. After all, the Austen family had done amateur theatricals in the barn at Steventon!
- Great dialogue! Conversations can be lifted from the page, though it is not always easy to speak them. Jennifer Ehle said Austen was the hardest dialogue she ever had to learn. "Shakespeare is a doddle compared to Jane Austen."
- Strong characterization.
- Dramatic exits and entrances.
- No living author to meddle in the screenplay or to negotiate with.
- Because she fleshes out the location and the story so well, she is her own script editor. Reread the scene of Darcy's proposal at Hunsford for all the staging Austen creates for Darcy—coming toward Elizabeth in "an agitated manner," leaning against the mantelpiece, walking "with quick steps around the room."
- Mythic, timeless themes.
- Visual entertainment: the countryside, the costumes (including a revival of interest in high-waisted dresses), the ballroom scenes.
- Happy endings.
- Name recognition.
- Can be made to serve the current politics whether during war or peace.
- The marriage plot.
- Gives people a sense that they know a book that they are expected (including by themselves) to have read. They believe they have achieved their goal of reading the book without actually having had to do so.
- Desire for difference, but familiar difference.
- Interest in "manners."
- Nostalgia . . . a longing for a "simpler" time.
- Filming her celebrates English national heritage for the British and allows for voyeurism for Americans.
- She does not describe love scenes explicitly, which allows for a lot of latitude in scripting them for film.
- In Austen, according to Nick Dear, author of the screenplay of *Persuasion,* we find "an invitation to discover the best of ourselves." We also get a comic dose of insipidity and other manifestations of the "worst of ourselves." (Fanny Dashwood is our favorite.)
- Men's neoclassical fashion of the time when Austen's novels are set emphasizes the male body, which shows off the actors to best effect.
- She provides opportunities for socially conscious representations of women's lives.
- On the contrary, she allows women today to recognize how far we have come.
- Because movie stars are already associated with her, she has cachet.
- Just need a small cast (unless you are filming a ball or two!).
- No animation required!
- Because we simply can't get enough of her. We're hooked.

Austen offers pleasures galore for moviemakers and movie watchers, but there are certain obstacles to filming Austen as well. While the novels may be subtle, dramatizing the novels may require exaggeration in behavior or depictions. It is difficult to convey Austen's irony. Films open up the world of the novels in different ways; and they serve different purposes. Many people love both the films and the novels. Many people come to the novels because of the films. Even those who don't think the films can do justice to the novels will probably watch them because it is hard not to want to see just what part of Austen they *do* capture. Austen herself appeared to understand the nature of adaptation. After all, she took one of the longest novels, Samuel Richardson's *The History of Sir Charles Grandison,* and reduced it to a play, a "playlet" as Paul Poplawski calls it in *A Jane Austen Encyclopedia.* Poplawski summarizes her adaptation: "Jane Austen's play takes some liberties with [the novel] and recasts it in a comic mode, but the main line of development is the same."

Film is its own medium; simply by providing the visual images to accompany what readers imagine, film complicates and sometimes reverses Austen. Several reasons exist for this complication and the resulting reversals. We will examine just a few, highlighting along the way some of the movies and television shows that stand out (for good or for bad).

Films Give Us Bodies

By depicting the actions of bodies, film can telegraph character while the novel must describe it. People we are not supposed to like speak with their mouths full (Mr. Kholi in *Bride and Prejudice,* Mrs. Elton in Miramax's 1996 *Emma,* Elizabeth Elliot in the 1995 BBC *Persuasion,* which was first made for British television and then released as a movie). Except when they represent characters such as Mr. Collins, the bodies that films give us are beautiful.

We see not only bodies but also the way actors sweat, smolder, snicker, smile, and sneer.

Bodies need to be clothed, so a heightened emphasis on clothing and what the characters are wearing accompanies filmmaking and film watching. We see the way Regency dresses act on women's breasts. We might not think, as readers, of what Lizzy Bennet's dress is like when she is proposed to by Darcy at the parsonage; with film we cannot help but notice.

The Miramax *Emma* shows Mrs. Elton as laughable because of what she is wearing (always just a little off, usually ostentatious, very colorful). Just as she points back at herself, her hats always point back to her.

In Nick Dear's *Persuasion,* Louisa and Henrietta's striking red cloaks are echoed in Mary Musgrove's garments in less ostentatious tones. On the walk that takes them to the Hayters', Mary's outer coat has a red interior lining that we can see when the wind blows it. Mary wears a red dress with a tame, white-printed, high-necked collar on the night that her son is injured (though she decides to attend dinner at Uppercross Great House nonetheless). Her efforts to maintain the appearance or attitude of youth despite her weak constitution and petulant manner are emphasized in these wardrobe choices. Contrast this to Anne, seen frequently in the same dress, or in very similar attire with not much variance in color. Other effective wardrobe choices cause the audience to link Lady Russell and Mrs. Croft in their minds. Despite the fact that the similarities in dress point out the similarities in age between the two women, the turbans, comfy-looking shawls, and handsome but not attention-grabbing jewelry all suffice to create around the two women an air of dignity, respectability, and knowledge of the world.

Director Roger Mitchell, in *Persuasion,* also shows us the boots that women wore at the time. It makes us wonder how women climbed, walked, and clambered about in those things!

Lydia as incarnated in the 1995 BBC *Pride and Prejudice* seems to represent the "id"—desire at its purest. She speaks through her body. "I'm so hungry," she proclaims at the beginning. She snorts, and is loud in other ways, too. It is she, still not fully dressed, who darts between rooms and encounters Mr. Collins. Unabashed, unashamed, she merely laughs and moves us. All of this prepares us for some scandalous behavior on her part.

Film often gives us not just bodies, but *movie stars'* bodies. Working with

Pride and Prejudice, *Focus Features, 2005.*

movie stars influences how the characterization occurs. In *Pride and Prejudice,* Elizabeth is not the most beautiful, but in the 2005 *Pride and Prejudice,* who can compete with Keira Knightley? (To begin with, we wanted to make her eat something more.) In the 1995 *Sense and Sensibility* directed by Ang Lee, Edward Ferrars is very like the persona Hugh Grant plays because he is played by Hugh Grant. We want Elinor to want him, and we forgive him for his deceptions. So, too, Colonel Brandon, played by Alan Rickman, conveys a smoldering physicality that makes it hard to imagine him as unattractive. The 2007 *Sense and Sensibility,* with a screenplay by Andrew Davies, gave us a Liam Neeson look-alike in David Morrissey as Colonel Brandon.

Extra Darcy

Louis Menand famously said that the 1995 BBC *Pride and Prejudice* gave us "extra Darcy." We are given extra emotions, extra action. From the screenwriter Andrew Davies's perspective, "the central motor which drives the story forward is Darcy's sexual attraction to Elizabeth." Darcy's erotic energy is established by focusing on his physicality; fencing, swimming, riding, bathing, walking. Indeed, the BBC dips Darcy into the water three times: a bath at Netherfield, washing his face after penning his letter at Rosings, and then his swim at Pemberley. Martine Voiret points out that the cravat worn by the men in the Austen films (the precursor of the tie) "begs to be untied; and it is." Darcy pulls his cravat off to swim. (In *Sense and Sensibility,* Brandon loses his, showing that both his wardrobe and his emotions are disheveled.)

Extra Darcy sometimes means less Elizabeth. In the novel, Elizabeth notices that Darcy is looking at her. She notices his notice. But in the 1995 BBC *Pride and Prejudice,* Darcy is looking at Elizabeth, but *the viewers are looking at Darcy.* We look at his profile, at how he looks out windows, or stands in front of a mirror. This has an impact on a moment of importance in the book: when Elizabeth gazes at the portrait of Darcy in Pemberly: "As she stood before the canvas, on which he was represented, and fixed his eyes upon herself, she thought of his regard with a deeper sentiment of gratitude than it had ever raised before." Encountering an artistic rendering awak-

Pride and Prejudice, BBC/A & E, 1995.

ens what she has thought she knows and challenges her to recast it. She is experiencing art touching her. This is her moment, a moment of elucidation. She recognizes his smile and in that recognition there is something more as well. But in the film version, this moment is shared with Darcy himself, hot and sweaty, riding a horse, with a need to dip into waters to wash away his awakened sensibility. John Wiltshire's *Recreating Austen* explains the significance of these juxtaposed images: "At this crucial moment then, the film replaces the key episode of the novel with a key of its own, a male writer's redefinition of its centre." Darcy's is an active struggle—riding, stripping off some clothes, diving, swimming. These actions are much more dramatic in expression than Elizabeth's—staring, thinking, reconsidering, *knowing*. Hers is an inward struggle. We are seduced by sheer action alone, if not by Colin Firth's body, into Darcy's drama. This focus transfers Lizzy's crisis of recognition to Darcy's struggle with his raw emotions.

This substitution of an outer struggle for an inner one has become the most famous scene in a film of all of Austen's novels. Colin Firth explained to Terry Gross of the radio program *Fresh Air* just how that came about:

It was almost an accident really that led to the whole wet shirt business and I think, probably, if anyone had connived it a phenomenon like that, they would have failed miserably. There was, if I remember it . . . the original script had it down that Darcy dives in completely naked and I suppose he might well have done that. He's on his own property and it's a hot day. But the BBC didn't consider that acceptable and then there was some talk of underwear and then we heard that nobody wore underwear (Colin laughs) in those days and then I think there was an attempt to create underwear, the kind of "If they had worn underwear, would they have looked like this?" And I went to be fitted with those and there was no way on earth . . . and I can tell you now, had I worn those, there would have been no heartthrob.

Instead, as Andrew Davies said "Colin burnt his way into the hearts of England's womanhood."

Extra Edward

Sense and Sensibility, *Columbia, 1995.*

The Ang Lee/Emma Thompson 1995 *Sense and Sensibility* gives us an affectionate, playful Edward (seen playing with Margaret, giving a handkerchief and an atlas to Margaret, riding horses with Elinor). It isn't just *extra* Edward, but *extroverted* Edward: he knows just what to do, he solves the problem of Margaret, he is deprecatingly funny. So, too, with the 2007 *Sense and Sensibility,* carried by *Masterpiece Theatre* in 2008, with a screenplay by Andrew Davies, who apparently likes to get his men wet. In this version, Edward, cravat loosened or lost, splits logs in the pouring rain to let out his emotions. The Edward of the novel is noticeably not someone who recommends himself "by any peculiar graces of person or address." As Joan Klingel Ray has observed, in the novel, Edward wouldn't have had the strength to chop wood.

In the novel, Edward never attempts to tell Elinor of his secret engagement; Emma Thompson wants us to think more kindly of him than Austen did, giving him some stammering lines in the stable at Norland that make it appear he is about to reveal this important information, but he is interrupted. The viewer may excuse Edward his failure; the reader does not.

Extra Brandon

Any Austen hero we are meant to like will be portrayed in a likeable way. So, as with Edward in the 1995 *Sense and Sensibility,* so, too, with Brandon: He greets Elinor and Marianne when they arrive at Cleveland, the home of the Palmers, though in fact he arrives after them. He finds the rain-soaked Marianne, and now it is his turn, Willoughby-like, to carry her heroically through the rain. In the 2007 Andrew Davies version, he accompanies them to Cleveland, and heroically rescues Marianne. In the novel, Marianne's illness is much less dramatic: she has walked around the wet grass, comes home, and doesn't take off her wet stockings. But the choice to have Brandon rescue a wet, faint, shivering Marianne, to carry her manfully in his arms through the downpour, gives Brandon a chance to look macho. That is not the only time: Again, in the 2007 version, his masculinity is expressed dramatically: he is shown dueling, and he is a falconer, whose ability to tame animals, it is implied, has something to do with his relationship with Marianne. Enhancing the men's roles and characteristics, especially those of Edward and Brandon, appears to reverse the reality of women's lives—women did not always get to marry heartthrobs but had to settle for men who were older (Brandon) and seemingly lackluster (Edward).

Extra Knightley

Although George Knightley shines perhaps more than any of Austen's heroes, without needing added luster, the Miramax *Emma* gives us extra Knightley, by adding some very cute lines. Jeremy Northam as Knightley is shown in front of the huge Donwell Abbey saying, "I just want to stay here where it's cozy." He also gets the line, after Emma's arrow falls way off target: "Try not to kill my dogs."

Films Give Us Scenery and Settings

Speaking of Donwell Abbey, films give us scenery and settings. It is said that in the recent spate of Austen films since 1995, the landscape, beautifully groomed and beautifully filmed, becomes a character as well. When Austen satirizes the picturesque, films will end up endowing the picturesque with luster simply because of the sumptuous settings selected. What Emma or Elizabeth or Anne Elliot see on their walks, we see. As a result, the voluptuous, the spectac-

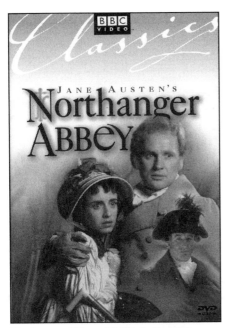

Northanger Abbey, *BBC/A & E, 1986.*

ular, the truly visible, are not the actors, themselves: it is the landscape.

So, too with settings. Was Rosings as grand as the 1995 BBC or 2005 *Pride and Prejudice* imply? Lady Catherine would almost have good reason for her imperiousness if it were. Did Hartfield have a greenhouse, as the Miramax *Emma* shows? That would have been very expensive because of the window tax at that time. Would footmen have attended Mr. Knightley's guests in his garden during their strawberry picking as in the ITV/A&E *Emma*? These images are all fantasies of luxury, serving an interest of film, not of the novel.

Yet, films help us see settings we might have difficulty imagining, for instance, the women in the spa waters of Bath in the 1986 *Northanger Abbey* di-

rected by Giles Foster. (This scene, as well as Katherine Schlesinger as Catherine Morland, makes that adaptation a favorite to revisit.) Or the claustrophobic feel to the rooms Mr. Woodhouse inhabits in the Miramax *Emma.*

The opening of the 1995 BBC *Pride and Prejudice* sets the pace for the movie, announcing, as we watch Darcy and Bingley gallop across the land, that this is a galloping story that won't let up.

Images may tell us too much, however, foretelling the outcome in a way the novel would not. For instance, the archery scene in the Miramax *Emma* shows us exactly whose hearts will be pierced by Cupid.

Streamlining the Plot

The 1972 BBC miniseries production of *Emma* shows what happens when a plot is *not* streamlined. It feels like a home movie. The creators of that program seemed to believe that no characters or lines of dialogue were expendable. If you are reading the book, you don't notice how long some of the scenes are. But with camera work so sparse, and actors who appeared to fear moving their heads, this *Emma* feels long. With no music, few camera cuts, many close-ups of people's faces, one feels as claustrophobic as sitting in Mr. Woodhouse's room with a fire burning on a summer night. There seems nothing to divert the viewer and at times we felt a desire to put our eyes out.

Unless their results are to be like this early BBC attempt to film Austen, screenwriters must streamline the plot in one way or another. Inevitably, this removes some (or all!) of the depth of the novel. Compressing a story usually involves inverting some events, putting people in scenes that they weren't in, and creating scenes that did not exist. Andrew Davies, adapter of four out of six of Austen's novels, explained his approach this way "Sometimes it's necessary to supply things that Austen somehow forgot to include, but to keep them very much in the spirit of what she did write." (Whether our screenwriter has gotten carried away by his own success is left to others to determine.)

Often the debate about whether a movie is faithful to an Austen novel or not rides on this very question: What is the spirit of what she wrote? How do *they* know what she forgot? Was she *really* writing romances? Doesn't Austen explore several other equally important themes, including the value of women's friendships? But streamlining the plot means casting out themes deemed subsidiary, and throwing oneself fully into romance. As romance becomes the central focus, it is often more elevated and celebrated than in the novels. As a result, the movies appear to adhere to conventions of romance that the novels condemn, or pair romance and courtship rather than showing them in opposition.

Streamlining may involve collapsing two events into one: so that in the Miramax *Emma*, strawberry picking at Donwell Abbey and the picnic to Box Hill become one event. It can mean eliminating: in the 2007 *Mansfield Park*, Fanny never goes back to Portsmouth. In the 1940 MGM *Pride and Prejudice,* there is no visit to Pemberly.

Unless the film will be many hours long, the minor characters that so entertain us in the novel must disappear. Who is expendable? In the 1940 and 2005 versions, Mr. and Mrs. Hurst are absent. (Though we have a fleeting glance of *Mr. Hill* in the 2005 version, bringing in biscuits for breakfast the day after the Netherfield Ball. The novel gives us *Hill*, the housekeeper. The film makers give her a husband.) Maria Lucas, too, becomes expendable for the trip to Hunsford in the 2005 version. The 1980 version of *Pride and Prejudice* eliminates Mrs. Jenkinson, such an important nonentity in the life of Lady Catherine! In *Bride and Prejudice* it's Kitty, Captain Fitzwilliam, and the Hursts. In the 1995 Ang Lee/Emma Thompson *Sense and Sensibility,* we lose Miss Nancy Steele and Lady Middleton (as well as her children). Thus, there is no Miss Steele listening at the door to Edward and Lucy's discussion, and justifying it by referring to times when she and Lucy would eavesdrop as children.

Establishing Your Parentage

Continually remade films evoke memories of earlier productions. The archery scene in McGrath's *Emma* refers to the archery scene in the 1940 *Pride and Prejudice*. It is not in either novel. Darcy plays billiards in both the 1940 *Pride and Prejudice* (with Bingham) and the 1995 BBC version (alone). In *Mansfield Park*, Fanny Price snuffs out a candle with her finger when she sees Henry Crawford standing outside her window,

Emma, *Miramax, 1996.*

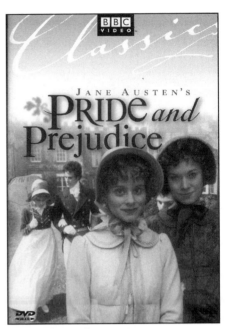

Pride and Prejudice, *BBC, 1980.*

recalling Darcy famously snuffing out his candle after being up all night (or so we suppose) writing his letter to Elizabeth in the 1995 BBC *Pride and Prejudice*. General Tilney is a falconer in the 1986 *Northanger Abbey*; Colonel Brandon gains the falconer glove and the skill in the 2007 *Sense and Sensibility*. It has been suggested that Darcy's fencing in that same adaptation draws upon the popular BBC classic serialization of *Clarissa* that had been made four years earlier. In it, Lovelace, the eighteenth-century rake, is shown fencing. In the 2007 *Sense and Sensibility*, Andrew Davies takes the sword he put in Darcy's hand and gives it to Brandon and Willoughby for their duel.

The unusual chair that sits not just two, but three, Bennet daughters can be found both in the 1980 BBC *Pride and Prejudice* and the 1995 BBC version.

Echoes of earlier performances and earlier depictions are found in more recent films (literally, for we are seeing both Mary Musgrove and Lucy Steele, both Mrs. Elton and Mrs. Hurst, both Mrs. Weston and Jane Bennet). This is not only because some of the actors re-appear (which they do) but also because the dresses themselves reappear. Mrs. Elton's pale green muslin gown when she is at Donwell for strawberry picking in the 1995 ITV/A&E *Emma* is the same gown Mrs. Hurst wore at Pemberly in the 1980 miniseries version of *Pride and Prejudice*. Meanwhile, Marianne Dash-wood wears a brown velvet grown with white lace in the 2007 *Sense and Sensibility*. Elizabeth Bennet (Keira Knightley) wore the same gown when she visited Pemberly for the second time in the 2005 *Pride and Prejudice*.

Depicting Interior Thoughts

Jane Austen's great innovation, tracing the consciousness of her characters, is difficult to transfer to film. Yet, to work with an Austen novel, filmmakers have to find ways to capture the subjective viewpoint. They choose a variety of methods:

- Voice-overs. This is the choice of Amy Heckerling in *Clueless*. The novel reports these thoughts: "Why was it so much worse that Harriet should be in love with Mr Knightley than Frank Churchill? Why was the evil so dreadfully increased by Harriet's having some hope of a return? It darted through her with the speed of an arrow that

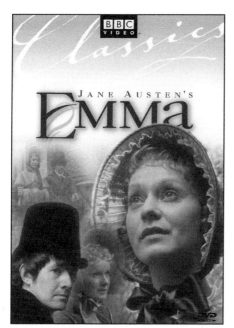

Emma, *BBC, 1972.*

Mr Knightley must marry no one but herself." *Clueless* cleverly captures this process of thought through a voice-over: "I mean, what is my problem? Harriet is my pal . . . I don't begrudge her a boyfriend. I really . . . Ooh, I wonder if they have that in my size?" "Oh my God, I love Josh."

- Talking to oneself, as does Lizzy when she reads Darcy's letter in the 1995 BBC *Pride and Prejudice*. Emma talks to herself in a mirror in the Miramax *Emma,* and after hearing that Miss Smith believes Mr. Knightley returns her affections in the 1996 ITV/A&E *Emma.*

- Dream sequences. In the 1972 *Emma,* the dream sequences are a lot of fun and let us know what is in Emma's head. They let us laugh at Emma. In the 1996 ITV/A&E *Emma,* Emma's worries about Mr. Knightley and Jane Fairfax are captured through a nightmare that places her in the church at the wedding of Jane and Mr. Knightley. In the nightmare, Emma cries out "but what about little Henry?" Then Emma startles awake from her dream. Catherine Morland also has nightmares in the 1986 BBC *Northanger Abbey* to represent her Gothic imaginings.

- Fantasies. Again, the same 1996 ITV/A&E *Emma* represents Emma's thoughts by showing them as fantasies, such as her imagining that Harriet Smith is the daughter of a baronet, the wedding of Mr. Elton and Harriet, Frank Churchill lifting Harriet onto his horse and cantering away as many young girls celebrate.

- Speaking directly to the camera, which was one of the choices Patricia Rozema used for her version of *Mansfield Park.*

- Writing in a diary, as does Emma in the Miramax *Emma. Bridget Jones' Diary*, living up to its title, shows Bridget writing the words she is thinking directly onto the screen.
- Ironic editing—using montage, or jump cuts—to capture the irony inherent in the thoughts.
- A collage of images that a person is bringing to mind: as when Darcy writes his letter to Elizabeth, and Emma thinks about and realizes who she has always loved in the 1996 ITV/A&E *Emma.*
- When a character writes a letter, the act itself conveys inner thoughts because the contents being written are voiced.
- Translating thoughts into a prayer spoken out loud: the Miramax version presents Emma's thoughts in this way.

- Using the symbolism of the scene to convey a thought or mood. Roger Mitchell's *Persuasion* shows the furniture in Kellynch Hall being covered, as the screenplay direction says, "It's a sad picture, as if the deceased house is being wrapped in a shroud." In the novel there would be no need to cover the furniture because the Crofts are moving in. But to telegraph what has happened to Anne Elliot, it is a very effective beginning.

But here is a challenge: how does one depict a character known for her silences? Someone like Anne Elliot, who only gains her voice in the latter part of the novel? If one gives her the first lines of the film, as does the 2007 *Persuasion,* the impact of her silence is never felt.

Admirers: An Interview with Karen Joy Fowler, the author of *The Jane Austen Book Club*

From *The Jane Austen Book Club*:
A partial list of things not found in the books of Jane Austen:
> locked-room murders
> punishing kisses
> girls dressed up as boys (and rarely the reverse)
> spies
> serial killers
> cloaks of invisibility
> Jungian archetypes, most regrettably, doppelgängers
> cats

Our own impartial list of things not found in Jane Austen:
> the supernatural
> swashbuckling (after all, any dueling occurs offstage)
> the sublime (though Kelly argues that a case could be made for it)
> Germanic composers (Mozart, Beethoven, Haydn). Doug argues that it is a
>   big deal that there is no Haydn, because Haydn was a London superstar.
> bedroom-comedy farces such as the *Marriage of Figaro*
> Scotsmen, excepting the juvenilia
> educated mothers
> moonlit walks on the beach

We talked with Karen Joy Fowler about her wildly successful book The Jane Austen Book Club. *One of us has read it more than three times, listened to it as a book on tape four times, and seen the movie two times. Each time, more Austenian references are found and delighted in! Alice Sebold says of* The Jane Austen Book Club, *"If I could eat this novel, I would." We understand the sentiment. Each chapter features the book club discussing one of the six Austen novels, and recapitulates through events that happen to the book club members a few key aspects of that novel under review . . . in a sort of kaleidoscopic way, or a jazz rendition of a given melody. Fowler takes elements in the novel but shades them, giving them different colors. The story of* Persuasion *has a fall and a pivotal declaratory letter; so, too, do these figure in the book club's reading of* Persuasion. *Colonel Tilney's frightening* Northanger Abbey *becomes a mansion in Bel Air, and like the novel, the chapter has a heroine who has read too many novels. But the entire book has an Austenian narrative arc, too, as Jocelyn, the Emma figure, the matchmaker/dog-breeder, finally discovers.*

"If I could eat this novel, I would." —ALICE SEBOLD

THE
JANE AUSTEN
BOOK CLUB

A Novel

KAREN JOY FOWLER

Q: Your book begins, "Each of us has a private Austen." The narrator tells us that Jocelyn's Austen wrote wonderful novels about love and courtship, but never married. Bernadette's Austen was a comic genius. Sylvia's Austen was a daughter, a sister, an aunt, someone who could love and be loved, but it didn't cloud her vision. Prudie's Austen changed each time she was read, and sadly died at the young age of forty-one. Allegra's Austen wrote about the impact of financial need on the intimate lives of women. Grigg's—well, we just don't know. But this discussion made us wonder, who was the narrator's private Austen?

A: Since the narrator is the book club, the collective voice, the narrator's viewpoint must be all of the above. Speaking, as I can, for the writer as opposed to the narrator, I can attest that the writer's private Austen is all of the above.

Q: What would you recommend to someone, like Grigg, who is just discovering Jane Austen?

A: I've read Austen so many times over the last forty years, that my own reading of her is now a very complicated one. As I read, I remember all those previous readings, so that I not only have the text itself, but the ghosts of all those earlier me's reading alongside. I honestly can't imagine what it would be like to be reading Austen for the first time as an adult.

But I usually suggest starting with *Pride and Prejudice,* which is the easiest of the novels. And the most buoyant.

Q: Each of the members of the Jane Austen Book Club was introduced to the love of reading in childhood. We learn of Jocelyn and the comics her parents brought to her at camp each Sunday; of how Allegra loved biographies of famous people's childhoods; Grigg's dramatic introduction to science fiction. Prudie read fairy tales and Sylvia was read European fairy tales and *The Lives of the Saints*. Bernadette was in a group named for a book, *Five Little Peppers*. She is taking some liberties with the facts of her life, so maybe

that is her way of saying this is what she read as a child. What was your experience of reading as a child and what books mattered to you then?

A: I was a passionate early reader. My family used to take a weekly trip to the library together and we'd all come home with our own books. I read those biographies with the orange covers about famous people's childhoods and I loved *The Bobbsey Twins* and later the Edward Eager books and the various Shoe books—*Ballet Shoes, Skating Shoes,* etc. *The Saturdays. The Green Poodles. The Trouble with Jenny's Ear.*

Before I could read myself, my parents read to me—Dr. Seuss and *Mary Poppins* and Winnie the Pooh. I spent half my childhood in one imaginary world or another.

Q: When did you first read Jane Austen and what book was the first one you read?

A: I don't actually remember. My best guess is that I was fourteen and read *Sense and Sensibility.*

Q: Do you remember what you felt reading it?

A: What I remember is that I found it easy to read and was quite pleased with myself over that fact. I should have been pleased with Austen—writing a book that went down so easy two hundred years later—but I'm afraid I thought the credit was all mine.

Q: The book is steeped in allusions to Austen's books in both subtle and explicit ways, some of which the movie makes even more explicit (perhaps to the disappointment of your most fervent readers): Jocelyn's Emma-like matchmaking; Allegra's first Marianne Dashwood-like fall introduces her to a Willoughby-like character, her second, like Louisa Musgrove's fall from the cob, brings Dr. Yep into her life. There is Bernadette and her Mrs. Bates-like glasses, Grigg as the heroine of a Gothic novel, the stable gossip being offered (and overheard!) as Prudie and Jocelyn watch the movie of *Mansfield Park* reminding us of Fannie Price not being allowed to ride once Mary Crawford arrives on the scene. We encounter a modern-day counterpart to Thorpe's fixation on his (Lexus-like) carriage; Grigg and Jocelyn's ride to the library dinner like Darcy's and Elizabeth's conversation as they danced; the play within the story when *Mansfield Park* is being read; the Bel Air mansion for Northanger Abbey; Prudie's French terms interspersed throughout the novel, like Frank Churchill's in *Emma*; an epistolary chapter (through e-mail); Daniel, like Wentworth, regaining his lover through a letter—and of course much more. It is all so delightful to discover, and then to find it layered into something else; there are echoes and reflections. Is there an allusion you put in that everyone has missed and that you are willing to reveal now? If not, are there a couple of allusions that when you think of them make you laugh?

A: What a good list! You've been really diligent! It was tricky, trying to lay in allusions subtle enough that you could believe the characters, in the process of rereading the Austens at that very moment, wouldn't notice.

Perhaps my own favorite concerns Bernadette's dance troupe, the Five Little Peppers. As Bernadette goes from being the tallest in the troupe to being the shortest, she is able to briefly be each of the five of the Bennet sisters, ending with the slutty Lydia when she runs off and gets married in Vegas.

Q: You have Prudie think, "The great thing about books was the solidity of the written word." Did you feel your words de-solidify (perhaps there is a better word than this faux one!) as they were translated into celluloid?

A: Since my own readings of Austen have changed so over the years, I'm not sure I'm entirely on board with Prudie's assessment. Reading is genuinely collaborative, and even if the words don't change, the reader does, which can profoundly affect the text. Prudie's own history is so tenuous, she appreciates books for their solidity, while the books I like best reward rereading by shifting around a lot.

Seeing my book on film was a bit like being in the head of a reader and watching what my book looks like from that perspective. And then you add the actors and the things they bring to the roles and what you get is sort of like the game of Telephone—my book passes through several filters and comes out recognizable, but transformed at the end.

The game of Telephone is a metaphor I seem to use a lot, by the way. Do you think in those long-ago days when we played it, there was genuine slippage or did someone simply change the word for the pure mischief of it? I suspect the latter.

Q: I sensed a change in the motives of some the characters as they were translated from book to film (for instance, Bernadette suggests the book club rather than Jocelyn); which, in fact, is similar to what some critics (including Prudie and Jocelyn) see happening with movie versions of Jane Austen's novels. Rather than point out those examples of the movie transforming the book, let me ask if you learned new things about your characters as you experienced the movie being made?

A: I wouldn't say that I learned new things about my characters, but that I did see alterations. In almost every case I understood why the change had been made. Because my book contains little information about Bernadette's current life and because the characters' backstories had to be trimmed or omitted for reasons of time and money, I think it was

necessary to give Bernadette more to do or she would have seemed slighted in terms of screen time.

An exception is Grigg's wealth. I don't see what was gained by making him a wealthy man and I liked it better when he had nothing to offer Jocelyn but his own good heart. And impeccable taste in books.

Q: What is the most startling thing someone has said to you about Jane Austen or her novels?

A: A woman told me once that she thought *Pride and Prejudice* was almost a great book and that it would be so easy to fix it. When I pressed her, she said she'd read the book too long ago to be more specific. I dislike the fixing of Austen in any case, but I was genuinely puzzled by this response, since it's difficult for me to see any way in which *Pride and Prejudice* could be changed. The other novels all present difficulties of the sort that I like a lot, but that I can imagine some other reader wishing to fix. But not *Pride and Prejudice*.

One notable consistency has been among the male Austen readers. I have yet to meet one who didn't read Austen for the first time because some woman—teacher, girlfriend, mother—made him.

Q: A historian has proposed that feminist consciousness-raising groups of the 1970s morphed into book clubs. A consciousness-raising group is mentioned during the first

meeting of the Jane Austen book club. Coincidence?

A: This historian and I are on the same page.

Q: Jane Austen was famously rejected by a publisher and the work of Allegra's lover Corinne is rejected by publishers. Did you experience any rejections in relationship to getting The Jane Austen Book Club published? If not, is there a different experience of rejection that you have had that is emblematic for you?

A: I've had the same editor for all my novels. She moved houses once, so I moved with her, but I've not faced rejection for a novel in a long time.

Getting my first novel, *Sarah Canary,* published was an ordeal, though. I collected some twenty-three rejections over three or four years. Those were dark days.

Q: Is there a Jane Austen-associated gift that you treasure?

A: My editor bought me an early edition of *Emma.* It's just a beautiful book and she had a beautiful box made to protect it. I can't remember ever getting a gift I loved more.

And a friend of mine attached a paperback copy of *Sense and Sensibility* to a wooden handle to make a Jane Austen book club for me. I take it to readings and threaten to whack people with it if they doze off. But I'm afraid to take it on a plane for fear it will be confiscated. Though there is something very appealing about the idea of hijacking a jet armed with nothing but *Sense and Sensibility* on a stick. I would force the plane to land in Bath and we would all take the waters there.

Q: What was the most surprising thing you experienced or learned about Jane Austen or her novels as you worked on your book?

A: Although I'd read her novels for years, I'd never paid any attention to her biography until after I wrote this book. I was surprised and delighted by the responses to her work that she collected from her family and friends. I wish I responded with such good humor to criticism. I'm inspired by Austen to try harder to do so.

And I was very taken by the work of William H. Galperin (in his book *The Historical Austen*) on *Sense and Sensibility.* He claims that the whole novel can be read with Colonel Brandon as the chief villain and now that he's pointed that out, I, too, can do so. It's an interesting reading.

Q: Grigg explains why he likes *Northanger Abbey* best of all, saying "I just love how it's all about reading novels. Who's a heroine, what's an adventure? Austen poses these questions very directly." I found I had some of those same thoughts reading *The Jane Austen Book Club*. In

fact, I created a formula like those old SAT comparison questions: *Northanger Abbey* : Gothic novels of the 1790s = *Jane Austen Book Club* : Jane Austen's books. Comment?

A: I suspect that Austen's feelings about the Gothics are more mixed than mine are regarding Austen. Even when I complain about something in her novels, it's an admiring, approving complaint. I never wish a word different than what it is. I feel she's often underestimated, particularly by people who haven't read her.

But with that caveat, I agree with your formulation. Certainly I was thinking a great deal about the role of reading in our lives, at least in the lives of the bookish among us.

Q: When did you last read Jane Austen?

A: I read all of it, including *Lady Susan* and the unfinished *Sanditon*, many many times as I wrote the book. I reread *Persuasion* yet again about four months ago.

Q: In working so closely with Jane Austen's novels, did you discover something about yourself, a sort of Austen-mediated self-revelation?

A: I noticed the ways in which I grew up in an Austen world. The conventional wisdom during my junior high and high school days was that the girl's role was never to pursue, but simply to wait to be chosen. We were taught to guard our reputations, and that a single misstep sexually would result in a lifetime of ruin and regret.

Thankfully it all turned out to be balderdash. I think of myself as a contrary, cantankerous person, so it was startling to see and concede how easily led I was regarding these things. I didn't start dating until college, so it was all quite theoretical.

I don't actually care much for the Austen as guidebook stuff. From the moment she began publishing straight through to today, there's been a concerted effort to insist that her books are filled with beneficial moralities. I feel it reduces a great writer. You can find useful moral lessons in Dickens and Shakespeare, too, but no one is writing the Shakespeare guide to dating.

P.S: Carol was waiting for a friend, who was late, to go to The Jane Austen Book Club *movie in Dallas. Deciding to do a little on-the-spot research, she approached two women and asked if they had read the book. One woman, a little startled, said "I didn't know it was a book." Inside, watching the movie of* The Jane Austen Book Club, *there is a scene in which Prudie and Jocelyn are at the movie of* Mansfield Park. *They hear someone say "I didn't know it was a book!"*

LARPing and JARPing

There is something in us that wishes to live within a world we are attached to—not just to participate as outsiders, but to really get into the guts of this other reality and make it our home. Jocelyn, the Emma-like founder of the Jane Austen book club, first encounters such reality-bending practices while attending an annual meeting of the Inland Empire Hound Club. The Hound Club's meeting coincides with a fantasy convention—much to Jocelyn's dismay. Here she encounters the novel's sole male protagonist, Grigg, who explains the seemingly bizarre behavior of an elevator passenger, who is acting as an invisible vampire.

What Jocelyn is unaware of is that the "vampire"—actually a dressed-up teenager—is engaging in a common role-playing activity called "LARPing," or, "Live-Action Role Playing." Role-playing games such as *Dungeons & Dragons* and *Vampire: The Masquerade* usually use pens, paper, dice, and a few rulebooks to create a story, but those more theatrically inclined tend to enjoy the LARPing aspect.

Jocelyn is equally unaware of her tendency to engage in "JARPing"—"Jane Austen Role-Playing." Of course, this is a theme of *The Jane Austen Book Club*, the meta-echoing of the Austen stories within the novel itself: Jocelyn's continual match-making, the least of which is among her dogs; Bernadette's Bates-like ramblings; Sylvia's role as a librarian who helps people consumed with knowing their genealogies à la Sir Walter Elliot.

JARPing shows up not just within *The Jane Austen Book Club*. The very existence of the popular sequel novels—*Mr. Darcy Takes a Wife*, the Jane Austen mystery series, and the Mr. and Mrs. Darcy mysteries, to name a few—shows that people want to continue living inside the worlds Jane Austen created and the world she lived in. Many of these, often quite sexually charged, are also probably fantasy fulfillment for those who have grown accustomed to viewing Colin Firth swimming in the pond at Pemberley.

Austenland

Sharon Hale's *Austenland* offers three aspects of JARPing: the love of Austen's writings, the love of the 1995 BBC *Pride and Prejudice* miniseries, and the fantasy of living during Austen's time. It is a playful, well-developed, sympathetic but not slavish response to *Pride and Prejudice*. A clue that the heroine will be able to work things out is the fact that she has read Austen *before* watching film interpretations of Austen. She read *Pride and Prejudice* first at sixteen, and has reread it a dozen times since. Her opinion of the novel? "Besides being witty and funny and maybe the best novel ever written, it's also the most perfect romance in all of literature and nothing in life can ever measure up." The problem? "It wasn't until the BBC put a face on the story that those gentlemen in tight breeches had stepped out of her reader's imagination and into her nonfiction hopes." A clue that she has something to work out is the shame she feels for her enthrallment to the BBC version. We learn that buying her own copy has probably helped put her local video store out of business; she hides her copy in a large plant in her apartment.

Her great-aunt's will sends our heroine Jane off to Pembrook Park, in Kent, England, where for three weeks she will stay as a houseguest—a houseguest living, not in the twenty-first century, but in Regency England. She will have to abide by their rules: no technological interlopers (no cell phones, no MP3 players, no computers), wear the dresses of the time, and learn to dance the dances of that period. Actors playing an aunt, several eligible young men, and servants will all help to create the fantasy, and Jane—in good JARPing fashion—must agree to keep in character to stay for three weeks. She is given instruction on how to dance, how to eat fish (no knives), play whist, and use the proper manners of the time. She must pretend to be an eligible young woman of 1816 and discover how she will withstand the attractions of a Wickham-like character and (perhaps) overcome her dislike of a Darcy-like character. She especially misses chocolate.

Confessions of a Jane Austen Addict

Laurie Viera Rigler's *Confessions of a Jane Austen Addict* is one great JARPing experience from beginning to end. Just how did Courtney Stone, a twenty-first-century thirty-something Los Angeles resident become Jane Mansfield of 1812? She goes from a broken engagement in the present time to awakening to bloodletting and threats of being institutionalized by her "mother," Mrs. Mansfield. She struggles to make sense of what she is doing there and with the stays, the dresses, the footwear, the chamber pots, the dirty coaching inn, the need for a chaperone; it is quite a struggle. *Mansfield Park* hasn't been written yet, so she has only two of Austen's novels to keep her sane. Perhaps the most touching moment is when she runs into Jane Austen herself in London. Haven't many people imagined what they would say to Austen?

JARPing and Filmmaking

The movie adaptations of the novels—and especially of Austen's life—make JARPing as plain as the nose on Mr. Collins's face. Because there is often a good deal of information, scenes, or a dialogue to be filled in, it is up to the ingenuity of the screenwriter to provide the viewer with the proper visual storytelling to coincide with Austen's verbal narration. The trick, then, is to endeavor to stay within the Austenian world as closely as possible. The movies run the gamut from exactness to the point of servility—the 1972 version of *Emma*—to freewheeling fancy. The latter is an apt description of the 1999 adaptation of *Mansfield Park,* which not only changes Fanny Price's character but also overlays Jane Austen's creative life onto it.

The 1999 *Mansfield Park* is five-star JARPing. It's an interesting film, though we won't reveal just how greatly Patricia

"A Witty, Entertaining Film...Thumbs Up!"

MANSFIELD
PARK

FOR EVERYONE WHO LOVED "EMMA" AND "SENSE & SENSIBILITY"
COMES THE STORY JANE AUSTEN LOVED BEST.

Mansfield Park, *Miramax Films/BBC, 1999.*

Rozema, writer and director, tampers with the plot. For many readers, Fanny is an unattractive character. She is frail and passive; some join with Austen's mother in viewing her as "insipid." It is difficult to build a movie around her, or so Rozema must have thought. Our film Fanny is a writer, a dreamer, a creator; she is active, not passive. She is Austen herself, writing her juvenilia. Using letters to Cassandra, passages from *Northanger Abbey,* biographies, and feminist analyses of Austen, Rozema creates a different Fanny, part Austen, part Brontë. Accepting and then refusing Henry Crawford s proposal, Fanny is Austen accepting a proposal from Harris Bigg-Withers and then the next day declining it. Rozema makes Fanny likeable, even admirable; after all, we *know* we would like Austen if we met her.

Perhaps it was this insertion of Austen into the novel that resulted in a novel being inserted in Austen's life, as in the 2007 movie *Becoming Jane,* in which Jane Austen is made into a pseudo-doppelgänger of Elizabeth Bennet. Though most of the characters are real, many of the events are not, and the romanticization whether for good or ill demonstrates our continuing desire to rework and relive the stories of Miss Austen. Its treatment of witty dialogue between the young Jane Austen and aspiring lawyer Tom Lefroy scans as another adaptation of *Pride and Prejudice.* Indeed this seems to be the film's premise, as Jane is frequently found dashing to her room after a night of banter with Tom to scribble down the next scene in her new work, *First Impressions,* later to become *Pride and Prejudice.* The need to believe that Jane Austen knew unrequited passion is to diminish her power as a writer, as though women could not write these things unless they had experienced them.

Rozema's interventions in Fanny's character seem to have paved the way not only for *Becoming Jane* but also for both the 2007 *Mansfield Park* with Billie Piper and *Miss Austen Regrets.* As the *Boston Globe* commented about the 2007 version, "Ultimately, this *Mansfield Park* makes Patricia Rozema's excellent 1999 version (in which Fanny is made into an Austen-like writer) seem stubbornly loyal to the author." Even Olivia Williams, who plays Jane Austen in *Miss Austen Regrets,* recognizes the JARPing aspect of that program, which gives

Jane Austen at least three potential lovers: "My ideal script would be quotations from the letters, brilliantly knitted together into perfectly natural scenes. Anything that you put into her mouth has to be brilliant, written by somebody who was as brilliant as Jane Austen, and that's impossible, so to have her speaking in a way that is lazily colloquial to me was a mistake."

Sex and Sensibility

When it comes to sexual expressions in Jane Austen movies, we arc truly in the area of JARPing. Martin Amis points out "as literary creations they *thrive* on their inhibitions. It is the source of their thwarted energy." Or as Jocelyn says more tersely in *The Jane Austen Book Club* (the movie), "Austen's all about keeping it zipped." But with romance driving the plot, the films give viewers the required kiss, or two, culminating in "*Mrs.* Darcy's" postcoital kiss at Pemberly in the 2005 *Pride and Prejudice*.

JARPing the end of the story

Ending a movie at Pemberly with two impassioned lovers is only one way that an ending is JARPed. Tampering may include the way that the 1972 BBC adaptation of *Emma* introduces the idea that John and Isabella Knightley will take over at Donwell. It concludes by showing a few of the new couples gathered at Hartfield to celebrate the arrival of the Westons' baby. Mr. Woodhouse almost has the last word (not allowing the postpartum Mrs. Weston to have

wine), "Emma, my dear, a glass of milk for poor Miss Taylor if you please." But Emma gets the last word of the show, "Father."

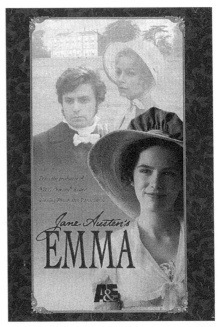

Emma, *ITV/A&E*, 1996.

A JARPing moment of discordance for many who love the novel, ITV/A&E's 1996 adaptation of *Emma* added a harvest festival in which all the tenants of Donwell Abbey, friends, and family sit down at a meal together ("Are we to sit down with hobbledehoys?" asks Mrs. Elton). Emma is introduced to Mr. Martin, and there is a grand dance that includes all the new couples—though the novel does not take us to such a scene. Egalitarian as Mr. Knightley may be, class structure in Regency England would not have looked favorably upon such an event. (Though Mr. Elton reassures his wife "I believe harvest suppers are traditional.") This JARPing, though, allows us to feel that all people are equal and that in the end all things work out for good. It also captures the idea of continuity and community.

Persuasion, *BBC/Sony, 1995.*

The 1995 *Persuasion* shows a logical, cohesive, and emotionally fulfilling ending that is not in the book. In this example of JARPing, Anne Elliot is shown alone in a room; only upon exiting the room does the viewer realize that she is aboard Captain Wentworth's ship and has taken to sailing with him, just as Mrs. Croft sails with her husband the Admiral. Due to Anne's expression of happiness and interest in the Crofts' situations and habits, and given Austen's ending of *Persuasion* ("and she lived . . . as a sailor's wife") this little piece of JARPing seems to complement Austen's story.

* * *

The very fact that almost everyone gets their just desserts in Austen is just a part of the reason why people enjoy JARPing so much. The world of Jane Austen is entrancing. For this reason, Jane Austen societies around the world still hold balls, readings, get-togethers, book clubs, and parties; movies are made of her novels; the novels themselves are bestsellers; and sequels are still written grafting further adventures onto her world. This is the magic of Austen, not the wand-waving magic of wizards in *Dungeons & Dragons.*

Homage to Jane:
Movies that Echo Austen

etropolitan (1990), produced and directed by Whit Stillman. A delightful, witty, comedy of manners that focuses on the lives of preppies in the middle of their first year at college, during the week before and after Christmas in Manhattan. It places the time and location in a very suggestive way by announcing: "Manhattan. Christmas Vacation. Not so long ago." *Not so long ago* . . . that is the clue, as we encounter intellectual discussions in upper-class living rooms about a variety of issues often dissecting bourgeois life or the nature of relationships. We meet Audrey, who reads Austen and loves *Mansfield Park.* Austen is named, debated, represented (next to a Raggedy Ann doll and a jump rope, in the Scribner's Fifth Avenue book store window we can see the *Oxford Illustrated Jane Austen* in 6 volumes). At first Tom dismisses Austen, especially *Mansfield Park,* because of Lionel Trilling's view of it. But later, Tom confides to Audrey, "I've been reading Jane Austen—*Persuasion.*

I like it. I was surprised." Next we see *Persuasion* on his bedside with a picture of Serena, a woman with whom he has been in love (his Mary Crawford).

We can see hints of Fanny Price and her cousin Edmund in these two characters. But sometimes it seems that Tom represents the Fanny character, rather than the Edward character. Like Fanny Price, Tom, a West Sider, is suddenly thrown into a different class, a different culture, that of the life of the upper class, well-off East-Side debutante and her friends. Audrey also represents Fanny. She, like Fanny for Edward, has always been in love with Tom. Central to the movie is an episode involving playing the came of "Truth."

While it is the exact opposite of a play as it requires honesty and openness instead of disguise and acting, for Audrey is it a questionable moment, it is *the* Mansfield Park moment. By the end of the movie, after a Henry Crawford-Maria Rushworth moment, Tom can be heard saying to Audrey, "it's not something Jane Austen would have done." (The movie of *The Jane Austen Book Club* will represent this thought at a pivotal moment by its clever substitution of "What Would Jane Do?" for Walk/Don't Walk on a street sign).

Jane Austen in Manhattan. From the formidable producers of English novels into lush films, *Jane Austen in Manhattan,* by Merchant/Ivory's favorite screenwriter, Ruth Prawer Jhabvala, confronts directly the issue of adaptation. It works with the play written by Jane Austen when she was very young, "Sir Charles Grandison, or the Happy Man." Opening with an auction at Sotheby's in which two people compete to buy the manuscript establishes that this is a manuscript that will be fought over. Whose interpretation will prevail? Pierre (Robert Powell) an avant-garde theater director who has a great deal of emotional power over his actors, or his mentor, Lilianna Zorska (played wonderfully by Anne Baxter)? A central theme in the movie is the seeming abduction of the young woman who plays the woman who is abducted in the play. It is funny and painful: the movie seems to ask who has the right to interpret Austen, and then, in its own way it provides a very open-ended answer.

Ruby in Paradise, written and directed by Victor Nuñez, features Ruby Gissing leaving rural Tennessee to seek her living on the Florida coast. One of her flawed suitors, Mike, lends her a

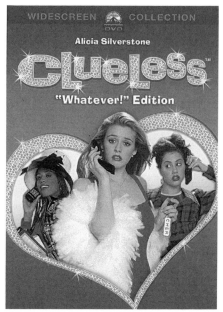

Clueless, *Paramount, 1995.*

copy of *Northanger Abbey.* Ruby thinks *Northanger Abbey* is a "neat story" and sees herself in Catherine Morland.

Clueless. Despite its transported setting, Amy Heckerling's *Clueless* is one of the most faithful Austen-related movies, because it captures Emma's dilemma of being caught between two worlds. *Clueless* is in the tradition of screwball comedies like *It Happened One Night* or *The Philadelphia Story.* Its *Emma* associations are both overt and covert. Teenage girls in *Clueless* often chose Empire-waist dresses, such as young women in the Regency period would have worn. We are not quite sure why in most scenes Josh (the stepbrother rather than the brother-in-law to her sister), is shown eating, but there you have it.

In the novel, Mr. Elton says to Emma: "I need not so totally despair of an equal alliance as to be addressing myself to Miss Smith!" In *Clueless*, the same response is captured in: "Don't you know who my father is?"

Emma's charitable acts are paralleled by Cher's decision to become involved in the Pismo Beach Disaster Relief. Heckerling changes Frank Churchill's secret; but he is still unavailable as a partner. Mr. Knightley's concern for the community, parish meetings, and his land is matched by Josh's breast cancer T-shirt and his work on getting a celebrity to plant a tree. It is a delightful dance in and through the *Emma* story.

You've Got Mail. With many allusions to an Elizabeth-Darcy parallel in the characters, the point is brought home at a pivotal moment in a café, when in a painful confrontation the novel *Pride and Prejudice* sits on the table.

Kandukondain Kandukondain is loosely based on *Sense and Sensibility,* transplanting the novel into a Bollywood film, well, actually a "Kollywood" movie (it is a Tamil-speaking, not a Hindi film). Rajiv Menon directs a movie that explodes with color and design. Two sisters struggle with the questions of love and marriage in very different ways.

Bride and Prejudice. Gurinder Chadha's *Bride and Prejudice* demonstrates that *Pride and Prejudice* translates extremely well to the genre of Bollywood, with Indian parallels in lively dances and formality in courting. The Bennets (the Bakshis), are Sikhs living in Amritsar. Darcy is an heir to a hotel chain and Wickham is a British backpacker (instead of being a soldier, he's a vagabond). For Mr. Kholi (Mr. Collins) his religion is everything American, from hip-hop to stocks and bonds. The alternative to Collin's boring sermonizing is Mr. Kholi's tedious secular worship of all things American. In this version, Lady Catherine is Darcy's mother; her house is a luxury hotel, and she wants Darcy to marry that old American ideal, a blonde. The multiracial elements recall the weight that the class issue would have held in the original *Pride and Prejudice*. In England of the twenty-first century, there would be no way to effect the original meaning of distance and travel that obtain in the novels. Instead, with the globalization of the distances being traveled (between Los Angeles, London, and Amritsar), the problem of distance and travel is restored. The various ways of traveling by carriage are replaced by whether one is flying first class or not for a ten-and-a-half-hour plane ride.

All the major scenes that appear in *Bride and Prejudice* appear as indebted to the 1995 BBC movie as to the book itself. And it dispatches the last half of the book in twenty minutes or less. But no matter; it is delightful, energetic, comedic, colorful!

Bridget Jones's Diary. Like *Bride and Prejudice,* Helen Fielding's *Bridget Jones's Diary* owes as much, or even more, to the 1995 BBC adaptation of *Pride and Prejudice* than it does to the book itself, especially with Andrew Davies cowriting the screenplay. Casting Colin Firth as Darcy makes the resonances with the film even more "real." At first there was some dismay that an American, Renee Zellweger, would play the quintessential Brit Bridget in this romantic comedy. But now people have "blue soup" parties, so all is well in the end. As the director, Sharon Maguire, says "Bridget and Darcy are home to each other."

Bridget Jones's Diary, *Miramax, 2001.*

Bridget Jones: The End of Reason, based loosely on *Persuasion,* might fall more in the category of JARPing.

Music in the 1995 BBC/A&E
Pride and Prejudice

Behind every action is an emotion; and, in a film, behind these emotions is music. Filmmakers use music to underscore certain aspects of a scene: the militaristic "Imperial March" in *Star Wars* at the approach of the Star Destroyers, or the "dawn of man" in *2001,* utilizing the sunrise-like opening of Richard Strauss's *Also Sprach Zarathustra.* Just as every prop, costume, and mannerism must be considered in making the film fit the period, so, too, should the music approach the sound and style of the time, although tempered by modern tastes. The ensemble chosen by Carl Davis in the 1995 film is an homage to that used by Ludwig van Beethoven's *Septet in E-flat Major.* For the majority of the score this small ensemble plays, though more instrumental forces are brought in at certain times to fill out the sound. This gives the film a "chamber ensemble" feel, the feeling of a close interaction of a handful of players, just like the story itself. It is classically balanced, appropriate, and with a hint of the pastoral—everything that society should be.

Though one may think a small ensemble such as this would be limiting compared to the Mahlerian super-orchestras of many modern film scores, the combinations available to a chamber group are varied and always fresh. Between the winds—clarinet, flute, bassoon, and horn, the strings—violin, viola and cello, and the pianoforte—a period predecessor of the modern piano with a little less resonance—there is quite a lot to be offered in terms of difference in timbre and expression.

Consider, for instance, the heroic opening as Darcy and Bingley dash across the plain near Netherfield. The French horns imitate the hunting horns of the day using perfect intervals—perfect fourths and fifths—which give rise to feelings of openness, spaciousness and nobility, the "perfect" match for these two as they survey the countryside. The French horn always carries with it the veneer of nobility, since the nobles are the one who use the horn in hunting.

A Plodding Melody

Compare this with the "Canon Collins," the plodding little melody in the bassoon that always announces the arrival of the obeisant clergyman. One of the bassoon's typical uses is to convey humor, which it certainly does here. A more telling function, however, is revealed when a closer look is given to the instrument's particular use in the orchestra of Mozart, Haydn, and Beethoven. In the classical orchestra, the bassoon would often be used in a role similar to that of the French horn, as the reedy timbre and ability to sustain long notes matched the similar sound and use of the horn. The bassoon would be used in those passages in which the horn would be too prominent and a softer, "shadow" horn was needed.

It makes perfect sense, then, for Mr. Collins to be the bassoon. Not only is his character a shadow of the more heroic gentlemen Bingley and Darcy, often portrayed by the French horns but he literally follows in the shadow of others, Lady Catherine de Bourgh specifically. In fact, the imitative nature of his music (a canon is a type of composition in which the lines play follow-the-leader, one voice stating a melody and continuing, while the other follows a step behind, like a round) also hints at his blind following as well as his repetitive speech and use of clichés.

Lady Catherine has her own specific music, in the style of the French opera overture. The halting dotted rhythms, slow tempo, and ornamentation give a feel of grandiosity and gravitas to the arrival at Rosings Park. The feeling of foreboding and tension inherent in the genre matches the Bennets' feelings when the haughty Lady Catherine visits Longbourn.

Opening and Closing

Not all characters have themes as specific as Mr. Collins and Lady Catherine (Lady Catherine, of course, would have demanded that they have their own themes if they had not been given them). A great deal of the music associated with the Bennets is based on the development and varied repetition of the opening title music played by the chamber ensemble. The opening theme is cheerful, energetic, and sequential; it keeps the listener interested and active. Conversation scenes, such as those between Jane and Lizzy, will use a varied form of this opening music. Slowing the melody down, adding in slightly different harmonies and utilizing a thinner musical texture—that is, fewer instruments—adds a certain patina of nostalgia to these scenes. This is also aided by the sequential nature of the melody: its first phrase is major, clear and bright, while the second phrase ever so briefly tonicizes, or moves to, a minor key, giving it a slightly clouded, wistful feel.

During the final wedding scene, this opening melody gives deference to the religiosity of the scene, building from a chant- or hymnlike beginning, and trading off between high strings and flute.

The slowly ascending line is literally a sine of religious fealty. The flute is the instrument that can come closest to imitating the sound of a perfectly balanced sine wave, which produces a completely neutral and balanced sound. This balance and equanimity would therefore be a symbol of perfection and purity: the strings and flutes move in slow, purifying waves just as the pious priest's speech does. After the wedding the theme takes on a bell-tolling character, and, once clear of the church, can finally break forth with ebullient gusto.

Darcy's Water-Music

Another well-crafted moment is Lizzy's encounter with Darcy at Pemberly. The famous scene in which Darcy dives into the pond is accompanied by the same "water-music" (which becomes his theme) that was heard when he was in the bath at Netherfield. At Pemberly, though, the texture is thicker—there are more instruments—which ups the level of intensity in the scene. The other factor in this is the use of dissonant notes—clashing notes that do not conform to the rest of the harmony and, in this style of music, require resolution. One such sharp dissonance is called a suspension, and results from a clash between two notes, one of which resolves to form a consonance. This release of harmonic tension makes the music all the sweeter upon resolution. One such suspension can be clearly heard when Darcy dives into the water, as if the tensions surrounding him have melted away upon the note's resolution.

There are also ascending chromatic notes, which add an extra dab of color to the music. Symbolically, however, the *downward* resolving suspensions and the *upward* resolving chromatic notes can represent the opposite forces acting upon Darcy—the strictures and niceties of family honor holding him back, while his own feelings surge upward.

Neither One Nor the Other

A beautiful elision takes place between the swimming scene and the cut to where Elizabeth is walking. A single horn note arises from the flowing texture of Darcy's music, holds as the transition is made to Elizabeth walking, and then begins to move into the title theme linked with the Bennets. But for a moment the horn bridges the gap between the two, and for that instant they are neither one nor the other. This magical ambiguity is not only suitable for the transition of feelings and temperament the two are experiencing but also expressively foreshadows their eventual union.

In understanding this music, it is important not to take each and every appearance of an instrument as symbolic in and of itself; the purpose of the instruments is primarily orchestral, and not narrative; otherwise, the bassoon that appears in Darcy's proposal scene would be taken as an intrusion of Mr. Collins in the proposal! A carefully prepared score, such as the one written by Carl Davis, can do wonders in bringing the emotional world of the characters to life.

Pride and Prejudice:
The Rejected Screenplays

Somewhere in Hollywood

Dramatis Personae:
Bill, the creative director for a film studio;

Beth, his assistant.

Bill (*leaning over and pressing intercom button*): Beth, Jane Austen is so hot right now, we need a script adaptation. Could you look in the slush pile and bring me what you find, also some coffee—hot.

(*Soon there is a knock at the door. Beth enters, with coffee in her right hand, and a large pile of scripts in her left.*)

Beth (*lifting up the first script*): There's *Positions of the Heart*.

Bill: Yeah, what's it about?

Beth (*quoting*): "As Lizzie, the instructor of a local yoga class, struggles to make a living, she meets the son of her landlord, who is hoping to break the lease. But un-

comfortable beginnings often yield flexible endings . . ."

Bill (*shaking his head*): I don't think I can be flexible about this; it won't work.

Beth: Okay, how about this? (*She takes the next one and reads its title*) *Love in Space: The Price of Pride.*

Bill: I've spaced out already.

Beth (*shooting him an icy glare*): "As the PemberPrize-250 hurtles through the dark reaches of outer space, Commander Bennet must secure the safety of his daughters, all the while guarding against the leechlike creatures, the Collinsians. Controlled by the robotic adversary, Lazy Catherine the Borg, these creatures threaten the happiness of Bennet's family; can the intrepid spaceman save the day?"

Bill: I don't know, but I'll save money not going to that one. Where do these come from, anyway?

Beth (*sighing*): Here's a proposal for an animated film: *A Pride of Prejudices*. (*continuing quickly so as to cut off Bill's attempts at ridicule*) "As Lizzie the Lion comes of age, she must choose who her mate shall be: the rude son of the Alpha Male, or the handsome and mysterious newcomer?"

Bill: I don't need no "Lion Fling" right now. What else is there?

Beth: *Court and Courtship: Pride of the Pre-Judicials* . . . "The Bar isn't the only thing these young women are studying as they make their way through their last year in law school." Then there's *CSI:*

Pemberly: "Something's rotten in Derbyshire . . . and it's not Wickham this time." (*she trails off and looks at Bill, who is staring at her.*)

Bill: (*realizes he is staring, is startled, and now speaks*): I'm sorry I was a little abrupt last night at the office party. People jostling and pushing, I'm really an introvert. (*Betsy takes off her glasses and turns toward Bill. He is taken aback, exclaiming*) I never noticed what fine eyes you have!

The plot thickens . . .

Persuasion

We open on Kellynch-hall, formidable country seat of the not-so-formidable Sir Walter Elliot. As solid as his copy of the *Baronatage of England* may be, with the names of all of his family handsomely nestled between its two covers, the weight of wealth behind the Elliot name is not quite enough to support the profligate pomp with which Sir Walter has been living out his latter days since the passing of his wife. The teetering towers of family finance housed under the splendid roof of Kellynch-hall, being made ever more rickety by the foolish Walter and his daughter Elizabeth, have for some time been kept from tumbling by the skillful maneuvers of Anne Elliot and a trustworthy neighbor, Lady Russell.

As Austen's novel opens, however, this fragile state of affairs is coming to its inevitable close. Like *Sense and Sensibility*, *Persuasion* begins with loss and relocation. There are cheaper pastures to be found, and to be found in Bath. To Sir Walter's horror, he is persuaded that he must do the unthinkable—Kellynch-hall must be rented out. All of Anne's pleas for prudence and penny-pinching had fallen too long on deaf ears. But, after all, "she was only Anne." In losing Kellynch-hall for a time, at least, Sir Walter will represent the loss of something even more—the prestige he cherishes, and moral authority.

Our heroine, "only Anne" is not trapped by her name in the *Baronatage* nor by the silly thoughts of her father. Anne, after all, possesses "the art of knowing our own nothing beyond our own circle."

Of course there would be no need for advertisements; Sir Walter could be sure of that. Kellynch-hall could be rented, but only to the most perfect of tenants. The neighborhood certainly need not witness his distress, and advertisements might bring *undesirable* applicants, especially with all of the *navy* folk home from the newly ended wars with France. Sir Walter ponders the offensive and disruptive nature of military fortunes, granting wealth to those whose only claims to it are bravery and service for king and country. Half of them have hardly names at all, and not a baronet in the whole lot of them, as far as Sir Walter can see. Such prospects for Kellynch-hall. No, indeed. There would be no advertisements on display for such riffraff. Lady Russell, Anne, and sensible lawyer Mr. Shepherd must be content to wait for precisely the right sort of tenant to appear, with precisely no encouragement of an open offer or notice of the expected vacancy at Kellynch-hall.

Behind Sir Walter's and Elizabeth's noisy sufferings at the prospect of leaving Kellynch-hall, behind the racket and din of the packing of crates and arguing lawyers, are the private sorrows of Anne Elliot. No longer in the sparkle of youth at twenty-seven, Anne Elliot is nevertheless possessed of an "elegance of mind" and "sweetness of character" that cause her to rather bear what ills she has than be the cause of others that she knows not of. Quietly, she sees herself at the brink of a Bath that she knows will be unpleasant; so far removed from the tranquillity and privacy of Kellynch-hall will be the bustle, crowds, and stone coldness of the city. Her father's silliness grows more and more worrisome, compounded by Elizabeth's adoption of an unlikely and inappropriate companion in the young widow, Mrs. Clay. The constant welcome presence of Mrs. Clay in the family circle points to Anne's lack of standing. They've chosen Mrs. Clay over Anne. What are Mrs. Clay's motives for remaining in such close proximity to widower Sir Walter and his titled name?

But all of this, all of the worries of a family fraught with disappointment, pale in comparison to Anne's largest regret. We hear of this as if by accident when the names of the prospective tenants for Kellynch-hall are announced. Unfortunately for Sir Walter, an acceptable gentleman has been found in the person of a naval Admiral Croft. He and his wife are put forward as the most likely candidates and are begrudgingly accepted by Sir Walter. What these names mean for Anne is something entirely different. It is Mrs. Croft who evokes Anne's memory. Mrs. Croft was formerly Miss Wentworth, a last name that has been very dear to Anne.

We hear the history of Anne's relationship with a Frederick Wentworth, a naval captain who had lived for some time some years ago near Kellynch-hall while home from active service. He had been captivated by a more youthful Anne Elliot and had proposed. Though their relationship had long been one of affection, a young officer with nearly nothing to recommend himself and no fortune of note was deemed an insufficient companion for an Elliot daughter. Sir Walter vowed to provide no dowry, and Lady Russell had flung herself into a campaign against marrying early and poorly to the ruination of one's future. Anne had conceded. The engagement plan was ended, and now the only thoughts left for Anne on the subject were that, soon, "*he*, perhaps, may be walking here."

Little does Anne suspect that her dealings with Captain Wentworth are far from over. The youngest Elliot daughter, Mary, now the wife of Charles Musgrove, declares her need for Anne at Uppercross Cottage, as her present ill health, while not so severe as to keep her away from dinner parties at the Great House, is certainly unpleasant enough to cause a wish for a companion. This event deposits Anne into the set of people that will concern her for the majority of the novel. At Uppercross Cottage are Mary and Charles Musgrove and their children, Charles and Walter. At the Great House at Uppercross dwell Charles Musgrove's parents and sisters. The Miss Musgroves, Henrietta and Louisa, share in the good fortune of being captivated by the new visitor to the house when, inevitably, Captain Wentworth comes to call on them.

Inevitable indeed must the acquaintance be, due to both the nearness in distance and familial connection between Kellynch-hall and Uppercross.

*Anne Elliot, overhearing Captain Wentworth and Louisa Musgrove:
"Her own emotions kept her fixed; she had much to recover from before
she could move." Title page illustration from the 1833 volume of*
Northanger Abbey/Persuasion *published by Richard Bentley. Courtesy
of the Burke Jane Austen Collection, Goucher College Library.*

Nevertheless, it pains Anne. To be so often in the company of her former beau but to receive little but the slightest of polite attentions from him is for some time unbearable. To make this situation even worse, Anne is constantly pressed by the other members of the party, when in private, to take part in their game of guessing which of the Miss Musgroves Captain Wentworth will eventually marry. Though Anne does not suspect an interest on his part in either of the girls, their attentions to him are pointed; even Henrietta, who enters into the acquaintance with her affections previously involved with her cousin Charles Hayter, participates.

Anne is given a variety of circumstances in which she may view these growing attachments—walks on the hills, dinners at Uppercross, and, most importantly, a holiday to the seaside town of Lyme-Regis. Captain Wentworth goes to visit Captain Harville, a former naval comrade, and brings with him Henrietta, Louisa, and Charles Musgrove, and, out of politeness to Charles, Mary, and, out of necessity to Mary, Anne. A number of interesting events conspire here. The first of these is the party's introduction to a Captain Benwick, a nice-ish sort of man with a tragic history. He was formerly engaged to Fanny Harville, sister to the aforementioned Captain Harville, but their marriage was never to be. Fanny died while Captain Benwick was still at sea, and her death has left him somewhat morose and nose-deep in Byron and Scott. Nevertheless he seems to be somewhat stirred by the members of the Uppercross party, particularly in his conversation with Anne. He becomes a fixture in their company during their time at Lyme. The other introduction of note here is an introduction, in the proper sense, only for the reader, for the characters catch only momentary glimpses of Mr. Elliot, a cousin, who is to inherit all that may be inherited from Sir Walter Elliot upon his death. We don't know yet what his role may be in the story—will he be a Willoughby to Anne's Marianne, a Henry Crawford to Anne's Fanny, or a Darcy to Anne's Elizabeth?

Mr. Elliot is to become a character of great importance, but his first appearances in the novel are soon overshadowed by a more momentous event. The playful and flirtatious Louisa Musgrove hits upon a game to her liking while on a walk with the rest of the young party on the Cobb, a sort of pierlike structure of stone jutting out into the water. This structure has two levels, the lower of which is accessed by a narrow set of stone steps called "Granny's teeth." Louisa has found, to her great satisfaction, that throwing herself off these steps to be caught by Captain Wentworth invariably ends with her being in the arms of Captain Wentworth. She wishes to jump a second time, and though Wentworth calls no, she throws herself off and falls, to the accompaniment of cries of caution and alarm, onto the hard stone of the lower Cobb. She is unconscious.

Granny's Teeth, Lyme Regis. When Tennyson visited Lyme Regis, he wanted to see first of all the place where Louisa Musgrove fell from the Cobb.

Only Anne has the presence of mind to call for a surgeon and to send Captain Benwick, who knows the area best. The Anne Elliot revealed in this chapter is one in charge of the situation and vital to its best outcomes. This singles Anne out from the fray, particularly in the mind of Captain Wentworth, and it is this picture of her that this group of people is left with, as her departure for Bath follows closely on the heels of this event. We can assume that Austen will con-

> "By this time the report of the accident had spread among the workmen and boatmen about the Cobb, and many were collected near them, to be useful if wanted, at any rate, to enjoy the sight of a dead young lady, nay, two dead young ladies, for it proved twice as fine as the first report."
>
> —*Persuasion*

tinue to mix her up with the Musgroves, the Harvilles, the Crofts, the Elliots, and Wentworth, with many complications, and she does not disappoint.

Dear reader, *Persuasion* is "that great rarity, a novel which is too short," as Richard Jenkyns says. The displacement of Sir Walter Elliot from Kellynch-hall suggests that a new order is coming to town—one in which men who have earned their merit displace those who have merely inherited their situation.

Before we are introduced to a naval officer in *Persuasion* we know we will like him. We will like the naval officers we meet in *Persuasion* because we know Sir Walter's prejudice—based on shallow peerage-oriented values—against them. The Crofts, as they take over Kellynch-hall, find one affectation in specific most revealing and unnecessary: Sir Walter's large looking-glasses from the dressing-room: "—Such a number of looking-glasses! oh Lord! there was no getting away from oneself," Admiral Croft blurts out to Anne. "'I should think, Miss Elliot' (looking with serious reflection), 'I should think he must be rather a dressy man for his time of life.'" A "little shaving glass"— which he finds a great improvement— suffices for the Admiral. In a few short lines, Austen has captured the essence of meritocracy: she shows how the simplicity of the new naval men of action replaces the navel-gazing of the old way.

Captain Wentworth, too, may have things he must learn from the new order, including the possibility of a woman who knows when to steer the carriage, who can argue with liveliness with her brother. Wentworth is shown to be conventional in his beliefs about women.

His sister, Mrs. Croft, however, "had a squareness, uprightness, and vigour of form, which gave importance to her person." She had been at sea with her husband. She looks "as intelligent and keen as any of the officers around her." Her manners are "open, easy, and decided, like one who had no distrust of herself, and no doubt of what to do; without any approach to coarseness, however, or any want of good humour." She shares with Admiral Croft "in everything."

Persuasion is often cast as an "autumnal" novel because it is the last completed novel before Austen died in 1817. Of course, Jane Austen did not know she was dying when she began it on August 8, 1815, nor when she was working on it in 1816. She also started another novel, *Sanditon*, and resurrected her never-published *Northanger Abbey*.

It is also considered autumnal because Anne Elliot has lost her "bloom," or so thinks her former admirer, Captain Wentworth. Yet, the book does not so easily map onto Austen's biography.

Claudia Johnson points out that elements of *Persuasion* are like *Sense and Sensibility*. They both open with displacement of the family and Anne, like Elinor, endures a silent love. Moreover, like Darcy, Wentworth is given the opportunity to propose a second time. These elements would argue against it being an "autumnal" novel.

Virginia Woolf said, "of all great writers she is the most difficult to catch in the act of greatness." But Austen's greatness is on display throughout the novel, culminating in a letter written in haste. Her greatness is also on display, for Austen changed the ending, and we are able to see how she improved on the original one she conceived, for it exists in manuscript form.

Anne Elliot, *only* Anne, finds her voice, something she must and can accomplish for herself. She moves from silence to eloquence, from shyness to bold assertion. From the fall in Lyme Regis, she springs forth, ready to help make a new world order.

Mrs. Bennet Was Right:
The Marriage Plot in Austen Novels

"Single Women have a dreadful propensity for being poor—which is one very strong argument in favor of Matrimony."
—Jane Austen to her niece
Fanny Knight, March 13, 1817

A very angry Mrs. Bennet tells her least favorite daughter: "But I tell you what, Miss Lizzy, if you take it into your head to go on refusing every offer of marriage in this way, you will never get a husband at all—and I am sure I do not know who is to maintain you when your father is dead.—" About this, Mrs. Bennet, frantic about marrying off her daughters, was right, as Austen wrote to her niece, "Single Women have a dreadful propensity for being poor."

Austen is called a social realist because romance or lack thereof provided an opportunity to show the vulnerability of women. In Austen, we find the effects of adultery on women, we learn of seduction by rakes, of the burden of pregnancy for an unmarried woman, and the problem of poor single women.

Consider the alternative to marriage for a young woman such as Charlotte Lucas. Jane Austen shows us plainly what is in store: Miss Bates, downwardly mobile, as Knightley furiously points out to Emma. Or Miss Nancy Steele in *Sense and Sensibility.* Charlotte Lucas understood this. As she explains to Lizzy, a certain practicality about marriage is essential: "I am not romantic, you know; I never was. I ask only a comfortable home; and considering Mr. Collins's character, connexions, and situation in life, I am convinced that my chance of happiness with him is as fair as most people can boast on entering the marriage state." Though Elizabeth does not feel she can ever be as close to Charlotte as she had once been, she also does not curtail their friendship.

Marriage for the most part was the only way a woman of the Regency era could hope to advance her station. Those lucky enough to be gifted with exceptional artistic abilities could ply their talents in hope of monetary advancement as long as doing so could be

The Wedding, 1794. *Courtesy of The Lewis Walpole Library, Yale University. 794.5.12.45.*

counted no more than a "hobby." In the indolent Regency society, work or "trade" of any sort would lower a woman's standing and threaten to bump her out of the gentry—hence Austen's desire to keep her writings anonymous.

Not only was marriage expected of men and women, it was nigh enforced by government regulations. Kristen Olsen's *All Things Austen* describes how bachelors encountered extra taxes on all their property, and a twofold tax on their servants. It soon became a question of mathematics— remaining single and losing money often lost out to getting married and gaining a (hopefully substantial) dowry.

In an effort to make sure their children lived a comfortable life, it was the parents' duty to put away money for their offspring's future. In the case of gentlemen, anything outside an allowance was mostly to be inherited upon the parents' demise, but in the case of a woman it took the form of her dowry. For men more concerned with ledgers than love, this often became, quite literally, the "selling point." Despite these few hardhearted males and the relative restrictiveness of Regency society, it was now becoming more common for couples to decide to marry for affection and not purely for money.

This, of course, does not say that money wouldn't have entered into it. Mrs. Bennet's initial views on Mr. Darcy's handsomeness seem directly related to his fortune, and the same can be said for Mr. Bingley and his £4,000—5,000 a year. As it was only at the risk of social demise that a woman would work (such as the lowly fate that awaited Jane Fairfax as a governess), it was prudent for her to choose a husband whom she thought would invest her dowry wisely, could care for her, and would be a tolerable companion.

Some families—especially those who felt themselves to be more blue-blooded than their neighbors, such as Lady Catherine de Bourgh—still kept the practice of arranging their children's marriages. As marriage between first cousins was not taboo, this was an efficient way for aunts and uncles to keep estates and investments within the family, a practice useful in expanding the bank account but not the gene pool.

One of the chief troubles in marrying for affection was that the appropriate marrying age for women was lower than that for men, which often resulted in underdeveloped sagacity on the part of the females. This, in turn, led to frequent attempts from impoverished suitors to convince their marks of their ardent love and devotion—ardent love, that is, for the hopefully substantial dowry which would be given to them. Wickham's sudden interest in Mary King can be attributed to her £10,000. In order to clinch

Gretna Green, *1802. Courtesy of The Lewis Walpole Library, Yale University 802.12.15.2.*

the deal, many young cads would convince their even younger loves that they should hightail it to Gretna Green, the closest Scottish town on the Scotland-England border. Scotland's marriage laws were incredibly lax compared to England's, which didn't allow the marriage of a minor without a guardian in attendance. In Scotland, however, the couple could become married when a legal witness observed their vows—no clergy needed whatsoever. Then, legally bound, the trickster could return to England and claim his winnings.

Women who avoided being taken in by a cad or promised away at birth might still have the trouble of not being talented, comely, or rich enough to attract an eligible bachelor. Charlotte Lucas is a prime example. It was to the advantage of gentlewomen to apply themselves to practicing music, drawing, and learning languages and developing manners, posture, and intelligence. There was little a woman could do, then, but to show off her wit, charm, talent, and beauty.

In the end, though, all a woman could do, as Henry Tilney realistically recognizes, is wait for a proposal and answer "yes" or "no." If measures became drastic enough, a common practice was to secure passage to British colonies in India or the Caribbean, where English women were in short supply, thus improving one's chances at catching a mate. Though often looked down upon, this practice was fairly common, and was utilized by Austen's aunt Philadelphia.

Actions such as these produced the feeling in neighbors that the woman had married beneath her station, a fact that could potentially shatter her social reputation. This explains Lady Russell's actions in *Persuasion* as she seeks to look out for the good of her young friend Anne Elliot. Of course, it was (almost) perfectly permissible for a man to marry below his station, save for where those de Bourghian holdouts held sway.

In Jane Austen's novels, the marriage plot is not front and center; it is there, but it does not hog space on the page. Some would even argue that the marriage plot is not the essential plot of the novels. As recent commentators such as Deborah Kaplan's *Jane Austen Among Women* have shown convincingly, the "friendship plot" that portrays strong friendships between women is equally compelling, *when* it is noticed. Consider Lizzy Bennet and Mrs. Gardiner, Anne Elliot and Lady Russell, and the sisters who are friends in *Pride and Prejudice* and *Sense and Sensibility.*

But when movies strip away all that is thought unrelated to the central plot, they also strip away the context for the marriage plot, and the ironic way in which it is often presented. Except for secondary characters such as Fanny Price's mother, Charlotte Lucas and Mr. Collins, and the Westons, there is no straight line from point a to point b: meeting the man and marrying him. Instead there are interrupted courtships—Jane and Bingley, Anne Elliot and Captain Wentworth, Miss Smith and Robert Martin, Edward Ferrars and Elinor, and extended secret engagements (we won't say whose).

While marriage was the only means for the typical gentry female to gain a comfortable life, Austen, however, does not chronicle and uphold the beliefs of marrying for money and reproduction. Instead, she is part of the gradual change in culture and philosophy that began to dictate that love was the governance of companionship, and not necessarily the possession of a good fortune.

Yes, Mrs. Bennet was right that by sending Jane to Netherfield by horse, something positive will come of it: Darcy ends up exposed to Elizabeth in all her wittiness. Of course, this is not what she meant. Mrs. Bennet, however, was wrong when she said "Netherfield holds nothing for Lizzy" or words to that effect. That is because Mrs. Bennet never had a full grasp of the marriage plot.

SIDEBAR

Was Lady Russell Wrong?

When she was nineteen, Anne Elliot ended her engagement to Captain Wentworth under the encouragement of Lady Russell. Like the young women in *Emma,* Anne Elliot is a motherless child, and Lady Russell has tried to step in when she can, or ought to, be of assistance. Wentworth at the time of the engagement was "a stranger without alliance or fortune."

More than anyone else, Lady Russell knew that her good friend, the late Lady Elliot, had made a mistake in marrying Sir Walter Elliot. Had, in a sense, thrown herself away. For Anne Elliot, "to throw herself away at nineteen—involve herself at nineteen in an engagement with a young man, who had nothing but himself to recommend him, and no hopes of attaining affluence, but in the chances of a most uncertain profession, and no connexions to secure even his farther rise in that profession; would be, indeed, a throwing away . . ."

John Halperin, one of Austen's biographers, sees "Persuasion" itself as one of the villains of the novels. (It appears more than twenty times in a novel with that name.) But, in fact, *Persuasion* was not Austen's name for the novel; she had thought of calling it "The Elliots." Perhaps because of the title, a little too much weight has been given to Anne's susceptibility to persuasion. After all, in the novel, there is another woman who married young, to someone who supposedly had more promise than Wentworth—the widowed Mrs. Smith. Her impoverished situation in Bath reminds readers that early love does not always promise financial security or ongoing fulfilling relationships.

Does Anne condemn Lady Russell? No. When she considers Lady Russell's influence in the decision of eight years earlier, Anne says:

"I have been thinking over the past, and trying impartially to judge of the right and wrong, I mean with regard to myself; and I must believe that I was right, much as I suffered from it, that I was perfectly right in being guided by the friend whom you will love better than you do now. To me, she was in place of a parent. Do not mistake me, however. I am not saying that she did not err in her advice. It was, perhaps, one of those cases in which advice is good or bad only as the event decides; and for myself, I

certainly never should, in any circumstance of tolerable similarity, give such advice. But I mean that I was right in submitting to her, and that if I had done otherwise, I should have suffered more in continuing the engagement than I did even in giving it up, because I should have suffered in my conscience. I have now, as far as such a sentiment is allowable in human nature, nothing to reproach myself with; and, if I mistake not, a strong sense of duty is no bad part of a woman's portion."

Yes, Lady Russell encouraged safety against risk. Certainly, Lady Russell lacks a "quickness of perception" and "a natural penetration." But another villain exists within the pages of Persuasion: Captain Wentworth's pride. He admits it himself, that, even after changing his circumstance, and having "a few thousand pounds" he failed to write to Anne to renew the engagement. Why? "I was proud, too proud to ask again." Indeed, when he reencounters Anne, Captain Wentworth behaves impetuously in encouraging two sisters to vie for his attention. He is also obstinate. "I shut my eyes, and would not understand you, or do you justice." Lady Russell did judge his character; but perhaps not all of his character; not the part that Anne had found most loveable. For besides being confident, he had "intelligence, spirit and brilliancy;" he was "full of life and ardor." Ironically, as Brian Southam points out in Jane Austen and the Navy, the characteristics that disappoint, worry, or alarm Lady Russell "are the very qualities of character which won British Captains mastery of the seas."

"You Should Be in Pictures": Jane Austen's Portraits

What did Jane Austen look like? Just as we first come to "know" Jane Austen, biographically, through her nieces and nephews, and her great-nieces and -nephews, we come to "see" her as they describe her appearance. According to Edward Austen Leigh, "She was tall and slender; her face was rounded with a clear brunette complexion and bright hazel eyes. Her curly brown hair escaped all round her forehead, but from the time of her coming to live at Chawton she always wore a cap, except when her nieces had her in London and forbade it."

Her nephew, James-Edward Austen, reported, "In person she was very attractive; her figure was rather tall and slender, her step light and firm, and her whole appearance expressive of health and animation. In complexion she was a clear brunette with a rich colour; she had full round cheeks, with mouth and nose small and well formed bright hazel eyes, and brown hair forming natural curls close round her face." Caroline Austen remembered of her aunt, "Hers was the first face I can remember think-ing pretty. Her hair, a darkish brown, curled naturally—it was in short curls round her face . . . Her face was rather round than long—she had a bright, but not a pink colour, a clear brown complexion, and very good hazel eyes. Her hair, a darkish brown, curled naturally, it was in short curls around her face. She always wore a cap." (Austen's niece may be remembering a Jane Austen who was already showing signs of Addison's disease, which includes the appearance of having a tan, if indeed that is what she died of.)

Her sister Cassandra's sketch of Jane was perhaps, in Jane Austen style, ironic in nature. (See next page.) Does the sketch help us imagine Austen or prevent us from doing so? She is attired plainly; she is not hesitant in her glance. Is she frowning or simply not smiling? Some see her pose, with her crossed arms and facial expressions as "confrontational," others as "defiant" or "caustic." What, though, is wrong with appearing that self-confident?

Such an image needed softening for the Victorian view of her that was being

Cassandra Austen's sketch of her sister Jane, 1810. Courtesy National Portrait Gallery, London.

created by a new generation of Austens. For J. E. Austen-Leigh's *Memoir* in 1870, he went to James Andrews of Maidenhead. Perhaps he asked Andrews to "soften her lines, her lips, add frills to her dress and cap, and give her a little more bosom to her chest" (though whether he would have said "bosom" in Victorian England is another thing altogether). "Oh yes, uncross those arms. Give her a different expression." And so Austen became endowed with a femininity seemingly lacking in the first image. Massaging her image this way seems to make her more acceptable, what with those pretty curls. (See the cover of this book.) The ladylike has replaced the sense of the self-confident Austen of Cassandra's sketch. Perhaps that is how people want her; or at least people who sell her image want her, because it is this image that shows up on bags, umbrellas, bumper stickers (and the *Bedside, Bathtub & Armchair Companion to Jane Austen* cover, too!).

She wrote so intimately about feelings, about feelings we ourselves know, we her readers seem to want a dear aunt

Jane whom we could invite to tea. Perhaps we share with the great-nieces and -nephews a Victorian sensibility: give us the gentle Jane. She *would* understand us.

Recently new attempts at portraiture have occurred and the former colonies get in the mix, too. Did she look like Anne Hathaway or Olivia Williams, the stars of *Becoming Jane* and *Miss Austen Regrets*? Even Jon Spence, the writer of the book *Becoming Jane,* is quick to reject Cassandra's drawing. "Cassandra's sketch, it seems to me, has been almost single-handedly responsible for creating a general idea of Jane Austen as a dry, homely spinster that no words of description from people who knew her when she was young ('handsome but with cheeks a little too full,' says one) have managed to dispel." Of course, he wants us to believe in a Jane Austen who maintained her love for Tom Lefroy, who could, in the twenty-first century be best represented by Anne Hathaway, but as Emily Auerbach points out, such complaints are reminiscent of Miss Bingley's complaint about Elizabeth Bennet: "I must confess that I never could see any beauty in her. Her face is too thin; her complexion has no brilliancy; and her features are not at all handsome. Her nose wants character . . . and as for her eyes, which have sometimes been called so fine, I never could perceive any thing extraordinary in them. They have a sharp, shrewish look, which I do not like at all; and in her air altogether, there is a self-sufficiency without fashion, which is intolerable."

What John Wiltshire calls *Recreating Jane Austen* is not only the process of transforming her novels into films but also recuperating a sense of who she is to us, the living readers experiencing her novels in the now of this time. For the Jane Austen Centre in Bath, Melissa Dring, trained both as a portrait painter and a forensic artist by the FBI, brought her forensic skills to the question of what Jane Austen looked like. For the crime of writing masterpieces, Jane Austen will be reconstructed. Tom Clifford, too, on the other side of the Atlantic, sought to capture a Jane Austen in a portrait that acknowledged Cassandra's original artistry and skill. He looked at the surviving portraits of Austen family

Image of Jane Austen in her garden at Chawton, courtesy of artist Tom Clifford. www.paintingport.com.

Sketch by Kelly Gesch.

her brothers and father. He decided to paint "a modern impression of what I feel Jane Austen may have looked like" and placed her in the west garden at her home in Chawton, near Alton.

Even the authors of this book have found themselves sketching. Cassandra Austen had done a watercolor in 1804. In this one, Austen sits outside, with her bonnet, and we see her with her back to us. We want her to have that bonnet, definitely; and perhaps her facial features aren't the important thing. We need to situate her somewhere; somewhere physical, a chair, at a desk, reading . . . why not position her on a path? She is not exactly here, there, or anywhere. Arising from insubstantiality, she resists being known. We are reminded that she belongs to our imagination and we will, all of us, continue to recreate her.

members; finding strong resemblances in Cassandra's drawing and portraits of

The Best Gifts for a Janeite

- The six novels as audio books. Her novels were often read aloud by her family. Reading the novels is wonderful, but *hearing* the novels deepens the experience of Austen! Listening to Miss Bates or Mrs. Elton, Mrs. Bennet or Anne Elliot, Darcy or Knightley—is a thrill that bears repeating.
- *Jane Austen's Letters,* collected and edited by Deirdre Le Faye. Extend your sense of Jane Austen's voice and life by reading her letters.
- A Jane Austen Action figure.

- Twenty-first century gruel: put together a bag with organic oatmeal and either pistachios and dried cranberries; walnuts and dried cherries; or almonds and dried blueberries. Add some nutmeg and cinnamon, shake, and tie with a ribbon. Cooking instructions: bring 2 1/4 cups of water and 1 cup of gruel to a boil, lower heat, and simmer and stir for five minutes. Remove from heat and let rest for five more minutes, then enjoy.
- The juvenilia. Enjoy Jane Austen in her Monty Python days!
- *Jane Austen for Dummies* by Joan Klingel Ray.
- To find out more about the world of Austen's novels: *All Things Austen: An Encyclopedia of Austen's World* in two volumes, by Kristin Olsen. (We don't know how she did it!)
- *The Annotated Pride and Prejudice,* edited and annotated by David Shapard. Probably more than you want to know, but it doesn't disappoint!
- Karen Joy Fowler's *The Jane Austen Book Club.*
- The 1995 BBC *Pride and Prejudice.*
- Claire Tomalin's biography *Jane Austen: A Life.*

- Stephanie Barron's Jane Austen detective novels.
- *Pride and Prejudice* Paper Dolls.
- Jane Austen Tarot cards. Yes, some of the images are derived from the movies (the 1940 *Pride and Prejudice* of all things!), but with Jane Austen as the high priestess, you can't go wrong.
- Sweatshirts, magnets, bumper stickers, and T-shirts at CafePress.com.

For those who would like to read some of the recent, interesting critical writings, you might chose among the following:

- Claudia Johnson, *Jane Austen: Women, Politics and the Novel*
- Mary Waldron, *Jane Austen and the Fiction of Her Time*
- Deborah Kaplan, *Jane Austen Among Women*
- Kathryn Sutherland, *Jane Austen's Textual Lives: From Aeschylus to Bollywood*
- Richard Jenkyns, *A Fine Brush on Ivory: An Appreciation of Jane Austen.*

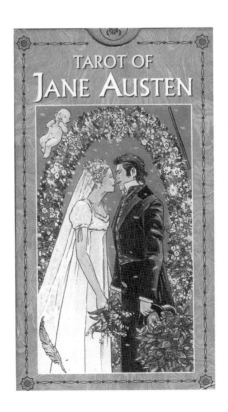

CAPSULE

Sanditon

Jane Austen began her unfinished final novel with the story of a place. This is not surprising. After all, what are *Mansfield Park* and *Northanger Abbey* if not places? Of course both of these houses turn out to embody much more than their simple existences as buildings in the course of the story, but what about *Sanditon*? What sort of house could it be with such an odd name? Surprisingly, perhaps, Sanditon is not a house. It is a town. And we don't get there immediately.

How like Austen to drop her poor reader (and her poor characters) into the wrong place first. Mr. and Mrs. Parker have found themselves in the wrong Willingden. They have been in search of a surgeon to entice away to their newly established seaside resort town of Sanditon. Happily for everyone involved they find instead Mr. Heywood and his wife and daughters. The lucky Miss Charlotte Heywood, despite her father's obvious ambivalence to any sort of seaside town or travel, is favored with an invitation to accompany the Parkers to their new community.

Much of the next section of this novel is spent introducing the reader

"Going after a doctor! Why, what should we do with a doctor here? It would be only encouraging our servants and the poor to fancy themselves ill if there was a doctor at hand. Oh! pray, let us have none of the tribe at Sanditon. . . . And I verily believe if my poor dear Sir Harry had never seen one neither, he would have been alive now. Ten fees, one after another, did the man take who sent him out of the world. I beseech you Mr. Parker, no doctors here."

The Anatomist, *Thomas Rowlandson, 1811. Courtesy of The Lewis Walpole Library, Yale University. 811.3.12.1.*

Sanditon is the one Austen novel that includes a scene in a Circulating Library. Charlotte goes there with the Parkers quite soon after arriving in Sanditon, as "Mr. Parker could not be satisfied without an early visit to the library and the library subscription book." The subscription book would reveal whether there were any new names as subscribers, and thus whether his seaside resort had attracted anyone to the town. The Circulating Library, 1804. Courtesy of The Lewis Walpole Library, Yale University. 804.10.1.1.

to the colorful cast of characters at Sanditon. First comes Lady Denham, a wealthy widow who seems to have gotten the best deal from her second marriage—a title without having to bear with the husband who brought it about (he died). Also in Sanditon are Lady Denham's nephew and heir Sir Edward, his sister, and the newfound relation that could ruin all of Sir Edward's hopes, a Miss Clara Brereton. News arrives of Mr. Parker's hypochondriac sisters, Susan and Diana, and brother Arthur, all three of whom, if impressions are correct, will be reported to be at death's door all together. This theme of constant

illness becomes the butt of many jokes in *Sanditon,* playing on the purported medicinal purposes of sea bathing. The ultimate irony, of course, is that Sanditon still has no medical surgeon to offer advice to the ailing who come there to soak up the sea and sun.

The fate of Charlotte Heywood as she arrives in town must certainly depend on her introduction into the best circles of the limited society Sanditon has to offer. Austen does not disappoint. Sir Edward is busy with his attempts to win the affections of her rival, Clara. Charlotte, in talking with him and watching him, realizes what he is doing.

Most seriously for her, his reading practices reveal him to be "downright silly." Quoting poets from Wordsworth to Burns, and novelists (including Sir Walter Scott, of whom Charlotte says "He felt & he wrote & he forgot"), Sir Edward reveals a mind unequal to the attempt. Rather than enlightenment, his reading gave him "only hard words & involved sentences," leading Charlotte to realize he has read "more sentimental Novels than agreed with him." He wishes to be a seducer of women (like Lovelace in Samuel Richardson's *Clarissa*), and believes his book learning will assist him.

Charlotte is a reader to our own purposes. After picking up a copy of *Camilla* at the Circulating Library, she puts it down again because "She had not *Camilla's* Youth, & had no intention of having her Distress."

Mr. Parker's "invalid" siblings arrive though days earlier they were too ill to travel. The elder sister, Diana, amuses Charlotte with her energetic meddling with others' lives, despite her status as an invalid. They bring news of possible future inhabitants of Sanditon, who arrive close on their heels. A Mrs. Griffiths brings with her three ladies under her care, one of whom is a West Indian "lady of large fortune" by the name of Miss Lambe—the first mixed-race character to appear in an Austen novel. What these auspicious arrivals will do to Charlotte's prospects and to the fate of the fledgling Sanditon must forever be conjecture, for here is the end of Austen's fragmentary novel.

Some see Austen going in a new direction in *Sanditon*; some don't. They see the same focus on "three or four families" in a village, and the same interest in place that so informs the six completed novels. Novel reading returns as a concern (with the only scene in an Austen novel in a circulating library), as does hypochondria (whether Mr. Woodhouse was a hypochondriac is one thing, but surely Mary Musgrove was). In a community attempting to rival Brighton for sea bathing, Sanditon is alive with money and investments, speculation and inheritance. Not yet successful in its goal of being a seaside resort (and one wonders if it can ever be), its financial calculations are out in the open. Money issues get a good airing in the fragment that exists.

With *Sanditon*, besides the emotions the novel itself calls forth as we sort through the delusions and opinions, maneuvers and machinations of this ensemble of characters, we experience another emotion as well: a sense of sadness for a novel, and a life, uncompleted.

Winchester Cathedral

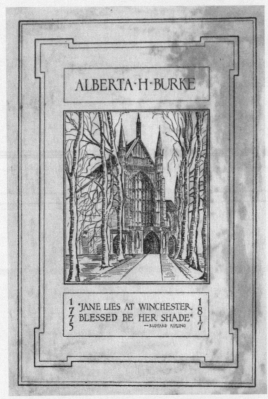

The bookplate of Alberta H. Burke, placed in her copy of the 1811 first British edition of Sense and Sensibility, *showing Winchester Cathedral. Throughout their lives, Alberta H. Burke and her husband Henry collected rare Austen editions, books related to Austen's life and times, and other material concerning Jane Austen. Goucher College received the Collection in 1975 as a bequest from Mrs. Burke to her alma mater. Courtesy of the Henry and Alberta Hirshheimer Burke Collection, Goucher College Library.*

Jane Austen died at 4:30 A.M. on July 18, 1817. Cassandra was with her when "she breathed her last." In a poignant letter to her niece Fanny, Cassandra describes how "I was able to close her eyes myself & it was a great gratification to me to render her these last services." Cassandra goes on to tell about the funeral plans: "The last sad ceremony is to take place on Thursday morning, her dear remains are to be deposited in the Cathedral—it is a satisfaction to me to think that they are to lie in a Building she admired so much—her precious soul I presume to hope reposes in a far superior Mansion."

On July 24, Cassandra stationed herself so that she could hear the mourners when they left the house. "Everything was conducted with the greatest tranquility, & but that I was determined I would see the last & therefore was upon the listen, I should not have known when they left the House." Cassandra was not attending the funeral; that is why she had to watch for when the pallbearers were leaving the house with Austen's body. Though Kristin Olsen in her *All Things Austen* explains that for "spinsters" their pallbearers might have been women wearing white, this tradition was apparently not followed here. Instead, Cassandra stayed at 8 College Street, where they have been living: "I watched the little mournful procession the length of the Street & when it turned from my sight & I lost her for ever—even then I was not overpowered, not so much agitated as I am now in writing of it."

The official mourners then proceeded to Winchester Cathedral, Jane Austen's burial place. The Cathedral is very, very old. The original Norman church, the no-longer-standing "Old Minster," dates back to Saxon times, somewhere around 648 C.E. St. Swithin, Bishop of Winchester during the mid-ninth century, was buried in the open near the "Old Minster." In 1079, during Bishop Walkelin's tenure, workers began laying a new foundation, and in 1093 the relics of St. Swithin were moved to the new building. On July 15th of that year, the old building was torn down. Its outline can still be seen on the ground next to the (relatively) newer structure.

The cathedral is the burial place of monks, kings, and saints, as well as the site of Richard I's coronation in 1194, Henry IV's marriage in 1401, and Queen Mary's marriage in 1554. So how in the world did Jane Austen end up here, of all places? Famous as she is now, any fame she had during her life would not have warranted a place for her among the royal remains.

Various theories exist. Some suggest that, as she died in the cathedral's Close (the area where the monks had lived) she was entitled to burial at the cathedral. Of course, as Paul Heningham of the Jane Austen Society of Australia points out, many common people would have died in the Close over the years, and none of them received this special treatment. Moreover, 8 College Street was not within the Close.

A more sensible theory suggests Jane and Cassandra's lifelong friend Elizabeth Heathcote may have had something to do with the special funeral arrangements. Mrs. Heathcote moved to the cathedral's Close after her husband's death, and was well acquainted with Winchester's Dean, the official who made the final decisions regarding burials.

Also suggested is that Henry and James Austen had a hand in convincing the Dean to allow their sister a final resting place in the Cathedral, or that it had something to do with the fact that their father was a clergyman. Unfortunately, none of the theories are conclusive. In the end it may have just boiled down to luck, or maybe the Dean secretly liked *Pride and Prejudice*.

Sleuthing Regency Dress
with Baronda Ellen Bradley

The Jane Austen Society of North America holds an annual convention. One of the many highlights of the several-day event is a Regency Ball, where members and guests can appear decked out in their own Regency finest. Perhaps best known of all the Regency dressers is Baronda Ellen Bradley, who wears Regency clothing from the time she leaves her house to attend the meeting until she returns. Each year, after much research, she commissions a new dress from her seamstress, Ute Forlano of Dragonfly Formals in Colorado Springs, to debut at the ball. We talked to Baronda about what Regency clothes teach us about Jane Austen.

Movies and academia have both fed the obsession with Regency dress. An interest in this clothing can be seen as Jane Austen "lite," but the social aspects—what they used and how they used it—were as important to them then as it is for us now. Your car and house are status symbols. Their elements speak of who you are and what your social status is. During the Regency period, your dress told a lot about you, what you could afford, what your aspirations were, and your standing within your family.

Jane Austen and her sister wore very simple clothes. At Chawton Cottage (Jane Austen's house) they have things Jane and her sister wore. They are very simple, like a beige print with brown, and a brown silk coat. It shows they were genteel women, but they were just getting by. They didn't have all the fine things, like lace at the sleeves, because it would get caught making bread or getting the donkey. The details tell what your status was.

"La! If you have not got your spotted muslin on!—I wonder you was not afraid of its being torn."
—Nancy Steele to Elinor Dashwood
while walking in Kensington Gardens

The material of the time was muslin, any kind of cottons (dimity, some gauzes, chintz, nankeen) and silks (sarcenet, other gauzes, Persian), basically, with linen and wool blends completing the options for outer dress. Spotted muslin likely referred to a kind of muslin with a pattern in thread darned upon it, like what was known as madras. Muslin in general, formerly loomed in India but more commonly a product of Scotland by Jane's time, is a sheer, loosely woven cotton fabric with a downy surface that is very easily torn during washing or just general wear. About ten yards of muslin, plus a sturdier fabric for lining, was needed for a dress because a light fabric has to be double lined. You chose thin material to cleanly show your curves. As a result, there would be an outer layer and an inner layer for the gown. At the end of the eighteenth century and the beginning of the nineteenth century, more and more material was put at the back of the dress; they were adding pleats in the back.

It's in the detail: "Six inches deep in the mud"

When Mrs. Hurst remarks to her sister Miss Bingley, in *Pride and Prejudice*: "I hope you saw her petticoat, six inches deep in mud," the petticoat she is referring to is something different from what we think of it. It was only during the mid-nineteenth century that petticoats, which we now think of as underwear, became something you would wear at the waist, more like our modern slip, with the cinch at the waistline. Before then, they were made of cambric or flannel, and of course, were narrow, and were commonly just a part of the dress skirt itself rather than an undergarment. If you were a well-to-do woman, then at the edge of it was embroidery—fancy handwork—so that when you sat down the bottom of your petticoat would show. It was in the little details, when you sat down, the lace showing from under your dress or from your sleeve, that was a strong determiner of what your class was, or what you wanted your class *to appear to be*. Another area where you can express yourself is to add a pelisse-robe overdress or cutout sleeves, where the second layer peeks through from under a layer that opens.

The influence of Beau Brummell, who so greatly shaped men's fashion at this time, can be seen in this emphasis on details: you distinguish yourself by looking undistinguished. People learned how to read the fine little elements in a dress like a language. Besides the lace on the petticoat (and during about a ten-year period, the hemline started to rise, accounting for those six inches Mrs. Hurst refers to!) and the lace on the sleeves, there was also "clockwork" on your stockings. Clockwork refers to an embroidered design on the ankle of one's stocking, originally to hide the seam where the triangular gore was inserted, but by Jane Austen's time, it was just for show: somebody might do it for you or you yourself embroidered it.

The fashion for what we call "bubble breasts" included some rules/hierarchy about when and where these would be exposed. During the daytime, you covered up the shoulder and breast area, but at nighttime, and at formal occasions where you would be more exposed, you would have a lower cut dress. I have read reports of there being one or two inches of material covering between your breast and the waist—which was at the bustline. Still that exposed a lot!

Popularly known as a corset, the small stays are shown as they would be worn, with a chemise underneath.

I have what are called small stays. Stays (the earlier word for what became more popularly known during this time as the French word, corset) take the bust and lift it up, giving the bubble breast that was so popular at this time: you see the top of the décolletage. A full corset would give the long narrow look, and wouldn't be what you'd wear while doing work about the house. But it wasn't a Victorian corset, the kind that we associate with the "wasp waist" and the rib-removal of later times. You might have a "busk"—a piece of whalebone or wood

going down the middle—to make sure you were always standing up straight. When you had a corset or stays popular during Jane's time, it wouldn't be a bra, per se. It was a lot more vestlike. The full-size ones would have more than one hundred pieces that would be stitched together, and were therefore very costly: you needed to protect your investment! So you didn't want to do anything that would get them dirty and you wanted to avoid getting body oils on the stays. That is why there would be a knee-length shift or chemise underneath the stays.

You'd cover yourself with a "fichu," which is nice, light material that you can tuck into your dress, or a chemisette, a piece more like our modern dickey and made of cambric or muslin. Or you would cover yourself with a shawl, or you'd wear a dress with a higher neck. Married women would always cover themselves.

A ficha from Baronda Bradley's collection. "I love having the contact with beautiful things that someone took hours and hours to make. I believe that by taking care of it, showing it, and wearing it, I am honoring the person who made this."

Piece by Piece: Creating a Regency Dress

Often, my dresses are the results of other period styles we've seen created by costumers' guilds, museums, or colleges, or more often, from actual pieces that come up for auction and so are online. Perhaps the most fun we have is buying pieces that are from that period, but in tatters, to study the styling and techniques. About the only things you can get nowadays are embroidered silks. We examine the fibers, the colors, and the patterns for our own inspiration.

When you look at the fabric from the time, you notice that the color palette was rather limited. They used anything in the red to purple, dark blue, browns, and indigos realm. There were no zippers, there were buttons and drawstrings—so that you could cinch something up. You might choose button-loop closures instead of button-holes, but both styles are authentic to the Regency period.

We study books on the materials that were available and the patterns that were on the material at that time. We examine a lace book to see what kind of laces were created in that era. *Accessories of Dress: An Illustrated Encyclopedia* is immensely helpful.

Little by little, going through all of these sources, it is like a mystery and you are trying to solve it through sleuthing: what parts and pieces could I incorporate, and how?

Baronda Ellen Bradley, clad in a Regency dress, with two nearby, poses in "a prettyish kind of a wilderness."

To create a Regency dress today, start by going to fabric stores, primarily interior decorating stores. If you go to Hancock or Jo-Ann Fabrics, they will have some cottons, but you don't get a whole lot of choice. At fabric stores, you know that you are going to find the raw silks (where you still have the nubs in them), the brocaded silks, the things you know they had available, though you will also find two-toned silk (where the threads are two different colors and they are woven against each other), which they did not have back then, but I still incorporate in my own dresses. I will take samples of the fabric I like with information about how much of the fabric they have in stock, and where I found it. Is there enough fabric for a hat? For a reticule? (A reticule is a purse.) Before the Regency period, when dresses were wider and had multiple layers, women would wear two big pockets under the dress on a string, but when they went to the Regency style and basically just had one sheath, women resorted to the reticule (alternately called a "ridicule").

So, I start with the fabric. Then my seamstress does a rough drawing. Perhaps I'll suggest a style, saying "I want a dress like Empress Josephine," or she'll suggest a style to me. I do try to pull in some of the French fashions and French ideas, even though Austen's contemporaries couldn't get some of the material because of the war. Yet, it was still in vogue, and if people could get things from across the sea, they tried to. People noticed when women were wearing foreign fashion styles and prints.

By the time you start, you're building on everything you already know. I took a sewing class on how to handle antique material and how to recover color. Covered buttons (taking a regular button and covering it with the material being used for your dress) were also poplular. I look for old pieces for buttons. I go to antique stores; a lot of horn was used back then, as well as coral and metal buttons.

* * *

The best thing about being in a Regency costume is everyone wants to come and look at it. It is an entry point for talking about my favorite author. As a result, I get to do a lot of education. When I was asked about the movie *Becoming Jane,* I had the opportunity to discusss that, other than two lines of truth, the rest of the movie was as "created" as my dresses. I got to talk about the film version versus the reality we know and how people are constantly making up and creating things to fill in the gaps. I have the opportunity to encourage people to have the curiosity to go and find out for themselves what's truth and what's ficion.

The Jane Austen Aptitude Test

True or False:

1. Austen did not like the name "Richard."

2. Austen put feminist statements only in the mouths of characters we are meant to dislike.

3. Mary Anne Evans created her nom de plume from her lover's first name and Anne Elliot's last name.

4. Some filmgoers went to see the movie *Sense and Sensibility* thinking it was a sequel to *Dumb and Dumber*.

5. Austen didn't write scenes between men without a woman present.

6. Tuesday is a popular day in Austen for dramatic things to happen

Math Problems:

7. For solving this math question assume

Petticoat extension = 6 inches and muddiness factor is $y = x^2$

If Lizzie ventures forth the three miles to visit her ailing sister Jane at Netherfield at three feet per second and there is a 50 percent chance of rain, factoring in a degree of muddiness of 2y, and her length of petticoat is constant, how fine will be her eyes upon arrival at Netherfield?

a. "very fine indeed!"

b. "brightened by the exercise"

c. "admirably fine"

d. "quite poor, like her indifference to decorum"

8. Create a mathematical formula that might represent a possible calculation of how Wentworth accumulated his wealth with "a" representing the prize money claimed for capturing an enemy vessel, "b" representing the prize money claimed for capturing an enemy vessel when an admiral was not nearby, and "c" representing the prize money for capturing enemy ships-of-war. For the purposes of the formula, you need to know that a captain could claim a quarter of the prize money of a captured enemy vessel and

three-eights of the prize money if an admiral were not nearby. In addition, a captain could get more prize money for capturing enemy ships-of-war. About 15 percent would be deducted for fees and other expenses.

9. Rank the following in order of their worth per annum:

Henry Crawford

Wentworth

Colonel Brandon

Darcy

Willoughby

Bingley

John Dashwood (from the Norland Property)

Rushworth

Mr. Bennet

10. Rank in order of wealth

Miss King

Augusta Hawkins

Miss Morton

Caroline Bingley

Miss Grey

Eleanor, Marianne, Margaret, *and* Mrs. Dashwood

Miss Woodhouse

Maria Ward

Georgianna Darcy

11. Rank, in order of minimum number of letters written (according to references in the novel), the following letter writers:

Lydia Bennet

Lady Catherine

Darcy

Georgianna Darcy

Lizzy Bennet

Caroline Bingley

Mrs. Gardiner

Mr. Gardiner

Jane Bennet

Colonel Foster

Mr. Bennet

Mrs. Bennet

Charlotte Lucas

Mr. Collins

12. Give a heroine's name in the form of a math equation.

13. Take the total number of dances Lizzy says Darcy danced at Meryton when reporting it to Colonel Fitzwilliam at Rosings and subtract the number of dances Darcy actually danced at the Meryton Assembly Hall.

Analogies:

14. Jane Bennet : Elinor Dashwood :: Lydia:_____

15. Collins : Elton :: Darcy : _____

16. Lizzie and Darcy at the Lucas dance: the Bingley ball :: the Collins parsonage : _____

What doesn't belong

17. Matthew Macfadyen, Hugh Grant, David Rintoul, Laurence Olivier, Colin Firth

18. Pemberly, Sotherton, Mansfield House, Barton Cottage, Donwell Abbey

19. Mrs. Norris, Lady Bertram, Georgianna Darcy, Emma, Miss Bates, Mrs. Grant, Jane Bennet, Lady Catherine

20. Fanny Price, Frank Churchill, Catherine Morland, Henry and Mary Crawford

21. Bingleys, Lucases, Hawkinses, Bennets, Coles

22. Elton, Collins, Edward Ferrars, Edmund Bertram

23. Mrs. Clay, Mary King, Caroline Bingley

Matching

24. Link the readers with what they were reading:

Mr. Collins	Voltaire
Harriet Smith	*Sir Charles Grandison*
Robert Martin	*Romance of the Forest*
Captain Benwick	*The Lady of the Lake*
Catherine Morland	Fordyce's Sermons
Mrs. Morland	"To the Memory of an Unfortunate Lady"
John Thorpe	*The Vicar of Wakefield*
Mr. Parker	*Clarissa*
Sir Edward Denham	*Tom Jones*

25. Link the person to the animal(s) he or she is associated with:

Mrs. Rushworth	a Newfoundland puppy and three terriers
Fanny Price	turkeys
Henry Tilney	pheasants
Mrs. Weston	pug
Charlotte Lucas	old gray pony
Charlotte Palmer	a pointer
Lady Bertram	poultry
Willoughby	hens

26. Which stars and directors had read the book in question before acting/directing?

a) Ang Lee (director of 1995 *Sense and Sensibility*)

b) Colin Firth (Darcy in 1995 BBC *Pride and Prejudice*)

c) Ewan McGregor (Frank Churchill in 1996 *Emma* directed by Douglas McGrath)

d) All of the above

e) None of the above

27. In *Emma*, the apple trees are blooming (incorrectly) in what month?

a) April

b) May

c) June

d) July

e) August

28. In *Emma* there are two characters only, besides Emma herself, who were present at the three dinner parties, at Randalls, at Hartfield, and at the Coles'. (1) Who were they? (2) Who (four) attended two? (3) Who (six) one only?

29. Which leading characters have no Christian names given them?

30. Why don't the Gardiners' children come with their parents to Longbourn at Christmastime? When Elizabeth arrives there the following March, we are told it had been a twelvemonth since she had seen her cousins.

Answers to the Jane Austen Aptitude Test can be found on pp. 213-218. A scoring guide is found on p. 218.

What Makes a Janeite?
Do you have what it takes?

Your score on the Jane Austen Aptitude Test determines what your barometric reading is.

If you got 1-5 questions right, your score is a 1.

If you got 6-10 questions right, your score is a 2.

If you got 11-15 questions right, your score is a 3.

If you got 16-20 questions right, your score is a 4.

If you got 21-25 questions right, your score is a 5.

If you got 26-30 questions right, your score is a 6.

What is your barometric reading?

1. Harriet Smith

Similar to Ms. Smith of Emma, you are easily "smith"-en: you like the idea of the works but haven't actually been initiated into the priesthood of the Austenians. Perhaps someone will show you the way.

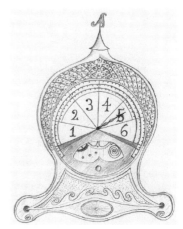

2. Catherine Morland and Emma "Woo"dhouse

Familiar enough with the novels to know the plots, you're still not knowledgeable enough to see past the archetypes—or your own misconceptions. You should read some "more"(land). Still, you're eager enough to try to "woo" others into reading the novels. Do you know how to spell "perfection?"

3. Marianne Dashwood

You'd "mari" any and all of the heroes (or heroines) if you had a chance—you know them all so well. Passionate and well-read concerning Austen, you're still just a little green in the ways of the world, but what can you expect from fiery youth?

4. Elinor Dashwood and Anne Elliot

Quite sagacious, you find yourself "dashing" to correct other's mistakes concerning the six great works, and "anne"-xious that they may not comprehend the masterful experience and miss out on the juvenilia. Quick, catch them before they fall!

5. Mr. Knightley

A proper Knight Errant for Austen, you uphold the characters and defend her works from all challengers. You are a true master of the text and your wisdom runs deep.

6. Janeite

Your comprehension and retention of the plotlines, even of the juvenilia, is a mystery to everyone else. Many believe you to be the second coming of Jane Austen herself. Will you write the "real" sequel to *Pride and Prejudice*?

Jane Austen in the Twenty-First Century

There was definitely no way that Jane Austen could have expected that *Emma* would ever be used in a scientific experiment. Medical science was slowly advancing during Austen's life. Gone were the days of the belief in "humours," the fluids believed to control health and mood by medieval physicians. But complicated DNA was nowhere near to being examined yet.

Despite this, *Emma* lives on to grant Jane Austen a hand in the experiments of the Human Genome Project, an attempt by the scientific community to map out and understand how deoxyribonucleic acid—DNA—works. These DNA strands, which form the "building blocks" of life inside all living cells, are made up of four chemical bases: adenine, thymine, guanine and cytosine, abbreviated A, T, G, and C.

A report released in the November 2006 issue of *Nature* described a new program created by Professor Simon Shepherd, who works as a Professor of Computational Mathematics at the University of Bradford. The program is able to pick out sequences and patterns in the seemingly infinite variations of proteins in strands of DNA. To test the program, Professor Shepherd fed it the text of *Emma*—with all the spaces taken out, resulting in one long string of letters. Without any programmed comprehension of the English language's syntax or vocabulary, the program was able to reconstruct 80 percent of the sentences. A feat indeed, especially considering some of Miss Bates's long-winded ramblings!

The private lives of genteel women of the regency would have certainly not allowed postings to web logs, or "blogs," which are like open-air forums and personal journals on the internet. Hundreds of blogs dedicated to Jane Austen exist. The blogs can be treasure troves of information—such as how many times Jennifer Ehle wears a specific dress during the course of the 1995 BBC *Pride and Prejudice* adaptation—as well as revelatory stories about how Jane Austen has affected the blogger's personal life.

The website Republic of Pemberly www.pemberley.com was created as a spin-off of an e-mail discussion group, austen-l. It is a Janeite's "haven in a world programmed to misunderstand obsession with things Austen." The site plays host to all manner of discussion groups, reviews, travel journals, and much more. Each of the novels can be found there and searched: who drove a barouche? What did Henry Tilney say about the picturesque? It is an outstanding website.

More online Austen can be found at the websites for the Jane Austen societies of North America (www.jasna.org), the United Kingdom (www.janeaustensoci.freeuk.com), and Australia (www.jasa.net.au). Each has a wealth of information, including how to become a member.

For help with understanding the timelines of any Austen novel, turn to the indefatigable Ellen Moody's website: www.jimandellen.org/austen/emcalendars.html. She has plotted the calendar for each of the novels, and provides excellent information regarding Austen's use of time.

For discussions on issues large and small, try www.austenblog.com.

A website devoted to beautiful photographs (and accompanying information) of the places associated with Austen is www.astoft.co.uk/austen.

YouTube

If all this weren't enough to entertain the private life of gentility, there is YouTube, the site on which anyone and everyone can share movie clips. Frequently used by creative college students with wacky ideas, there are some interesting spins

on Austenian themes to be found within. One short film retells the story of *Pride and Prejudice* in just five minutes—using only Barbie dolls. Another popular idea is to take the movie trailer for a Jane Austen film, use its sound and narration, and splice it together with clips from another movie. The results are often hilariously ridiculous. One, *"Pride" and Prejudice,* uses footage of lions spliced in time with the trailer for the 2005 *Pride and Prejudice*; another does the same, but with *Harry Potter* clips—and with Hermione Granger as Elizabeth. Alternatively, one could watch the trailer *Becoming Hermione,* a parody on the *Becoming Jane* preview. As both the *Harry Potter* films and *Becoming Jane* employ the incomparable actress Maggie Smith, this one was a no-brainer.

YouTube also offers videos from past "Austen Nights" and similar get-togethers, which feature music, dancing, and period costume. One such event is organized by Professor Amy Smith of the University of the Pacific in Stockton, California. Each year she has her students work on Jane Austen projects and then present them at a night filled with Regency high jinks. A short, homemade documentary on YouTube chronicles the 2005 event, which included a Jane Austen silent auction, a mock reality TV show using Jane Austen characters (in the form of dolls with faces of celebrities glued on), Austen-inspired board games (such as "Austenopoly"), a Jane Austen radio show, and even an up-to-date Austen play: *Sense and Homosexuality,* in which a male Marianne gushes over his new crush, Willoughby. Their favorite composer, is, of course, Sondheim.

Reactions to these posts on YouTube have been mixed. Amid all the adoring fans of Austen, there is always the one who ruins the party by bad-mouthing her in terms that would have curled even one of Captain Wentworth's sailor's beards. But one military graduate proclaimed to these dissenters that, yes, he loved Jane Austen, possessed her action figure, and believed that it took a "real man" to read her.

Real man or real woman, it appears that Austen is alive and well and living strong in the twenty-first century. But who knew she'd end up in Stockton, California?

If Jane Austen Had Been a Man

- He'd be called Austen.
- Austen lovers would be called "Austenites" or "Austenians."
- His status as a single, unmarried person would arouse little comment because it would be seen as a result of his devotion to his work, or else great discourses on the process of sexual sublimation producing great authors would appear.
- He would not be portrayed as an unselfconscious writer, barely aware of what he was doing.
- Brothers might have been portrayed more kindly in *Northanger Abbey*.
- He might not have noticed or cared about the fate of single women of little fortune.
- It would not be patronizingly said of him "he wrote about what he knew."
- The women in *Sense and Sensibility*, who had to live on £500 a year, would probably not have been an accurate representation of his own situation. (After 1805, Jane Austen, her sister, and mother had about £460 a year to live on.)
- His statement about working with a little bit of ivory would be seen as ironic.
- His family might not have rushed to claim his piety and religiosity upon his death.
- He would not have had to hide his authorship behind the title "BY A LADY."
- His own name would have been attached to his work before he died.
- He would have been able to negotiate directly with publishers using his own name.
- He would have written fewer letters, as letter writing was largely the province of females.
- But his sister might have destroyed more of his letters, not fewer.
- He might not have recognized, nor written about, the value of female friendships.
- He would not have been excluded from the world he created. (Compare the status of single, older men such as Colonel Brandon and Mr. Knightley to Miss Bates or Miss Nancy Steele, who will probably never get a proposal from the doctor.)
- It would be said that he ingeniously picked new ways to illustrate political topics, for instance, portraying the effects of wartime on civilian populations (*Pride and Prejudice*), a brief hiatus between wars (*Persuasion*), and the effects of colonization on England (*Mansfield Park*).

- Books providing information on nineteenth-century literature would not be entitled *What Jane Austen Ate and Charles Dickens Knew,* but instead *What John Austen Wrote With and Charles Dickens Knew.*
- He would have had a professionally painted portrait of himself—perhaps several of them at different stages of his life—rather than only his sister's simple watercolor-and-pencil sketch.
- He would have worn a smart high hat, rather than a spinster's mobcap.
- He might have entered the Royal Navy like brothers Frank and Charles, but been killed in battle before any of the novels were written.
- His grave in Winchester Cathedral would tell all about his novel writing, and there would be a life-size statue of him next to it.

Austen the Novelist

Each novel is a formidable engine of strategy. It is made to be—a marvel of designing and workmanship, capable of spontaneous motion at the lightest touch and of travel at delicately controlled but rapid speed toward its precise destination. It could kill us all . . . ; it fires at us, all along the way, using understatement in good aim. Let us be thankful it is trained not on our hearts, but on our illusions and our vanities.

—**Eudora Welty**

Jane Austen's writing desk, now in the British Library. Photographed at Jane Austen's House Museum, Chawton, England. © Jane Austen Society of North America, photo by Adrian Harvey. Courtesy of JASNA and Jane Austen's House Museum.

Jane Austen was a great novelist. We might think of Jane Austen as our best friend, as she seems to understand our own inner feelings so well, but that is because she was a great novelist. We might enjoy many, or all, of the movies and miniseries based on her novels, but that, too, is because she was such a great novelist that filmmakers and screenwriters, actors, and actresses are attracted to her: they want to recreate, reinvent, imitate, or upend her. The novels, however, are the springboard. We might think we can find the novels in her biography or her biography in the novels, but in this we might truly be tricking ourselves. We think we *know* her, when it is the novels we know. Again, it is because she was such a great novelist.

At her brother's Henry's feet lies the blame for many of the myths about Austen the novelist: that she wrote not for fame or profit, but for pleasure. "Her painstaking revision of the novels became not the perfectionism of a professional but the diffidence of a lady who could not trust her own judgement." Perhaps it was a little scary to be a brother who could not comprehend what his sister had accomplished; he tried to box her into a "type," but her novels prove him wrong.

The novelist Eudora Welty, who calls Austen "a highly conscious artist," is not the only one to disagree with poor Henry's attempts to tame Austen's professionalism. Welty says Austen "looked on the novel as a work of art" to which she gave "the concentration, the devotion, of all her powers."

Of course Henry knew otherwise himself: After all, Austen had been writing from the time she was eleven. In her teenage years, she wrote entertainingly, she wrote spoofs and takeoffs, she explored territory that included much violence. She recognized women's unstable situations in the world. She put her work aside and returned to it, to edit it again with fresh eyes. She tried to keep information private about her ideas and even her book titles, aware that a plot or a name could be lost to someone else for the lack of discretion. She was not discouraged by rejection (1797) or the failure of a publisher to actually publish the book he had contracted to publish (1803). She continued to write. She experimented with different forms of the novel. When the publisher refused to either publish or return her manuscript without being paid his £10 (1809), she continued to write. When she was already experiencing the symptoms of the disease that would kill her, she continued to write.

Once published, she tracked her earnings in her letters to others; she was happier when people bought her books rather than borrowing them; she revised her work, read it out loud, put it aside, came back to it. She is the very model of a serious novelist. She structured her stories carefully.

She read her writings to her family, knowing that they would be entertained. But she also developed a sense of herself as an author that involved trusting her own creative self more. She began to have as her goal, not entertaining her family with her writings but satisfying her self. Kathryn Sutherland believes Austen was moving "towards ever greater independence of creative judgment."

Henry also wants us to believe she wrote only what she knew, but actually she knew more than she wrote:

—an aunt arrested for shoplifting and jailed for several months

—a cousin-in-law guillotined

—people in the neighborhood who did unseemly things

—the death of a sister-in-law and her baby after giving birth on board ship

But she chose to avoid the melodrama, the plot that can only be resolved by a "car" accident or two.

"The Creator of the Modern Novel"

The novel had evolved up to Fanny Burney, Austen's immediate predecessor. And then along came Jane Austen.

She read the novels of her contemporaries; she was aware of what they had accomplished, and, being a genius, did what they could not do. The novelist Carol Shields says, "It is almost as though she reinvented and stabilized the wobbly eighteenth-century novel—which seemed unable to stare at itself, to *know* itself—and made it into a modern form."

What specifically did Austen accomplish?

- Her characterization is much more subtle and has much more depth than that of her predecessors.
- Her moral vision is more serious than theirs. They are all quite satirical, the earlier ones, but there is more depth to hers.
- She was a brilliant stylist. That is her most important contribution. In the history of the English language there are few writers who have equaled her in terms of elegance and sophistication of her style.
- And what turns them into masterpieces rather than just competent novels is the aesthetic beauty of the architecture of the novels, similar in terms of balance to a Mozart composition.

Add to all this, her use of "free indirect style." Instead of a giving a direct quote you give an indirect quote and somehow that shifts the perspective to one that is more ironic. (This simply means that instead of saying "Jane said, 'the tree is green,'" the statement is: "Jane said that the tree was green.") Free indirect style is commonly used in the novel; it gives a sense of irony or a sense of satire, a sense of overheard conversation. One of Austen's great strengths is a sense of social irony, and free indirect style allows for this ironic sense.

How did she accomplish it? Letters to her niece Anna critiquing her niece's novel-in-process is the closest we come to her talking about her writing. She advises:

- Don't let your heroine "act inconsistently."
- Don't be verbose: "the sense might be expressed in fewer words."
- Write realistically: Anna should not describe Ireland if she hasn't been there: "You will be in danger of giving false representations."
- As we would say nowadays, watch out for giving t.m.i.: "your descriptions are often more minute than will be liked. You give too many particulars of right hand & left."
- Edit your manuscript.
- Watch out for clichés: "Devereux Forester's being ruined by his Vanity is extremely good; but I wish you would not let him plunge into a 'vortex of Dissipation': I do not object to the Thing, but I cannot bear the expression;—it is such thorough novel slang—and so old, that I dare say Adam met with it in the first novel he opened."

A Genealogy of Publication

On the title page of *Sense and Sensibility* (see p. 25), the authorship is announced to be "BY A LADY." But after that, Austen dispensed with any kind of signifier except "author." Austen was proud of the association of the novels: *Pride and Prejudice* announces that it is "By

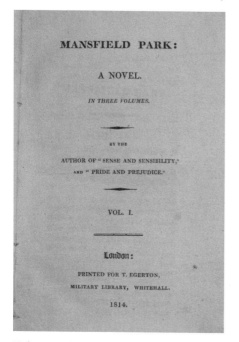

MANSFIELD PARK:

A NOVEL.

IN THREE VOLUMES.

BY THE

AUTHOR OF " SENSE AND SENSIBILITY,"
AND " PRIDE AND PREJUDICE."

VOL. I.

London:

PRINTED FOR T. EGERTON,
MILITARY LIBRARY, WHITEHALL.

1814.

Title page of Mansfield Park, *first published in 1814, showing the lineage of books by the same author. No longer "BY A LADY," but by an author. Courtesy of the Burke Jane Austen Collection, Goucher College Library.*

the Author of *Sense and Sensibility.*" The third book, *Mansfield Park*, is proclaimed to be by the *author* of "Sense and Sensibility" and "Pride and Prejudice." She becomes the authorizing author of the previous work, giving each new volume standing through its own literary genealogy. And perhaps, gaining readers of the earlier volumes because of their admiration for the one in their hands.

Perhaps we do not need to suggest to our readers to place her books in *your* hands. Perhaps you have and do. But if you never have, we encourage you to read her. Read this great novelist. You'll have to focus your attention in a way you don't have to in a movie. But it is worth it! Take the time to pay detailed attention and concentrate.

You might discover what many Austen lovers do, that in being made into film, the most important thing about Austen—the language—gets lost. It is said you can translate poetry, but what is lost is the poetry. You can translate Austen to film, but what is lost is Austen. Films may be faithful to the plot and to the characters; still, what is lost is the most valuable thing of the novels, her writing. As we said when we began, keep her by your bedside, your bathtub, and your armchair. And read her.

Last Words:
Acknowledgments

First, our thanks to Evander Lomke, Carol's editor for twenty years and the person to whom this book is dedicated—an amazingly supportive and challenging editor, who made this book possible. Carol, and her entire family, have been lucky enough to call him not only "editor" but also "friend."

A wonderfully generous community of Austen scholars, photographers, and Austen lovers has supported our efforts, including members of the Jane Austen Society of North America. In specific: Joan Klingel Ray, former President of JASNA; Marsha Huff, current President of JASNA; Rosalie Sternberg, President of JASNA of North Texas; Mary Lou White, formerly of Book Adventures, and Baronda Ellen Bradley. We also thank both of JASNA's publications, *Persuasions* and *Persuasions On-Line*.

For taking the time to share their thoughts with us through interviews and conversations: Joan Klingel Ray, Mary Lou White, Baronda Ellen Bradley, Anne Timmons, and Karen Joy Fowler.

We also wish to acknowledge: Josephine Donovan, author of an incredible book, *Women and the Rise of the Novel, 1405-1726,* for sharing her thoughts on the novel and Austen's contribution to the novel. The section on "Austen the Novelist" is indebted to an e-mail conversation with her, especially the list of what Austen accomplished and the ideas about what is lost in translation; Joan Klingel Ray, not only for her interview and general willingness to help with the book but also for some of the ideas found in the section "If Jane Austen Had Been a Man." Joan Klingel Ray has also offered a defense of Lady Russell.

The staffs of several libraries have been extremely helpful in obtaining information and/or images for the book:
- The staff at the Richardson Public Library, Richardson, Texas, who once again tackled all manner of research for a project of ours; and in specific, the interlibrary loan staff.
- Susan Walker and Brian Palmer of The Lewis Walpole Library, Yale University.
- Wendy Zieger of the Bridgeman Art Library.

- Tara Olivero, Special Collections Librarian and College Archivist, Julia Rogers Library, Goucher College, who helped me obtain scans from The Henry and Alberta Hirshheimer Burke Collection of rare first editions of Jane Austen.

Photographers, too, have been very generous in their support of this book. We thank Elaine Maylen, Allan Soedring, and Geoff and Mercia Chapman.

Thanks too, to Helen Trompeteler, Picture Librarian of the National Portrait Gallery, Tom Clifford for his image of Jane Austen in her garden, and Tony Kentuck, for his cartoon "Pride and Prejudice II." CafePress and their artists for "Shelves in the closet" sweatshirt, "Jane Austen kicks ass" T-shirt, "Got Jane?" magnet, "Eat Drink Austen" magnet, "Janeite" bumper sticker, "Jane Austen is my co-pilot" bumper sticker.

Finally, Bruce Buchanan, who endures deadlines as Emma does Mrs. Elton, because it is necessary, even if unpleasant, and they do depart, though often overstaying their welcome.

We have made every effort to contact holders of copyrighted works. If we have missed any copyright holders, we invite them to contact the publishers so that a full acknowledgment may be given in subsequent editions.

We also wish to acknowledge quotations that were not explicitly attributed in the text itself, and other valuable sources for ideas:
- The idea that Austen was "born, or rewarded, with fairy gifts—not one, but two entirely separate ones. She had the genius of originality, and she had the genius of comedy. And they never fought each other at all, but worked together in a harmony," is from novelist Eudora Welty.
- Information on Austen and her publishers was found in Kathryn Sutherland's *Jane Austen's Textual Lives: From Aeschylus to Bollywood* and Jan Fergus, "The Professional Woman Writer" in *The Cambridge Companion to Jane Austen.*
- James Thomson observed that "the real actors in *Sense and Sensibility* [Ang Lee's version] are the landscape and the houses. . . . So voluptuous that it regularly upstages the actors, so emphatically stitched together from some twenty different counties."
- Maria Jerinic in "In Defense of the Gothic: Rereading *Northanger Abbey,*" complained about the title *What Jane Austen Ate and Charles Dickens Knew*: "Why not 'what Jane Austen wrote with'? Why does Dickens get to 'know' and Austen only to 'eat'?"
- Kathryn Sutherland in *Jane Austen's Textual Lives: From Aeschylus to Bollywood* argues that "A case can be made for linking *Northanger Abbey*; possibly in a second drafting, *The Watsons,* and the revision and completion of *Lady Susan* with the disrupted Bath and Southampton years."
- Claudia Johnson, *Jane Austen: Women, Politics and the Novel* makes several points that we have incorporated into the book: that Lydia makes Lizzy's impertinence acceptable. In addition, we draw upon her insight that by showing that the Gothic is in fact the inside out of the ordinary, that the abbey does indeed present a disconcerting

double image, particularly forbidding and arrogant to one who, like Catherine Morland, does not have entrée, *Northanger Abbey* does not refute, but rather clarifies and reclaims, Gothic conventions in distinctly political ways." It was Paul Morrison who said, "Horror, like charity, begins at home" and Ronald Paulson, that the French Revolution changed the Gothic novel.

• Richard Jenkyns in *A Fine Brush on Ivory*, proposes that the plot of *Pride and Prejudice* is like a Rolls-Royce.

Jane Austen's letters are quoted from *Jane Austen's Letters,* collected and edited by Deirdre Le Faye, published by Oxford University Press, 1995.

Besides pictures fully credited on the page upon which they appear, we wish to acknowledge:

p. 42: *Godmersham Park, Kent, the Seat of Thomas Knight Esq.*, pub. in 1785 (engraving) (b/w photo) by Watts, William (1752-1851)
Private Collection/The Bridgeman Art Library.

p. 83: *The Pump Room*, Bath (aquatint) by Nattes, John Claude (c.1765-1822) (after)
© Victoria Art Gallery, Bath and North East Somerset Council/The Bridgeman Art Library.

p. 85: *Lansdown Crescent*, Bath, 1820 (colour litho) by Cox, David (1783-1859) (attr. to)
Private Collection/The Bridgeman Art Library.

p. 105: *Walking Dress*, 1814 (color engraving) by English School (19th century)
Private Collection/The Bridgeman Art Library.

Answers to the Crossword Puzzle

ACROSS

1. ARREARS
5. ARDOR
10. HOE
11. O
12. TEAR
13. A
14. HE
15. AUI
18. CM
20. SWIFT
22. A
23. MINE
24. LAP
26. LODE
27. RUSTIC
29. RATIN
31. DO
32. LIEU
33. ROS
34. MP
36. AM
37. ELIZABETH
38. OR
39. REX

41. ROI
42. CO
43. PREJUDICE
52. CD
53. YS
54. RARA
55. ALAS
56. OE
57. ROMAN
58. MISSEW
60. LEES
62. SEA
64. USES
65. R
66. EMMAS
68. EE
69. MIX
70. TO
71. T
72. AINT
73. J
75. ERA
76. UNCLE
77. WICKHAM

DOWN

1. AHHA
2. ROE
3. RE
4. SO
5. AT
6. RES
7. DAWLISH
8. ORION
9. R
13. ATE
15. AISLE
16. UNTIL
17. IEIEI
18. CL
19. MAREB
21. FD
23. MU
25. PARE
27. ROMEOS
28. CUZ
30. TOT
31. DARCY
34. MOOCOW

35. PRIDE
40. X
41. R
43. PROSAIC
44. RAM
45. ERAS
46. JANEE
47. U
48. DAM
49. ILIUM
50. CASSI
51. ESSEX
57. REMAN
59. ES
60. LET
61. EM
63. AE
65. ROAM
67. SNL
70. TRA
73. TE
74. JW
75. EH
76. U

Answers to The Jane Austen Aptitude Test

True and False

1. True. For some reason, Austen disliked the name "Richard." In *Northanger Abbey*, we are told that Catherine Morland's father "was a clergyman, without being neglected, or poor, and a very respectable man, though his name was Richard." And in *Persuasion*, the only child we learn of who dies in a novel, is "poor Richard" Musgrove. Whether this is an allusion to Benjamin Franklin's *Poor Richard's Almanac,* or to the first name of the publisher who failed to publish *Northanger Abbey,* we do not know.

2. False. Austen did not put feminist statements only in the mouths of characters we are meant to dislike. While Lady Catherine is the person who voices the all-important position "no occasion for entailing estates from the female line" in *Pride and Prejudice,* and Mrs. Elton makes a feminist statement or two in *Emma,* in *Northanger Abbey* and *Persuasion,* other, more positive characters pronounce feminist insights. Catherine Morland says about history "I read it a

little as a duty, but it tells me nothing that does not either vex or weary me. The quarrels of popes and kings, with wars or pestilences, in every page; the men all so good for nothing, and hardly any women at all—it is very tiresome: and yet I often think it odd that it should be so dull, for a great deal of it must be invention." Anne Elliot in *Persuasion* cautions Harville: "if you please, no reference to examples in books. Men have had every advantage of us in telling their own story. Education has been theirs in so much higher a degree; the pen has been in their hands. I will not allow books to prove anything." Even Darcy may be seen as voicing feminist thoughts. After Darcy proposes the second time, he says, "As a child, I was taught what was right; but I was not taught to correct my temper. I was given good principles, but left to follow them in pride and conceit. Unfortunately, an only son (for many years an only child), I was spoilt by my parents, who, though good themselves (my father particularly, all that was benevolent and amiable), allowed, encouraged, almost taught me to be selfish and overbearing—to care for

213

none beyond my own family circle, to think meanly of all the rest of the world, to wish at least to think meanly of their sense and worth compared with my own. Such I was, from eight to eight-and-twenty; and such I might still have been but for you." This monologue "contains many phrases by which feminists had earlier made their charges against the male sex: 'spoilt,' 'selfish,' 'overbearing,' 'taught to think meanly of [women's] sense and worth compared to [their] own' are accusations that could be found in any radical or moderate feminist tract." Allison Sulloway, *Jane Austen and the Province of Womanhood*.

3. Maybe true. Mary Anne Evans ("George Eliot") "said she chose George as a tribute to Lewes, and Eliot because it was 'a good, mouth filling, easily pronounced word'; but it also had resonances of a hidden female tradition—George reminding us of her beloved George Sand, and Eliot perhaps a nod to Jane Austen, since it was about the delayed blossoming of Anne Elliot in *Persuasion* that she was reading aloud that spring." Jennifer Uglow, *George Eliot*. In fact, Ellen Moers (*Literary Women*) finds an uncanny association between *Emma* and George Eliot's *Adam Bede* and recommends reading them together. "*Adam Bede* appears to be the novel that Austen rejected; it seems to hover below the surface of *Emma* waiting to be born in the hands of another woman novelist, forty years later."

4. True. Some filmgoers went to see the movie *Sense and Sensibility* thinking it was a sequel to *Dumb and Dumber*. What can we say? They needed more of the former and less of the latter.

5. False. See Edmund's conversation with his father in *Mansfield Park*. "Edmund's first object that morning was to see his father alone." *Mansfield Park*, opening of chapter 20, or vol. II, chap. 2.

6. True. Tuesday is the day of the week for important happenings in Austen. Emma Watson's first ball and dance with Mr. Howard is on a Tuesday; the Netherfield Ball is on a Tuesday, the Cole's party is on a Tuesday, Frank Churchill leaves Highbury on a Tuesday, Anne Elliot's concertgoing and frustration at trying to communicate with Captain Wentworth is on a Tuesday. These and other examples are discussed at http://www.jimandellen.org/austen/tuesdays.html

Math Problems

7. b. "brightened by the exercise"

8. $((a-15\%) \times 1/4) + ((b-15\%) \times 3/8) + ((c-15\%) \times X/8) = £25,000$, where a = the total value of captured enemy vessels with an admiral in the vicinity, b = the total value of captured enemy vessels without an admiral nearby, c = the total value of enemy ships-of-war, and X/8 the percentage received for enemy ships-of-war.

9. Rushworth (£12,000)

Darcy (£10,000)

Bingley (£4,000—£5,000)

John Dashwood (from the Norland Property) £4,000

Henry Crawford £4,000

Mr. Bennet £2,000

Colonel Brandon £2,000

Wentworth £1,250

Willoughby £600—700

10. Miss Grey £50,000

Miss Morton £30,000

Miss Woodhouse £30,000

Georgianna Darcy £20,000

Caroline Bingley £20,000

Miss King £10,000

Eleanor, Marianne, Margaret *and* Mrs. Dashwood, £10,000

Augusta Hawkins £10,000

Maria Ward £7,000

11. Letter Writers: (minimum letters they are known to have written)

Jane Bennet (11)

Lizzy Bennet (8)

Lydia Bennet (7)

Mr. Bennet (6)

Mr. Gardiner (5)

Caroline Bingley (4)

Mr. Collins (3)

Darcy (3)

Mrs. Gardiner (3)

Colonel Foster (2)

Charlotte Lucas (2)

Georgianna Darcy (1)

Lady Catherine (1)

Mrs. Bennet (1)

Jane Bennet (11): to Lizzy, to Caroline Bingley, to Caroline Bingley, to Mrs. Gardiner, to Lizzy from London (at least 2 letters), plus "all the letters" sent to Lizzy at Hunsford (at least 2), 2 to Lizzy in Derbyshire, to Mrs. Gardiner.

Lizzy Bennet (8): to her mother from Netherfield, to Mrs. Gardiner, to Mrs. Gardiner, to Jane, to Mr. Gardiner, to someone (while at Hunsford), to Mrs. Gardiner, to Lydia.

Lydia Bennet (7): at least 2 from Brighton to her mother, at least 2 to Kitty, to Mrs. Forster, to Kitty, to Lizzy.

Mr. Bennet (6): to Mr. Collins, to Lizzy at Hunstford ("He wrote last week to hurry my return"), to Longbourn, to Mr. Gardiner, to Mr. Gardiner, to Mr. Collins.

Mr. Gardiner (5): to Mrs. Gardiner, to Colonel Forster, to Lizzy, to Mr. Bennet, to Mr. Bennet.

Caroline Bingley (4): 2 to Jane from Netherfield, one from London, and one to express her delight in her upcoming wedding.

Mr. Collins (3): to Mr. Bennet in thanks (though there was a promised second thank-you note that is never mentioned as having been received), to Mr. Bennet on Lydia's elopement, to Mr. Bennet about Lizzy.

Darcy (3): to Georgianna, to Lizzy, to Lady Catherine.

Mrs. Gardiner (3): to Lizzy (excludes her notes to her friends upon leaving Derbyshire).

Colonel Foster (2): to Mr. Bennet, to Mr. Gardiner.

Charlotte Lucas (2): to Lizzy, at minimum, reference is to "first letters" from Hunsford.

Georgianna Darcy (1): upon learning Darcy's good news.

Lady Catherine (1): to Darcy.

Mrs. Bennet (1): to Lizzy.

We know from the references in the novel that at least this number of letters was written by each correspondent. In many cases there were probably more: for instance, Lydia's letters to her mother or her sister Kitty. Though her letters were always short, we can assume she wrote more often to Mrs. Bennet and Kitty and that they wrote back. Austen, however, does not enlighten us on this point. Similarly, we don't know how many letters Charlotte sent to Elizabeth, but we know there had to be at least two, as they are referred to as her "early letters" from Hunsford.

12. M = A. Emma.

In the Cambridge edition of *Emma,* editors Richard Cronin and Dorothy McMillan cite scholar Mark Loveridge. Loveridge suggests that Mr. Weston's puzzle at Box Hill ("What two letters of the alphabet are there, that express perfection?" and answer "M. and A.— Em-ma") is a reference to a metaphysical equation contained in the volume *Enquiry into the Original Ideas of Beauty and Virtue,* written by Francis Hutcheson and published in London in 1728. In his book Hutchison suggests that "M" equals the "moment of Good," while the other variable "A" is "Ability," thus: "Benevolence, or Virtue in any Agent, is as M/A, or $M+1/A$, and no *Being* can act above his *natural* Ability; that must be the Perfection of Virtue where M=A." Hence, M and A equal perfection.

13. $(4-2 = 2)$. We are told by the narrator, "Mr. Darcy danced only once with Mrs. Hurst and once with Miss Bingley, declined being introduced to any other lady, and spent the rest of the evening in walking about the room." Elizabeth tells Colonel Fitzwilliam, "The first time of my ever seeing him in Hertfordshire, you must know, was at a ball—and at this ball, what do you think he did? He danced only four dances!" However, dances were grouped in pairs, so that when Darcy danced a pair of dances with Mrs. Hurst and a pair with Miss Bingley, Lizzy might have counted that as four dances, not two. Whether this calculation magnified the harm of his slight of her, we do not know.

Analogies:

14. Jane Bennet : Elinor Dashwood :: Lydia: [Margaret]

(oldest to youngest sisters)

15. Collins : Elton :: Darcy : [Knightley] (unsuccessful suitors; successful suitors)

16. Lizzie and Darcy at the Lucas dance: the Bingley ball :: the Collins parsonage : a [walk]

she says no to Darcy, she says yes to Darcy

What doesn't belong

17. Hugh Grant (all the other actors played Darcy)

18. Barton Cottage (all the others are big manor houses)

19. Georgianna Darcy (all the others are aunts)

20. Catherine Morland (all the others were raised by someone other than their parents)

21. Bennets (all the others are families who made their money in trade)

22. Edmund Bertram (all the others are clergy who don't marry the first person they propose to)

23. Caroline Bingley. She is the only one who doesn't have freckles. Did you think "they are in competition with a character for the love of a man?" For Caroline Bingley only imagined an interest on Darcy's part.

24. Link the readers with what they were reading:

Mr. Collins—Fordyce's Sermons.

Harriet Smith—*Romance of the Forest*

Robert Martin—*The Vicar of Wakefield*

Captain Benwick—*The Lady of the Lake, Giaour*

Catherine Morland—"To the Memory of an Unfortunate Lady" by Alexander Pope

Mrs. Morland—*Sir Charles Grandison*

John Thorpe—*Tom Jones*

Mr. Parker—Voltaire

Sir Edward Denham—*Clarissa*

25. *Link the person to the animal(s) he or she is associated with:*

Mrs. Rushworth—pheasants

Fanny Price—old gray pony

Henry Tilney—a Newfoundland puppy and three terriers

Mrs. Weston—turkeys

Charlotte Lucas—poultry

Charlotte Palmer—hens

Lady Bertram—pug

Willoughby—a pointer

26. e. None of the above.

27. d. July. Jane Austen's brother wrote to her, "Nae, I wish you could tell me where you get those apple-trees of your that comes into bloom in July?"

28. Questions 28 and 29 (and answers) are taken from Sheila Kaye-Smith and G. B. Stern, *Speaking of Jane Austen*.

answer:

Mr. Knightley and Mrs. Weston

Mr. Elton, Mr. Woodhouse, Mr. John Knightley, Mr. Weston

Mrs. John Knightley, Frank Churchill, Jane Fairfax, Mrs. Elton, Mr. and Mrs. Cole.

29. Kaye-Smith and Stern's answer: "Mrs. Smith, Mr. Rushworth, Mr. and Mrs. Bennet, General Tilney, Mr. Gardiner (Mrs. Gardiner has only the initial M.), Mr. Weston, Colonel Brandon." They left out Colonel Fitzwilliam, Mrs. Norris, and included Mr. Gardiner, though he signs his letter to Mr. Bennet, "Edward Gardiner."

30. The narrator does not tell us. Perhaps because young children would have been too much for Mrs. Bennet's nerves.

Scoring:

Whether you answered true or false for question 3, give yourself credit for a right answer. Also, if you attempted a formula for question 8, how Captain Wentworth accumulated his wealth, give yourself credit for a correct answer, since we cannot know exactly how he did; ours is but an example of how it might have been figured. If you were able to identify at least five people missing a Christian, or first name, for question 29, give yourself a point. Also, if you answered question 30 about the Gardiner's children, but it differed from ours, that is fine. Give yourself a point for that as well. For the others, well, those are little less flexible in scoring.